## CREDITS

**Authors**
Khristine Annwn Page and Patti Schulze

**Editors**
Kari Brooks, Wendy Sharp

**Production Coordinators**
Kate Reber, Myrna Vladic

**Compositors**
Rick Gordon, Emerald Valley Graphics
Debbie Roberti, Espresso Graphics
Myrna Vladic, Bad Dog Graphics

**Indexer**
Emily Glossbrenner, FireCrystal Communications

**Cover design**
Steven Soshea, Macromedia, Inc.

**Technical Review**
Julie Hallstrom, Dreamweaver Technical Support
Don Booth, Dreamweaver Technical Support
Francois Richardson, Dreamweaver Technical Support

Many thanks and blessings to John Robinson, Richard Gann, and Jim Spadaccini, whose teachings and friendships have opened many doors for me; to Mary, Rick, and Richard Page for their endless love, support, and guidance; to Marjorie Baer, Wendy Sharp, and Kari Brooks for their superb editing skills and incredible patience; to Laura Tempest Schmidt for being the ultimate sister and friend and making me smile when I think of you; to Bryon Kennedy for being there, for being magnificent, for your friendship, love, and encouragement; and to the Fates for Inspiration.

# table of contents

# introduction

Macromedia's Dreamweaver 4 combines visual layout tools with text-based HTML editing features for the creation, management, and maintenance of Web sites. It gives beginners immediate access to the tools needed for creating Web pages, while allowing developers familiar with hand-coding to work directly with the code when needed. This flexible program makes advanced techniques accessible and easy to use. The integration of powerful design, code, and reference features gives both beginners and advanced users an advantage.

This Macromedia training course leads you step by step through the projects in each lesson, presents the major features and tools in Dreamweaver 4, and guides you towards developing the skills you need to create Web sites. This approximately 21-hour curriculum includes these lessons:

**Lesson 1:** Learning the Basics
**Lesson 2:** Working with Graphics
**Lesson 3:** Creating Links
**Lesson 4:** Elements of Page Design
**Lesson 5:** Adding User Interactivity
**Lesson 6:** Managing Your Site
**Lesson 7:** Using Libraries
**Lesson 8:** Using Templates
**Lesson 9:** Creating Frames
**Lesson 10:** Creating Layers
**Lesson 11:** Using Style Sheets
**Lesson 12:** Using Find and Replace
**Lesson 13:** Creating Forms
**Lesson 14:** Animating with Timelines
**Lesson 15:** Extending Dreamweaver

Each lesson begins by outlining the major focus of the lesson and introducing new features. Learning objectives and the approximate time needed to complete all the tasks are also listed at the beginning of each lesson. The projects are divided into short tasks that explain the importance of each skill you learn.

This training course also features these elements:

**Tips:** Alternative ways to perform tasks, and suggestions to consider when applying the skills you are learning.

**Notes:** Additional background information to expand your knowledge, and advanced techniques you can explore in order to further develop your skills.

**Boldface terms:** New Dreamweaver vocabulary that is introduced and emphasized in each lesson.

**Menu commands and keyboard shortcuts:** There are often multiple ways to perform the same task in Dreamweaver; the different options will be pointed out in each lesson. Menu commands are shown with angle brackets between the menu names and commands: Menu > Command > Subcommand. Keyboard shortcuts are shown with a plus sign between the names of keys to indicate that you should press the keys simultaneously; for example, Shift+Tab means that you should press the Shift and Tab keys at the same time.

Appendix A contains a table with special characters, regular expressions, and their meanings for use with Dreamweaver's Find and Replace feature, covered in Lesson 12. At the end of the book are Appendixes B and C, which provide shortcuts for Dreamweaver commands for use on Macintosh and Windows systems, respectively.

The files you will need to complete the projects for each lesson are located in the DW4_Lessons folder on the enclosed CD. Inside the Lessons folder are folders titled with the name of the lesson—Lesson_01_Text, for example—that contain the subfolders and files necessary to perform the tasks in the respective lesson. Which subfolders are included will depend on the projects in the lesson. Common subfolders include: *Completed*, which contains the completed files for each lesson so you can compare your work and see the end result of the project; *Images*, which contains all the images necessary for the lesson; and *Text*, which includes text documents you will need to import into Dreamweaver. The files you will use for each of the projects are listed at the beginning of each lesson.

2

## AUTHORIZED TRAINING FOR MACROMEDIA

Each book in the Macromedia Training from the Source series includes the complete curriculum of a course originally developed for use by Macromedia's authorized trainers. The lesson plans were developed by some of Macromedia's most successful trainers and refined through long experience to meet students' needs. We believe that Macromedia Training from the Source courses offer the best available training for Macromedia programs.

The instructions in this book are designed for Web designers, Web developers, and others interested in creating Web pages. This course assumes you are a beginner with Dreamweaver but are familiar with the basic methods of giving commands on a Macintosh or Windows computer, such as choosing items from menus, opening and saving files, and so on. For more information on those basic tasks, see the documentation provided with your computer.

Finally, the instructions in this book assume that you already have Dreamweaver 4 installed on a Macintosh or Windows computer, and that your computer meets the system requirements listed on page 5. This minimum configuration will allow you to run Dreamweaver 4 and open the training files included on the enclosed CD. If you do not own Dreamweaver 4, a demo version is included on the CD. You will be able to complete the lessons with the training version of the software, but the demo version will function only for 30 days, after which the program will no longer launch without a serial number. Follow the instructions in the downloaded Read Me file to install the demo version of the software.

Welcome to Macromedia Training from the Source. We hope you enjoy the course.

## WHAT YOU WILL LEARN

You will develop the skills you need to create and maintain your own Web sites as you work through these lessons.

**By the end of this course, you will be able to:**

- Format text in different sizes, colors, and styles
- Use HTML styles to speed up your text-formatting process
- Import and clean up text from text files, Word documents, and spreadsheets
- Insert graphics and control their appearance
- Create and manage internal and external links throughout your site
- Learn how to make changes directly within the HTML code
- Place text and graphics within tables to achieve more control over the layout
- Make use of image rollovers and other interactive elements
- Use the Site window to manage your files and folders
- Develop library items in order to use the same elements quickly and repeatedly
- Create templates to set the look and feel of a site
- Create frames and target links to develop a clear navigation
- Make your pages accessible and redirect visitors according to the browser version they are using
- Incorporate different types of files such as Flash Objects and Flash Text
- Insert a background graphic or change the background colors of your pages
- Specify text attributes using cascading style sheets to gain control over the appearance of text
- Use the extensive Find and Replace feature to make changes in single documents or throughout the entire site
- Create forms to collect information from visitors
- Create animations and control the placement of objects with layers
- Test and run reports on your Web pages to verify their compatibility with multiple types of browsers
- Customize and extend Dreamweaver's capabilities to suit your needs

## MINIMUM SYSTEM REQUIREMENTS

### Macintosh

- Power Macintosh
- Mac OS 8.6, 9.x, or later
- 64MB of application RAM
- 135MB available disk space
- CD-ROM drive
- Color monitor capable of 800 x 600 resolution
- A Web browser (an Internet connection is not necessary)

**NOTE** *If you are running Mac OS 9.1, you will need to install the Dreamweaver 4.01 updater. This update is included on the CD. It fixes several conflicts between Mac OS 9.1 and Dreamweaver 4. If you are running an earlier version of the Mac OS, installing the updater is still recommended.*

### Windows

- 166MHz Intel3M Pentium processor or higher
- Windows 95, Windows 98, Windows 2000, Windows ME, or Windows NT 4 (with Service Pack 3) or later
- 64MB of application RAM
- 110MB available disk space
- CD-ROM drive
- Color monitor capable of 800 x 600 resolution
- A Web browser (an Internet connection is not necessary)

**NOTE** *It is recommended that you install the Dreamweaver 4.01 updater. This update is included on the CD.*

5

# learning the basics

## LESSON 1

Dreamweaver 4 is an HTML (Hypertext Markup Language) editor that gives users visual design and editing capabilities combined with the ability to work directly with code. Dreamweaver helps speed production time for your Web sites and provides tools for the management and maintenance of those sites.

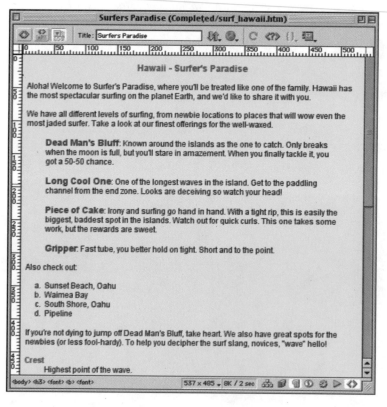

In this lesson, you'll create a page like this one while learning to format text and test your pages.

In this lesson, you learn the basics of HTML layout and production in Dreamweaver 4, and you become familiar with the program's interface and tools. You begin to use the main site-management features by setting up a local site for the pages that you create.

You learn how to import text in different file formats. You also work with text and document settings to create a simple Web page and test your work in different browsers—a vital part of creating accessible Web sites.

You can find an example of the completed lesson in the Completed folder inside the Lesson_01_Text folder on the CD-ROM.

## WHAT YOU WILL LEARN

**In this lesson, you will:**

- Identify the tools and become familiar with the Dreamweaver interface
- Set up a new local site and specify preview browsers
- Create, save, and title a new document
- Specify a background and default text colors
- Place text on a page
- Position and format text
- Use the Assets panel to save colors and apply them to text
- Create and apply HTML styles
- Create and modify Flash text

## APPROXIMATE TIME

This lesson should take approximately two hours to complete.

## LESSON FILES

**Media Files:**
*Lesson_01_Text/Images/background.gif*
*Lesson_01_Text/Images/fish.gif*
**Starting Files:**
*Lesson_01_Text/Text/surfing.txt*
*Lesson_01_Text/Text/biking_adventures.htm*
**Completed Project:**
*Lesson_01_Text/Completed/surf_hawaii.html*

## EXPLORING THE TOOLS

When you open Dreamweaver, you'll notice the document window where you design your page. You may also see several additional panels for adding or changing text and objects on the page. Visible panels might include the Objects panel, the property inspector, the HTML Styles panel, and the Reference panel. You can access these panels, as well as others, from the Window menu. If you've opened Dreamweaver before, Dreamweaver places the panels exactly where they were the last time you quit the program. A check next to an item in the Window menu indicates the panel is open, but the panel could be hidden beneath another panel or the document window.

**NOTE** *If a panel is selected but still doesn't appear, choose Window > Arrange Panels to reset all open panels to their default positions. The Objects panel moves to the top-left corner of the screen, the property inspector moves to the bottom of the screen, and all other open panels move to the right of the screen. No overlap occurs.*

### 1) Move the mouse pointer over the document window. Rest the pointer over a button to see its name.

The document window is where you do most of your work. It gives you an approximate representation of your page as you add and delete elements. The title bar shows the document's title and file name. The toolbar lets you select the document view and enter the document title. In the bottom-left corner of the document window is the tag selector. The tag selector always starts from the <body> tag, hierarchically displaying HTML tags that apply to the currently selected element.

**TIP** *You can use the tag selector to select and navigate the elements in your page by using the elements' HTML tags. This tool allows you to move quickly through the page, to see what element you are working with, and to select other elements easily. Get used to working with the tag selector, as it will be particularly helpful when you begin working with tables in Lesson 4.*

The mini-launcher bar, located in the bottom-right corner of the document window, gives you immediate access to many panels while taking up minimal space on your screen. You'll become familiar with many other customizable options in the document window as you work through the lessons in this book.

TOOLBAR          DOCUMENT TITLE BAR          VIEW OPTIONS MENU

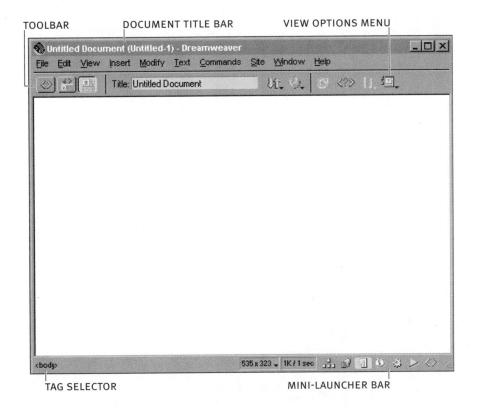

TAG SELECTOR                          MINI-LAUNCHER BAR

**2) Move the mouse pointer over the Objects panel. Rest the pointer over a button to see its name.**

The Objects panel contains many of the objects or elements that you can add to your page, including images, tables, special characters, forms, and frames. To insert an object, drag the object's icon from the Objects panel to its place in the document window. You can also place the insertion point in your document where the object should appear and click the object's icon in the panel. When you click the icon, the object appears in the document at the insertion point.

You can access several other panels from the category pop-up menu at the top of the Objects panel. The objects you need to create a form, for example, are in the Form Objects panel. You can also access these objects and elements through the Insert menu.

9

*Depending upon the element you select, a dialog box may appear, giving you options for the element's properties and placement. You can bypass most of those dialog boxes and insert a placeholder object instead. This method may be useful if you are working on pages for which photographs or artwork are forthcoming.*

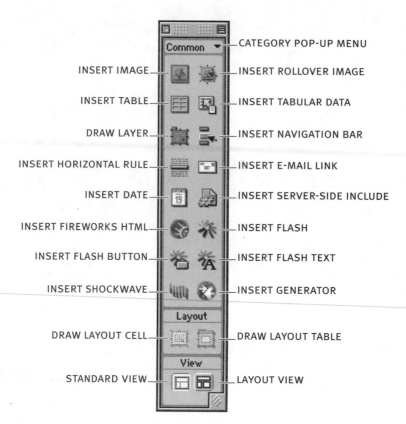

CATEGORY POP-UP MENU

INSERT IMAGE —————— —— INSERT ROLLOVER IMAGE

INSERT TABLE —————— —— INSERT TABULAR DATA

DRAW LAYER —————— —— INSERT NAVIGATION BAR

INSERT HORIZONTAL RULE —— —— INSERT E-MAIL LINK

INSERT DATE —————— —— INSERT SERVER-SIDE INCLUDE

INSERT FIREWORKS HTML —— —— INSERT FLASH

INSERT FLASH BUTTON —— —— INSERT FLASH TEXT

INSERT SHOCKWAVE —— —— INSERT GENERATOR

DRAW LAYOUT CELL —— —— DRAW LAYOUT TABLE

STANDARD VIEW —— —— LAYOUT VIEW

### 3) Move the mouse pointer over the property inspector. Rest the pointer over a button to see its name.

With the property inspector, you can view and change the attributes of selected text or of an object on the page. The inspector is context-sensitive—it changes based on what you have selected in the document window. Depending on the selected object, additional properties may be available but not visible. To see all the properties, click the expander arrow in the bottom-right corner of the inspector window.

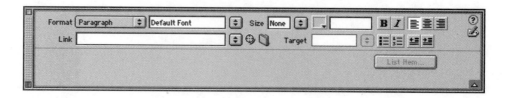

## WORKING WITH PANELS

Many of Dreamweaver's panels can be **docked**—combined in tabbed windows. Docking maximizes your screen area while giving you quick access to the panels you need.

### 1) Click the Reference panel to make it active. If it is not visible, choose Window › Reference.

The Reference panel is a new resource in Dreamweaver 4 that gives you quick access to information about specific tags, objects, or styles while you are working in code view. You will use the Reference panel later in this lesson while you edit HTML in code view.

### 2) Drag the Assets tab (located just to the right of the Reference tab) out of the window.

The Assets panel is now a separate window. You can undock any panel by dragging its tab out of a set of docked panels.

### 3) Drag the Assets panel toward the Reference panel.

Notice that the Assets panel snaps to the Reference panel. The document window and panels align to one another or to the sides of your screen. This arrangement helps you better manage your workspace.

### 4) Drag the Assets panel over the Reference panel. When the border of the Reference panel highlights, drop the Assets panel.

You have now rejoined the two panels into a docked set. You can separate or combine most of Dreamweaver's panels to create a custom workspace that fits your needs and working style.

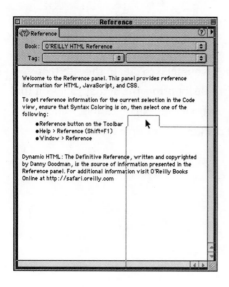

11

## ORGANIZING YOUR SITE

Before you begin creating your Web pages, you should have some idea what the pages will contain.

You should develop the concept first. Ask yourself and your client some basic questions: Why is the Web site needed? What are you trying to communicate? Who are the potential viewers of the pages? What do you want your visitors to take away with them?

Also consider what browsers your users are likely to have. Are they likely to have the most updated version with all the latest plug-ins? Or are they more likely to have older computers and older browsers? The browser question might determine whether you can use cascading style sheets or layers on your pages.

In addition, you need to develop an outline of the site. Web sites depend on file management; a Web site with poor file structure is confusing to navigate and hard to use. A good Web site should be intuitive and should create a positive user experience. To make such a site, plan its structure before you build any HTML documents. An outline or storyboard will give you an idea of the scope of the project. By developing the concept and outline at the beginning, you are taking the first step in setting up the file structure you need.

Finally, you have to gather the text and graphics for the Web pages. After you collect all the necessary materials, you are ready to start using Dreamweaver to create your site. For the lessons in this book, all the work described in this section has already been done for you.

## DEFINING A LOCAL SITE

Before you begin to create individual Web pages, you need to create the site that contains those pages. This local site on your hard disk mirrors the actual pages on the Web server. The local site is the structure you set up within the local root folder; it is where you do all your initial development and testing. To set up a local site, you need to create a folder on your hard drive.

### 1) Copy the DW4_Intro folder from the CD-ROM to your hard drive.

This folder contains all the files and folders you will use for the lessons in this book, and it will be the root folder of your local site. When you begin work on other sites, you will want to create individual root folders for each of those sites. The names of those folders can be the names of the sites or any names you choose.

**NOTE** *You should not save your local folder within the Dreamweaver application folder. If you ever needed to reinstall Dreamweaver, your work would be overwritten and lost.*

### 2) Choose Site > Define Sites.

The Define Sites dialog box opens. The dialog box displays all the sites you may have defined and lets you create new ones. You can also edit existing sites through this dialog box.

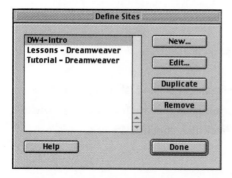

### 3) Click New to create a new site.

The Site Definition dialog box appears.

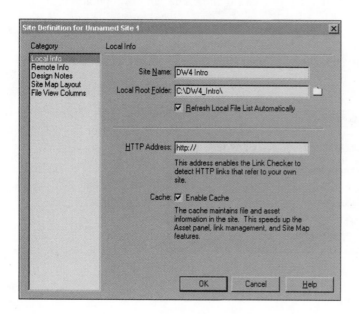

### 4) Type the name of the site in the Site Name text box.

The names you assign to your sites can be anything that identifies them. The names are for your reference only. For the purposes of this lesson, type *DW4 Intro* in the Site Name text box.

### 5) Click the folder icon next to the Local Root Folder text box.

The Local Root Folder text box specifies the folder on your hard drive where the files for this site are stored. This folder is the local equivalent of the root folder on the remote site. Dreamweaver will use this local root folder to determine the paths for documents, images, and links in your site. You will learn about paths and links in Lesson 3.

### 6) Locate the DW4_Intro folder on your hard drive.

For Windows: Select the DW4_Intro folder and click Open. Then click Select to use the DW4_Intro folder as your root folder.

For Macintosh: Select the DW4_Intro folder and click Select.

### 7) In the Site Definition dialog box, select Refresh Local File List Automatically.

When you check this checkbox, Dreamweaver updates the site list whenever you add a new file to the site folder. If you don't check this checkbox, you'll need to refresh the local files manually.

### 8) Select Enable Cache and click OK.

When you check the Enable Cache checkbox, a local cache is created, improving the speed of linking and site-management tasks. Although you usually will want to select this option, keep in mind that re-creating the cache can slow operations on very large sites.

### 9) If a message box appears, click OK; then click Done to close the Site Definition dialog box.

You should always create and work within local sites. If you don't, you may have problems with links, paths, and file management. (Dreamweaver's tools for these features are covered in later chapters of this book.) You can create a site by creating a new folder and designating it as your root folder, or you can create a copy of an existing site by selecting and designating as the root the main folder that contains the entire site.

## SPECIFYING PREVIEW BROWSERS

As you develop your Web pages, you will want to view your efforts in a browser—in fact, in several browsers. In Dreamweaver's Preferences dialog box, you can specify which browsers you want to use to preview your pages. To simplify the preview process, you can use keyboard shortcuts for viewing your pages in two browsers, called the primary and secondary browsers.

**1)  Choose File > Preview in Browser > Edit Browser List.**
The Preferences dialog box opens. When you click a browser name in the browser list text box, the checkboxes below the list will show whether it is the primary or secondary browser. If you have more than two browsers, it will leave both boxes unchecked to show that it is neither.

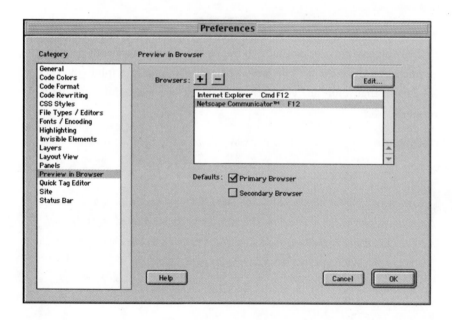

**TIP** *Alternatively, you can choose Edit > Preferences and select Preview in Browser in the Category list, located on the left side of the dialog box, to open the same Preferences dialog box.*

### 2) Click the plus (+) button to add a browser to the list.

When the dialog box appears, browse your hard drive to find a browser application. Check the Primary Browser checkbox if you want to launch this browser by pressing F12 when you preview your pages. Check the Secondary Browser checkbox if you want to preview your document by pressing Control+F12 (Windows) or Command+F12 (Macintosh). (You'll be using these shortcuts often, so memorize them now.)

To remove a browser from the list, select the browser name in the list and then click the minus (–) button.

To change a browser choice, select the browser name in the list. Then click Edit and locate a different browser.

### 3) Click OK when you are done adding browsers.

Dreamweaver's visual representation of your page simulates how it will appear in the browser. You will see differences in how the pages are displayed in different browsers, however, and you'll notice differences even between different versions

## CREATING AND SAVING A NEW PAGE

Whenever you create a new page, the first thing you should do is save your document.

### 1) Create a new empty page by choosing File > New.

Don't wait until you have text or graphics on the page to save—save your pages as soon as you open new documents. This way, when you do import graphics or other media, all the paths that reference where those elements are located in your site will be made properly.

In Windows, you can also choose File > New Window in the Site window to create a new page.

**NOTE** *Dreamweaver adds the extension .htm (Windows) or .html (Macintosh) to the file name automatically when you save. These are the default extensions, but either can be used. You can change this extension by choosing Edit > Preferences and selecting the General category. Make your change in the Add Extension when Saving text box.*

**2) Choose File > Save to save the file. Locate the folder Lesson_01_Text where you will save this file. Type *surf_hawaii.html* in the File Name text box at the bottom of the Save As dialog box and click Save.**

**TIP** *For Windows users only, if your system is set to automatically add the appropriate extension after you save, you do not need to include the .htm in the File Name text box.*

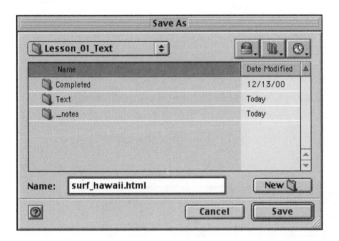

Naming your files for use on a Web server is a little different from naming your files for your hard drive. First, you need to know what operating system the server will be using—Windows NT, UNIX, or Macintosh. The naming structure is different on each of these platforms. UNIX, for example, is case-sensitive, which means that myfile.htm does not equal MYFILE.HTM. Your best bet, if you don't know the server type, is to use lowercase names for your files. Here are some other rules to follow:

Don't use spaces in file names. Use the underscore or dash character to simulate a space to separate words.

Use letters and numbers but no special characters, such as %, *, or /.

Avoid beginning your file names with numbers.

Make sure that you don't leave a space at the end of the file name. If you do, the browsers substitute %20 for the spaces.

**TIP** *Keep folder names short. Remember that the folder name becomes part of the URL you type to get to the page. You should follow the naming guidelines in this section for folders as well as files.*

## GIVING THE PAGE A TITLE

Every HTML document should have a title. The title, used primarily for document identification, is displayed in a browser's title bar and as the bookmark name. Choose a short phrase that describes the document's purpose. The title can be any length, but you can crop it if it's too long to fit in the browser's title bar.

Get into the habit of adding the title to each page that you create before you add text or graphics to the page. If you forget, Dreamweaver makes the title "Untitled Document"—and you should not keep that page name.

**1)  In the Title text box at the top of the document window for surf_hawaii.html, type *Surfer's Paradise*. Press Enter (Windows) or Return (Macintosh) or click in the document.**

If you don't see the Title text box at the top of the document window (below the menu bar), choose View > Toolbar.

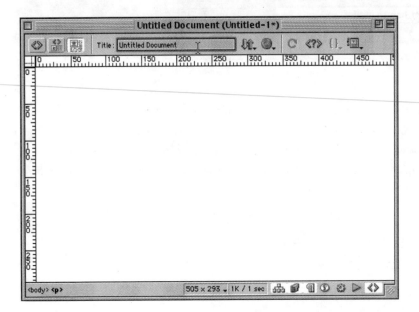

**NOTE**  *Dreamweaver gives you several visual cues if you haven't titled your page. Look at the document title bar, which displays the title and the file name. If you see Untitled Document (filename.htm), you haven't titled your document. You'll also see Untitled Document in the title area of the document window.*

## SPECIFYING A BACKGROUND COLOR

In Dreamweaver, you can change the background color of a page easily by using a panel of colors known as the Web-safe color palette. You access that panel from the Page Properties dialog box to change the background color for surf_hawaii.html in this exercise.

### 1) Choose Modify > Page Properties.

The Page Properties dialog box appears.

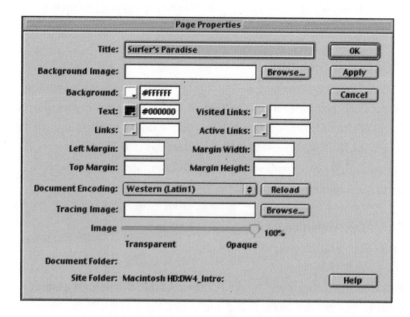

### 2) Click the color box next to the Background text box. In the color picker, move the cursor over a color swatch.

A color picker opens. Notice that when the panel opens, the cursor changes to an eyedropper.

The swatch's hexadecimal equivalent is shown at the top of the color picker.

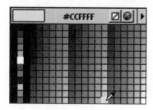

**NOTE** *You can also move the eyedropper over the document window and choose a color from items there such as text and images.*

**3) Click a pale blue color to select it, or type *CCFFFF* in the Background text box.**

You do not need to include the number sign (#) before the hex color code.

**4) Click Apply to view the color change in your document.**

Choosing Apply allows you to view your changes without closing the Page Properties dialog box.

**TIP** *To view more colors, click the arrow located in the top-right corner of the color picker and choose a color picker from the pop-up menu. Keep in mind that other color pickers may not contain cross-platform Web-safe colors.*

## USING A BACKGROUND GRAPHIC

You'll add a background graphic to the surf_hawaii.html in this exercise. A background graphic generally is a small graphic that tiles behind your page by repeating itself to the width and height of the browser window. You can define both a background color and a background graphic for your pages. On slow connections or in slow browsers, you may see the background color displayed first. The background graphic then appears and remains on-screen, overriding the background color.

**1) Choose Modify > Page Properties.**

The Page Properties dialog box appears.

**2) Click Browse next to the Background Image text box. Locate the fish.gif graphic in the Images folder to use as your background and click OK.**

You see an example of a background image tiling in the document window.

You don't need the background graphic for the rest of the exercises in this lesson, so follow the remaining steps to delete it.

**NOTE** *If you have not saved your file, the entire path name of the graphic is displayed in the text box. When you save your file, the path name changes to the location of the graphic relative to the HTML file. It is always best, however, to save your file before importing any graphics—even background images. You learn more about path names in Lessons 2 and 3.*

**3) To delete the background graphic, choose Modify > Page Properties to display the Page Properties dialog box. Delete the file name in the Background text box and then click OK.**

Your changes are applied to the document.

## SPECIFYING THE DEFAULT FONT COLOR

When you change the background color or add a background graphic, you might also need to change the color of the text that is displayed. Black text won't display on a black background, for example. In the following steps, you'll change the font color in the surf_hawaii.html document.

**1) Choose Modify > Page Properties.**

The Page Properties dialog box appears.

**2) Click the color box next to the Text text field.**

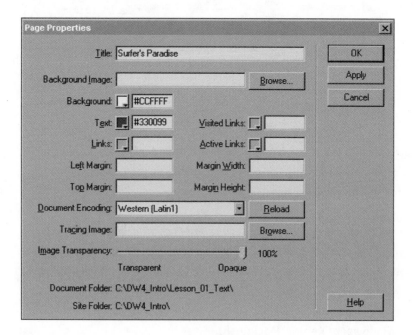

A color picker opens.

**3) Select a color for your text—dark blue would look good—and click OK.**

You could also type the hex color code directly into the text box. The Page Properties dialog box closes, and you return to your document.

## PLACING TEXT ON A PAGE

In this exercise, you'll add some text to your page and see the changed color.

You can add text to surf_hawaii.html by typing it directly in the page.

**1)  In the document window, type *Hawaii – Surfer's Paradise*. From the property inspector's Format drop-down menu, choose Heading 3.**

You have tagged the text as a level3 heading.

HTML has six levels of headings—numbered 1 through 6—with heading 1 having the largest font size.

Headings are displayed in larger or bolder fonts than normal body text. Tagging a paragraph as a heading automatically generates a space below the heading. You cannot control this spacing.

**NOTE** *In many documents, the first heading is identical to the title. In multiple-part documents, the text of the first heading should be related information, such as a chapter title. The title tag should identify the document in a wider context (including both the book title and the chapter title, for example).*

**2)  Press Enter (Windows) or Return (Macintosh).**

You have created another level3 heading line by default.

**3)  From the Format drop-down menu in the property inspector, choose Paragraph.**

You've tagged the line as a paragraph—that is, regular body text.

**4)  Save the file.**

Whenever you modify your document, notice the asterisk (*) that Dreamweaver inserts near the file name at the top of the document window. This asterisk is a reminder that the file has been modified but not yet saved. The asterisk disappears once you save the document.

## IMPORTING TEXT

You can add text to a page by copying and pasting from an existing document. If the text is from an application that supports drag-and-drop copying (Microsoft Word for Macintosh, for example), you can open both Dreamweaver and that application and then copy and paste or drag the text into Dreamweaver.

Dreamweaver can also open files created in word processing or page layout applications, provided that those files were saved as ASCII text files. For example, Dreamweaver can open a Microsoft Word document if you save the file in Microsoft Word as text (.txt) or HTML. Text files (.txt files) always open in code view in Dreamweaver. After you open a text file in Dreamweaver, you can copy and paste the text you need into another file. Alternatively, you can save the text file you opened in Dreamweaver as a new HTML file, but you will need to add the .htm or .html extension when you save the new document.

Simple document formatting, such as paragraphs and line breaks, can be retained, but you need to know a little about the differences in the ASCII format on the Windows and Macintosh platforms. Files created in Windows use an invisible control character called a **line feed** to indicate a new line within the text. Macintosh computers do not use the line-feed character. If you open a Windows text file in SimpleText on a Macintosh, you'll see a small rectangle at the beginning of each new paragraph, indicating the line-feed character.

If you open a Macintosh text file in Windows, all the paragraphs merge because of the missing line-feed character.

Knowing this situation, you can change your preferences to match the file format of text files you receive and want to open in Dreamweaver.

**1) Choose Edit > Preferences to display the Preferences dialog box and select Code Format in the Category list. From the Line Breaks drop-down menu, choose CR LF (Windows).**

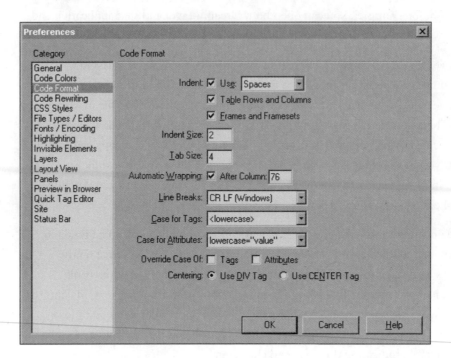

In the Line Breaks menu, your choices are CR LF (Windows), CR (Macintosh), and LF (UNIX). If you are using a Macintosh, change this setting to CR LF (Windows). If you are working in Windows, make sure that you have the same setting.

**2) Click OK.**

The Preferences dialog box closes.

**3) Open Lesson_01_Text/Text/surfing.txt. Select and copy all the text. Then open the surf_hawaii.htm file. Position the insertion point below the "Hawaii – Surfer's Paradise" heading and insert the copied text.**

You can use the Edit menu to copy and paste the text (choose Edit > Copy and/or Edit > Paste), or you can use the familiar keyboard commands: Ctrl+C (Windows) or Command+C (Macintosh) and Ctrl+V (Windows) or Command+V (Macintosh).

**4) Save the file.**

When you use this method to import text, you may need to check that your document uses the correct kind of line breaks (paragraph breaks vs. line breaks), as discussed in steps 1 and 2 of the next exercise.

## CREATING A LINE BREAK

If you want to create a single line break in the text, you need to insert a line-break character. This technique is useful for an address line, for example, when you want a new line for each line in the address without the extra spacing of a paragraph.

**1) In surf_hawaii.html, find the paragraph that begins "Besides helping you find...." Position the insertion point before the text "Big Kahuna Surf and Swim Shop." Then press Shift+Enter (Windows) or Shift+Return (Macintosh).**

The text after the insertion point moves to the next line. A new paragraph has not been created, so no additional spacing appears between the two lines.

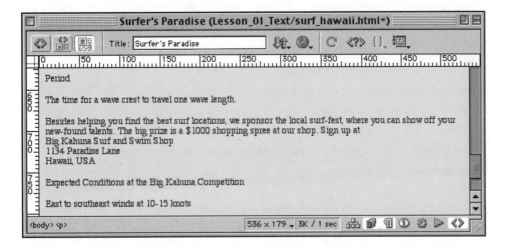

**2) Move the text "1134 Paradise Lane" to the next line and "Hawaii, USA" to a new line. Position the insertion point before the text "Sign up at" and press Enter (Windows) or Return (Macintosh) to insert a new paragraph.**

If you use two line breaks, you can simulate the appearance of a new paragraph. Because you are not actually creating a new paragraph, however, you may have difficulty when you apply formatting to it.

## CENTERING AND INDENTING TEXT

You may want to center some text, such as a heading, to make it more prominent.

**1) In surf_hawaii.html, position the insertion point in the heading "Hawaii – Surfer's Paradise." Click the Align Center button in the property inspector.**

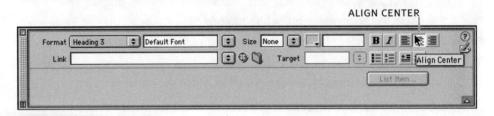

The heading is centered.

Many times, you'll want to indent the text on the page. You can use the Text Indent and Text Outdent buttons in the property inspector for this purpose. When you use Text Indent the text is indented at the both left and right margins of the page. You cannot control the amount of indentation because the browser automatically determines it.

**2) Select the first six body paragraphs of surf_hawaii.htm and click Text Indent in the property inspector or choose Text > Indent.**

All the text on the page is indented. But your page might look better if only the list in the middle of the page were indented. In the following steps, you'll remove the indent from the first two paragraphs.

**3) Select the first two body paragraphs of the document. Click the Text Outdent button in the property inspector or choose Text > Outdent. Save the file and preview it in the browser.**

The four paragraphs you formatted appear indented in the browser window.

**TIP** *If you try to indent one paragraph and nearby paragraphs become indented as well, check to see whether you are using paragraph breaks or double breaks. Place the mouse pointer at the beginning of the paragraph you want to indent. Then press Delete (Macintosh) or Backspace (Windows) until you reach the end of the preceding paragraph, and press Return (Macintosh) or Enter (Windows) to create a paragraph break.*

## MAKING LISTS

Dreamweaver creates two types of basic lists: ordered and unordered. An **ordered list** consists of list items that are ordered numerically or alphabetically. You have the option of using Arabic or Roman numerals or uppercase or lowercase letters. **Unordered lists** are often called bulleted lists because each list item has a bullet in front of it. The bullet symbol Dreamweaver displays by default can be changed to a disc, a circle, or a square.

In this exercise, you'll make two lists: one ordered and one unordered. Then you'll revise the list styles by using the List Properties dialog box.

**1) In surf_hawaii.html, select the four lines of text "Sunset Beach, Oahu"; "Waimea Bay"; "South Shore, Oahu"; and "Pipeline." Click the Ordered List button in the property inspector or choose Text > List > Ordered List.**

The selected text is indented and numbered.

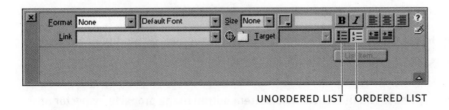

UNORDERED LIST    ORDERED LIST

You can change the numbering scheme of ordered lists by modifying the list's properties. You'll do this in the next step.

**2) Click any line in the list. Click the List Item button in the property inspector or choose Text > List > Properties.**

Select only one line in the list. If you select multiple lines, the List Item button is dimmed and not available for you to use. If the List Item button is not visible, click the expander arrow in the bottom-right corner of the property inspector.

The List Properties dialog box opens.

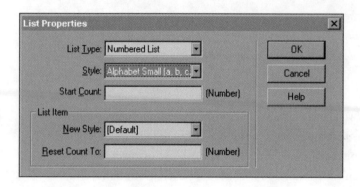

**3) From the Style drop-down menu, choose Alphabet Small (a,b,c). Then click OK.**

All items in the list are alphabetized.

Creating and modifying an unordered list is a similar process. You'll try it in the following steps.

**4) Select the text starting with "East to southeast winds" and ending with "Water temperature at 76 degrees Fahrenheit." Click the Unordered List button in the property inspector or choose Text > List > Unordered List.**

The selected text is indented and bulleted.

You can change the default bullet symbol of unordered lists by modifying the list's properties, just as you did with the ordered list.

**5) Click any line in the list. Click the List Item button in the property inspector or choose Text > List > Properties.**

The List Properties dialog box opens.

28

## 6) From the Style drop-down menu, choose Square. Click OK.

All items in the list now use the square bullet symbol.

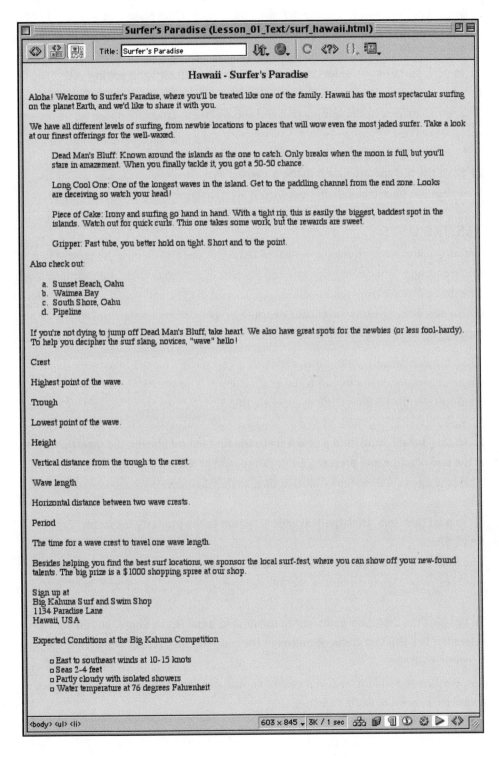

## MAKING DEFINITION LISTS

A **definition list** consists of a series of terms and their definitions. The word or term to be defined is left-justified; the definition is indented and placed on the next line. For this type of list to work, a term and its definition must be separate paragraphs.

**1) In surf_hawaii.html, select the text starting with "Crest" and ending with "The time for a wave crest to travel one wave length." Choose Text > List > Definition List.**

The terms are now at the left margin, and their indented definitions are on succeeding lines.

**2) Save the file and preview it in the browser.**

Now that you have created all these lists, it's a good time to save your document.

## NESTING LISTS

You can create lists within lists, or **nested lists**. You can also change the type of lists that are nested. You can have an ordered list within a definition list, for example. By default, bullets are displayed as filled circles, open circles, and squares (in that order) as you nest lists. Dreamweaver calls the bullet types default, bullet, and square. The corresponding HTML terminology is circle, disc, and square.

Some browsers display open square bullets. Netscape 4.7 for the Macintosh displays open squares, for example, but Internet Explorer 5.0 for the Macintosh displays filled squares. In Windows, the squares are filled.

**1) In surf_hawaii.html, add a new item to the first list by placing the insertion point at the end of a line and pressing Enter (Windows) or Return (Macintosh).**

This step adds another item after that line, at the same level.

**2) To nest this item, click the Text Indent button in the property inspector. Type *North Shore*.**

The item indents to the next level. You don't need to have a nested list in this file, however, so you'll get rid of it in the following steps.

**3) Position the insertion point within the nested item, North Shore, but do not select it. Click the Text Outdent button in the property inspector. Then delete the North Shore item.**

Just as when you indent text, you cannot control or adjust the spacing of outdented text, lists, or nested lists.

## CHARACTER FORMATTING

Occasionally, you need a word or phrase to look different from the surrounding text. You might want a word to be bold or italicized to set it apart from other text.

**In surf_hawaii.html, select the word "Crest" in the definition list you created in the preceding section. Click the Bold button in the property inspector or choose Text › Style › Bold.**

The selected text now has bold formatting. You can apply italic formatting in the same way.

## REPEATING A COMMAND

Many times, you repeat the most recent formatting you did on another paragraph or other selected text. The Repeat command reduces that task to a simple keystroke. The first two items listed in the Edit menu are the Undo and Repeat commands. You'll want to remember these keyboard shortcuts:

Undo—Ctrl+Z (Windows) and Command+Z (Macintosh)

Repeat—Ctrl+Y (Windows) and Command+Y (Macintosh)

**1)  In surf_hawaii.html, select the word "Trough" in the definition list. Press Ctrl+Y (Windows) or Command+Y (Macintosh).**

Because you used the Bold command most recently, it is applied to the selected text.

**2)  Repeat the bold formatting on the other terms in the definition list.**

You can also access the Undo and Redo commands through the history palette.

## CHANGING THE FONT

To make your page more interesting and easier to read, you may want to change the font used to display the text. Although a great deal of information is available concerning how type is used for print, not all of that knowledge translates to the Web. You have to consider the fact that users are free to change the screen size or to change the font size and color of the text. The way type flows on a page can change from user to user. Also, a dramatic difference occurs between font sizes in Windows and on a Macintosh. Macintosh computers display text approximately 75% smaller than the same text on Windows computers.

If you are accustomed to print, you might be frustrated by the lack of typographic control, such as line and letter spacing, in HTML. You also can't control widows (single words on a line) in Web text, and you can't control line spacing in paragraphs. You should remember that text support on the Web is still very primitive. You need to work within the constraints of the medium.

**TIP** *Generally, sans-serif fonts are easier to read on a computer screen than serif fonts.*

You can change the font for the entire page or for selected text on the page. In the following exercise, you change the font of a single line.

**1) In surf_hawaii.html, select the text "Hawaii – Surfer's Paradise." From the property inspector's Font drop-down menu, choose Arial, Helvetica, sans-serif.**

For users to see your page as you designed it, the font you choose must be installed on the user's computer. Do not make the assumption that all fonts are loaded on everyone's computer. The combinations of fonts (such as Arial, Helvetica, sans serif) will instruct the browser to change the selected text to another font, depending on the fonts installed on the computer. If the first choice in the font list is not available, the browser attempts to use the second choice and then the third. If none of the fonts in the list are available on the user's computer, the text is displayed in the browser's default font.

The font combinations are useful but may not always include the specific fonts you want to use. You can change the font combination by choosing Edit Font List from the property inspector's Font drop-down menu or by choosing Text > Font > Edit Font List to display the Edit Font List dialog box.

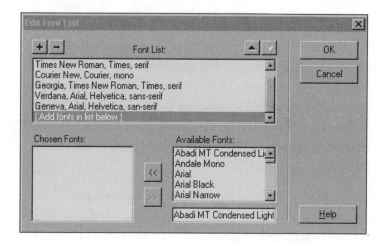

You can choose among several font options. To add or remove fonts, select the font and then click the directional buttons between the Chosen Fonts list and the Available Fonts list. To add or remove a font combination, click the plus (+) or minus (–) button in the top-left corner of the dialog box.

To add a font that is not installed on your system, type the font name in the text box below the Available Fonts list, and click the directional arrow to add it to the combination. Adding a font that is not installed on your system is useful, for example, for specifying a Windows-only font when you are authoring on a Macintosh.

To move a font combination up or down in the list, click the directional arrow buttons in the top-right corner of the dialog box. You can change the font of multiple paragraphs, as well as a single line or phrase, which you'll do in the following step.

**2) Select the remainder of the text on the page. From the property inspector's Font drop-down menu, choose Arial, Helvetica, sans-serif.**
All the text now has the same font.

**3) Save the file and preview it in the browser.**
The text will now display with the fonts you selected in your browser, depending on what fonts you have installed on your computer.

**TIP** *If you don't like a font, you can remove the font settings and return the type to its default setting. Simply select the text that uses the font you want to remove. In the property inspector, choose Default Font from the Font drop-down menu, or choose Text > Font > Default Font.*

## CHANGING FONT SIZE

In HTML, the options for changing the font size on the page are limited. You have more control when you use cascading style sheets (CSS), which are covered in Lesson 11.

**1) Select the four indented paragraphs near the top of the page. From the property inspector's Size drop-down menu, choose –1.**
You'll notice the sizes are listed as 1 through 7, +1 through +7, and –1 through –7. Selecting just the number (1 is smallest, 7 is largest) sets the absolute size. Picking a plus or minus number chooses the font size relative to the base size of the font. For example, +1 makes the font size one size larger than the base size.

The default base size for text in your browser is 3. If you choose +3 for the font size, you are effectively changing the size to 6 (3+3). The largest size for the font is 7, and the smallest is 1; any font size larger than 7 displays as 7. If you set the font size to +6, 3+6 is larger than 7 and displays as 7.

> **TIP** *You can also choose Text > Size, Text > Size Increase, or Text > Size Decrease to pick the size from the submenus.*

## CHANGING FONT COLOR

You can easily change the color of your text in Dreamweaver.

**1) Select the text "Hawaii – Surfer's Paradise." Click the Text color box in the property inspector.**

The color picker appears, with the Web-safe color palette selected.

TEXT COLOR

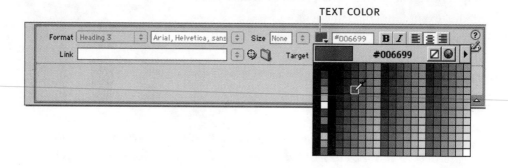

**2) Choose a blue color (#006699).**

The Color Picker window closes automatically after you click a color, and Dreamweaver applies the color immediately. You can also access the color picker by choosing Text > Color, which gives you access to several Color Picker windows.

## SAVING COLORS AS FAVORITES

All colors used in your site are located in the Assets panel. To ensure that the colors you use are consistent across your site, you can save commonly used colors in the Assets panel as favorites.

**1)  In the Assets panel, click the Colors icon in the left column to see the asset colors.**

**TIP**   *If the Assets panel is not open, choose Window > Assets.*

COLORS

SITE SELECT

LIST OF SITE COLORS

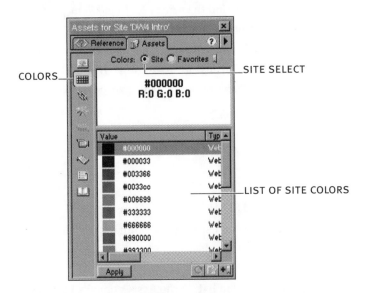

**2)  At the top of the Assets panel, click the Site radio button. Select #006699 from the list of colors. Click the Add to Favorites icon in the bottom-right corner of the Assets panel.**

The blue color of your text is now one of your favorites.

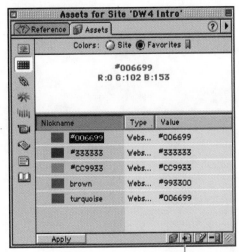

ADD TO FAVORITES

**LEARNING THE BASICS**

## CREATING HTML STYLES

As you design your Web pages, you will want to use font changes to make your pages more interesting. You can easily change the font, including its size and color, but if you want to use the same color, the same font, and the same size for all your pages, you would have to remember the settings from page to page. HTML styles save the text and paragraph formatting from selected text, making it easy for you to apply that style to other paragraphs in your document or to any document in your site. If you change or delete an HTML style, text originally formatted with that style does not change.

**N O T E**  *To apply formatting that updates your pages, use cascading style sheets, which are covered in Lesson 11.*

The following exercises demonstrate using HTML styles on a page. You will format some text, define several HTML styles, and then apply those formatting styles to other portions of the document.

**1)  Select "Crest," the first term in the definition list. In the Assets panel's Favorites list, select #006699 and click Apply at the bottom of the Assets panel.**

You applied a bold format to the word "Crest" earlier. Now you've changed the color to blue.

The remaining definition terms on this page need the same formatting, as will any other lists you create in the site. You'll use an HTML style for this purpose.

**2)  Choose Window > HTML Styles.**

The HTML Styles panel opens.

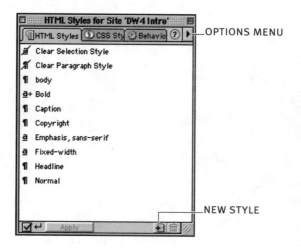

OPTIONS MENU

NEW STYLE

**3) Click the New Style button at the bottom of the panel, or choose New from the Options drop-down menu.**

The Define HTML Style dialog box appears.

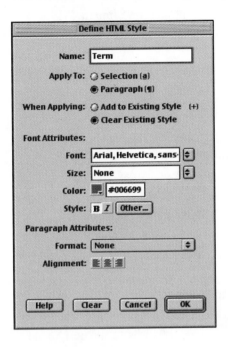

**4) Type *Term* in the Name text box. In the Apply To list, select Paragraph. Then click OK.**

The dialog box closes, and your new style appears in the HTML Styles panel.

**NOTE** *The dialog box lets you make any necessary changes in the format of the styles. Any changes you make in this dialog box, however, are not applied to the original text. If you want to make changes in the original text, you need to apply the style directly to that text.*

**5) Select the heading "Hawaii – Surfer's Paradise." Make a new HTML style for this paragraph, naming the style Level3. Click OK.**

This paragraph already has color applied and is centered on the page.

**6) Select the text "Dead Man's Bluff." Change the font and the text color and make the words bold. Make a new HTML style for this text, naming the style Boldit. In the Apply To list, choose Selection.**

Applying a style to a selection means you have to highlight all the appropriate text before applying the style. Applying a style to a paragraph means you have to place the insertion point within the paragraph—you don't have to select each word in the paragraph.

37

## APPLYING HTML STYLES

Now that you have several HTML styles defined, it's time to try applying them.

**1) With the HTML Styles panel open, select the definition term "Trough."**

In this case, the style to be applied is a paragraph, so make sure that you place the insertion point within the text.

**2) Click Term in the HTML Styles panel.**

The style is applied to the paragraph.

**3) Apply the Term style to the remaining definition terms in the list.**

The style is applied to the rest of the terms.

**4) Select the text "Long Cool One." In the HTML Styles panel, click Boldit.**

This time you are applying a selection style, so make sure that you highlight each word. After you click Boldit, the style is applied to the selected text.

**5) Apply the Boldit style to "Piece of Cake" and "Gripper."**

Selection styles like the one you are using are designated by a lowercase, underlined "a" in the HTML styles panel. Paragraph styles, on the other hand, are designated by a ¶ (paragraph) symbol.

**6) Select the text "Expected Conditions at the Big Kahuna Competition" and apply the Level3 style.**

You have applied to your document a variety of HTML styles that can help you save time and maintain consistency throughout your site.

The HTML styles you create can be used in other projects or shared with other users. When you create an HTML style, a file named Styles.xml is saved in a folder named Library. You can copy the Styles.xml file and move it to other site folders.

## EDITING HTML STYLES

After you've created styles, you can use the Define HTML Style dialog box to revise or delete them.

**1) Click the HTML Styles panel.**

Clicking the HTML Styles panel makes it active.

If the HTML Styles panel is not visible, choose Window > HTML Styles. Make sure that no text is selected in the document window.

**2) Right-click (Windows) or Control-click (Macintosh) the Level3 style name in the panel. Choose Edit from the drop-down menu.**

The Define HTML Style dialog box opens.

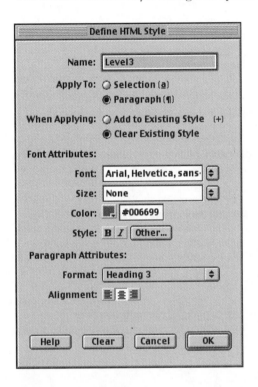

**TIP** *You can also double-click a style name to open the Define HTML Style dialog box.*

The Define HTML Style dialog box allows you to edit or delete styles. If you make a change, such as Font Attributes, and click OK, any new selections created with the style (or selections to which you apply the style) reflect the change you made.

**NOTE** *The change you make in a style does not affect the current text that has that formatting. If you want current text to reflect the new formatting, you have to reapply the style.*

Deleting a style can be a little trickier. First, you must make sure that no text is selected in the document and that the Auto Apply checkbox in the bottom-left corner of the HTML Styles panel is not checked. Then you have to select the style you want to delete and click the trashcan icon in the bottom-right corner of the panel.

If you forget to turn off the Auto Apply option and have any text selected, you might see that text on the page change to the HTML style you selected to delete. If this happens, clear the text formatting by using the following steps.

### 3) Select the formatted text.

If you are clearing a paragraph style, you can place the insertion point anywhere in the paragraph.

### 4) In the HTML Styles panel, select Clear Paragraph Style or Clear Selection Style.

All formatting is removed, regardless of how it was applied.

## ADDING SPECIAL CHARACTERS

When you work in Dreamweaver, you sometimes need characters and other information that you cannot access directly from the keyboard. These special characters have specific HTML codes or alternative keyboard commands that may be difficult to remember.

### 1) Click the arrow at the top of the Objects panel and choose Characters from the drop-down menu.

The Character Objects panel appears. This panel contains the most commonly used special characters.

### 2) From the Character Objects panel, drag the copyright character to the bottom of the page. To the right of the copyright character, type *2000, Compass Adventure Travel*.

COPYRIGHT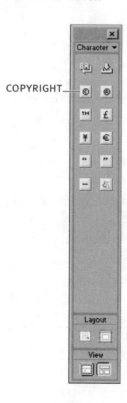

The Character Objects panel doesn't provide an all-encompassing list. If the character you want to use isn't available in this panel, you can still select it by choosing the Insert Other Characters icon or Insert > Special Characters > Other. The following steps tell you how.

### 3) Click the Insert Other Characters icon or choose Insert > Special Characters > Other.

The Insert Other Character dialog box opens.

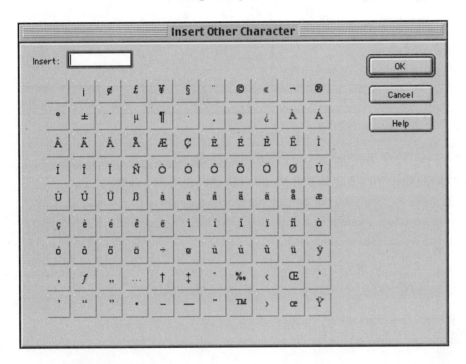

### 4) Click the character you want to use, and then click OK.

The character appears on the page.

**NOTE** *Other special characters are listed in the appendix. Type the HTML code for the special character in the Insert text box and click OK.*

## SWITCHING DOCUMENT VIEWS

As you develop your pages, you may need to view the HTML source code generated by Dreamweaver. Perhaps a stray line break is ruining the effect you are trying to achieve, but you can't locate it in the document window. By looking at the HTML source code, you can find and remove the line break easily.

Dreamweaver gives you three views of your document: design view, which shows all the objects (text, images, tables, and so on) that you have added to your page; code view, which shows only the HTML source code; and a combination of both code and design views. In the following exercise, you'll look at each of these views.

### 1) If the toolbar is not visible, choose View > Toolbar.

The toolbar is displayed at the top of the document window.

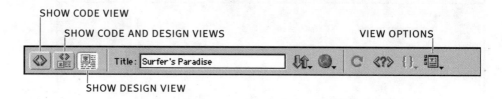

SHOW CODE VIEW

SHOW CODE AND DESIGN VIEWS

VIEW OPTIONS

Title: Surfer's Paradise

SHOW DESIGN VIEW

### 2) Click the Code View button in the toolbar or choose View > Code.

In code view, you don't see the visual elements of the page as they would actually appear in a browser window. Instead, you see the HTML code in a text editor that includes controls for extensive coding.

The Refresh Design View feature updates the design view (the visual representation of your page) to reflect any changes you make in code view.

The Reference feature allows you to select a tag and use the Reference panel to obtain more information on what the tag does—a good way to learn more about HTML.

The Code Navigation feature lets you work with JavaScript or VBScript functions. You'll learn more in Lesson 5 about how you can choose the functions from this drop-down menu or use it to set break points for testing your scripts.

The View Options menu provides options that adjust the display of code view. These options are different depending on the view you are using. You can add line numbers for each line of code, enable wrapping to eliminate horizontal scrolling and make the code easier to view, and so on. You can customize any of these options by choosing Edit > Preferences > Code Format.

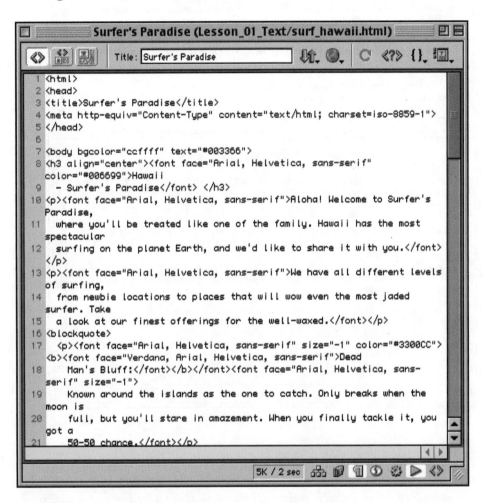

```html
1  <html>
2  <head>
3  <title>Surfer's Paradise</title>
4  <meta http-equiv="Content-Type" content="text/html; charset=iso-8859-1">
5  </head>
6
7  <body bgcolor="ccffff" text="#003366">
8  <h3 align="center"><font face="Arial, Helvetica, sans-serif" color="#006699">Hawaii
9    - Surfer's Paradise</font> </h3>
10 <p><font face="Arial, Helvetica, sans-serif">Aloha! Welcome to Surfer's Paradise,
11   where you'll be treated like one of the family. Hawaii has the most spectacular
12   surfing on the planet Earth, and we'd like to share it with you.</font> </p>
13 <p><font face="Arial, Helvetica, sans-serif">We have all different levels of surfing,
14   from newbie locations to places that will wow even the most jaded surfer. Take
15   a look at our finest offerings for the well-waxed.</font></p>
16 <blockquote>
17   <p><font face="Arial, Helvetica, sans-serif" size="-1" color="#3300CC"><b><font face="Verdana, Arial, Helvetica, sans-serif">Dead
18     Man's Bluff:</font></b></font><font face="Arial, Helvetica, sans-serif" size="-1">
19     Known around the islands as the one to catch. Only breaks when the moon is
20     full, but you'll stare in amazement. When you finally tackle it, you got a
21     50-50 chance.</font></p>
```

5K / 2 sec

**NOTE** *You can also open the code inspector, which gives you the same options and controls as code view. The difference is that the inspector opens in a separate window.*

**3) Click the Code and Design Views button in the toolbar or choose View › Code and Design.**

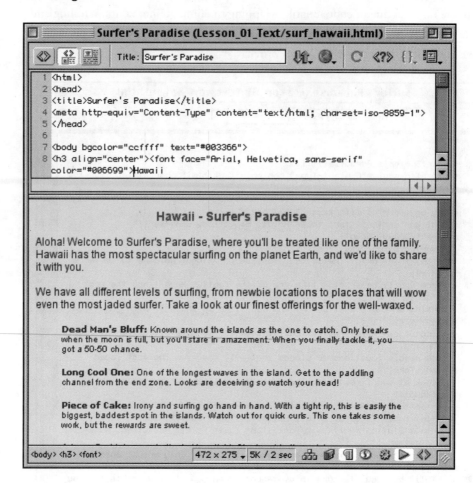

In this view, you can see both the design and the code that creates the code. You can resize the code pane by dragging the border between the design and code panes. To change the location of the code pane, click the View Options button in the toolbar (located at the right end), and choose Design View on Top from the drop-down menu. This menu also contains other options for adjusting the view, including rulers, visual aids, and the grid.

**4) Click the Design View button in the toolbar or choose View › Design.**

Your screen changes to design view, showing all the visual elements of your page approximately as they will appear in the browser. As in the other document views, you can access several view options through the toolbar.

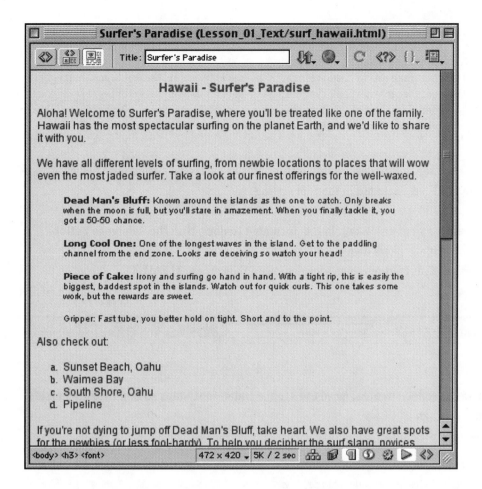

In the following exercise, you'll format some text and then change the HTML inserted by Dreamweaver.

### EDITING HTML IN CODE VIEW

You can edit the HTML by hand, and Dreamweaver will not overwrite those changes. If a change is made that appears to be wrong, Dreamweaver will highlight it to call the code to your attention. There may be many times when you need to adjust the code by hand, as demonstrated in the following steps.

**1) Select the list from Sunset Beach to Pipeline. View the page in Microsoft Internet Explorer. Look carefully at the font for the numbering.**

The font is different from the text. Netscape Communicator displays the font as expected. In this exercise, you will change the placement of the font tags so that you get the same result in Internet Explorer and Netscape.

**2) Look at the HTML code. You should see the following:**

```
<ol type="a">
<li><font face="Arial, Helvetica, sans-serif">Sunset Beach, Oahu</font></li>
<li><font face="Arial, Helvetica, sans-serif">Waimea Bay</font></li>
<li><font face="Arial, Helvetica, sans-serif">South Shore, Oahu</font></li>
<li><font face="Arial, Helvetica, sans-serif">Pipeline</font></li>
</ol>
```

The <li> tag, which defines the list numbers or letters, is outside the <font> tag and therefore is not included in the font styling.

**3) Select a single <li> tag. In the document toolbar, click the Reference button.**

The Reference panel displays information about the tag have selected and its function. This feature is a good way to learn more about HTML.

REFERENCE BUTTON

**4) In the code-view area, move the <font> and </font> tags so that they are outside the <li> tags.**

The result should look like this:

```
<ol type="a">
<font face="Arial, Helvetica, sans-serif"><li>Sunset Beach, Oahu</li></font>
<font face="Arial, Helvetica, sans-serif"><li>Waimea Bay</li></font>
<font face="Arial, Helvetica, sans-serif"><li>South Shore, Oahu</li></font>
<font face="Arial, Helvetica, sans-serif"><li>Pipeline</li></font>
</ol>
```

**5) View your page in Internet Explorer and see the results.**

If you make a mistake while editing HTML, Dreamweaver does not correct the mistake, but it highlights the errors in bright yellow. You have to then make the corrections yourself. This feature is one of Dreamweaver's advantages (known as RoundTrip HTML), because you can add special tags that your Web server recognizes, but that are not standard HTML, and Dreamweaver will leave them alone.

## CLEANING UP WORD HTML

You may get content for your pages from a variety of sources. Clients or colleagues might send text or changes by e-mail or send the content in a Microsoft Word file. If the format of the Word document is fairly simple, you can use the copy-and-paste method to import your text into Dreamweaver. If the Word document has formatting such as bullets or tables, you may want to save the document as a Web page (choose File > Save As Web Page in Word 97 or later) and open the resulting HTML file in Dreamweaver. Word may insert some unnecessary tags, however. You can clean up this code in Dreamweaver in one step. The tags that Dreamweaver removes are required to display the page in Word but are not needed in HTML or the browser.

**1) Choose File > Import > Import Word HTML.**

The Select Word HTML File to Import dialog box opens.

**2) Select the Biking_Adventures.htm file from Lesson_01_Text/Text and click Open.**

This HTML file was saved from a Word 2000 document. Dreamweaver opens the file and then opens the Clean Up Word HTML dialog box automatically.

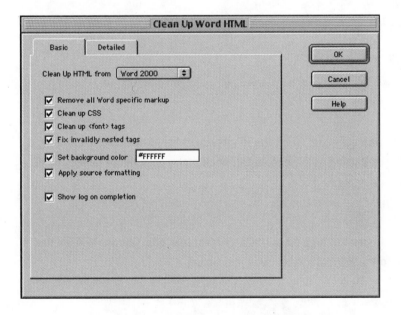

Dreamweaver attempts to determine what version of Word was used to create the HTML. If Dreamweaver is unable to determine the version, you need to choose the correct version from the drop-down menu. For this exercise, choose Word 2000.

The dialog box has two tabs, Basic and Detailed, with several options to check for each. For this exercise, you can use the default setting (all options checked).

### 3) Click OK.

Dreamweaver displays a dialog box listing all the changes that it made.

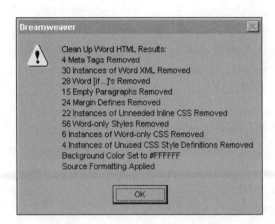

### 4) Click OK again to close the dialog box. Save and close the file.

**TIP** *You can also open the Clean Up Word HTML dialog box by choosing Commands > Clean Up Word HTML.*

## ADDING HORIZONTAL RULES

A **horizontal rule** is a line that goes across the page and provides a visual division between sections of your page.

### 1) In the Common Objects panel, click the Insert Horizontal Rule button and drag a horizontal rule to the bottom of the document, or click the bottom of the document and choose Insert > Horizontal Rule.

If the Common Objects panel is not visible, choose Window > Objects.

### 2) In the property inspector, type *90* in the W (width) text box. Choose % from the drop-down menu to the right of the text you just typed.

The horizontal rule extends across 90% of the browser window regardless of the browser width. The rule is displayed as a shaded bar centered on the page.

**NOTE** *Choose pixels from the menu to specify an absolute width. If you choose this option, the rule is not resized when users resize the browser window.*

### 3) Deselect Shading. Type *3* in the H (height) text box.

Deselecting the Shading checkbox displays a solid bar. The horizontal rule is 3 pixels high.

### 4) From the Align drop-down menu, choose Left.

The thick, unshaded bar moves to the left but still extends across 90% of the browser window.

### 5) Save the file and preview it in the browser.

Notice how the horizontal rule appears. You can make changes by selecting it and modifying the properties in the property inspector.

## ADDING A DATE AUTOMATICALLY

Sometimes you need to keep track of the date when you last modified a page on your site. Dreamweaver lets you place a date and time on your pages to track this information. Dreamweaver can update the date and time automatically every time you save, so you don't have to do it manually.

In the following exercise, you'll add an automatic date.

**NOTE** *This date is not a dynamic date that changes according to the date and/or time when a user is accessing the page. This date simply tells your users when your pages have been updated.*

### 1) Place the insertion point where you want the date to appear.

This information is displayed at the bottom of a page.

### 2) Click Date in the Common Objects panel or choose Insert > Date to place the current date on the page.

The Insert Date dialog box opens.

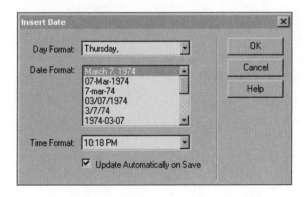

**3) From the Day Format drop-down menu, choose Thursday. From the Date Format drop-down menu, choose March 7, 1974. From the Time Format drop-down menu, choose 10:18PM. Check the Update Automatically on Save checkbox to update the date on your page each time you save your document. Click OK.**

The current day, date, and time are displayed. This information will change every time you save the document. You can change the date format if it is updated automatically. The following steps tell you how.

**4) Click the date in your document. In the property inspector, click Edit Date Format.**

The Edit Date Format dialog box opens. This dialog box is the same as the Insert Date dialog box and is where you will make any necessary changes.

**5) Make the appropriate changes and then click OK.**

Your changes are applied to the document.

## ADDING FLASH TEXT

When you add a heading to your page, your options are to use text and format it as a heading tag or to create a graphic and insert it into the page. Text formatted as a heading will load quickly because it is text, but your font and size choices are limited. Using graphics as headings solves the font-choice problem, but you may not have access to a graphics program or just not enough time to create the graphic you need.

Flash text provides the best of both these options. You can use any font you choose and create the text within Dreamweaver. The text you create is a small Flash file (.swf).

**1) Position the insertion point in the center of a new line at the bottom of the document. In the Common Objects panel, click the Flash Text button.**

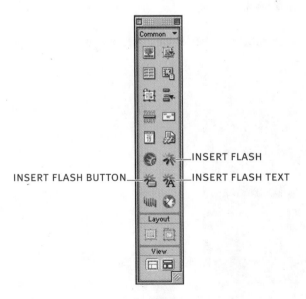

INSERT FLASH BUTTON — INSERT FLASH
INSERT FLASH TEXT

Make sure that you don't click the Flash Button or Flash Object button.

The Insert Flash Text dialog box appears.

### 2) From the Font drop-down menu, choose Comic Sans MS.

If Comic Sans MS is not available on your machine, choose another font.

### 3) From the Color drop-down menu, choose a maroon color. From the Rollover Color drop-down menu, choose a blue color. For Bg Color, type *CCFFFF*, or use the eyedropper and click the background in the document window.

When the user moves the cursor over the text, the color changes. This changed color is set in the Rollover Color menu, while the Color menu controls the base color of the text. The Bg Color text field sets the background color.

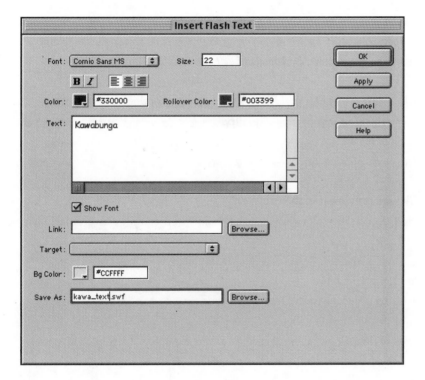

### 4) In the Save As text box, type *kawa_text.swf*, and then click OK.

The Insert Flash Text dialog box closes.

### 5) In the property inspector, click Play to start the Flash animation.

This step enables you to view the animation within Dreamweaver as it would appear in a browser.

**6)  In the document window, place the mouse pointer over the Flash text.**

The text changes to the rollover color you chose.

**7)  In the property inspector, click Stop.**

The Flash text no longer changes when you roll over it in Dreamweaver. To preview it, you must either click Play again or preview the document in a browser.

**8)  In the document window, select the Flash text and resize it by dragging one of the handles.**

It doesn't matter what size you make the Flash text. Because the text is Flash text and not normal body text or a bitmap graphic, you can resize it directly in the document window.

**NOTE**  *Resizing graphics (discussed in Lesson 2) within Dreamweaver is not recommended. But you can resize the Flash text image that you create because it is a vector graphic. Vector graphics are scalable; bitmap graphics (such as GIFs and JPEGs) are not.*

Because the Flash text is a vector graphic, you can increase or decrease the image size without concern about loss of image quality.

**TIP**  *Hold down the Shift key to constrain the proportions while you resize the Flash text.*

**9)  Save the file and preview it in the browser.**

The text will roll over to the color you chose as it did when you previewed the Flash file in Dreamweaver.

## MODIFYING FLASH TEXT

Changing Flash text objects within Dreamweaver is easy.

**NOTE**  *Although creating and working with Flash text is quick and easy, always consider whether your audience is likely to have the correct plug-ins.*

**1)  In the document window, double-click the Flash text.**

If you can't select the text, first click Stop in the property inspector.

The Insert Flash Text dialog box opens.

**2)  Change the options to your liking; then click Apply to see the results of your changes. When you finish, click OK to close the Insert Flash Text dialog box.**

The edited Flash text is placed on the page, and the .swf file has been updated.

## WHAT YOU HAVE LEARNED

**In this lesson, you have:**

- Familiarized yourself with Dreamweaver's Objects panel; property inspector; document window; and other tools, windows, and panels (pages 8–11)

- Prepared to create a Web site, set up a local site, and defined the local root folder (pages 12–15)

- Specified preview browsers and used the keyboard shortcuts throughout the lesson to test your page (pages 15–16)

- Created a new page, saved the document with proper naming conventions, and gave the page a title (pages 16–18)

- Specified a background color and default font color (pages 19–21)

- Learned how to import text in different ways and clean up Word HTML (pages 22–24, 47–48)

- Positioned text by using paragraphs, breaks, and alignments (pages 25–27)

- Created three list types and modified their properties (pages 28–30)

- Applied text formatting of style, size, and color by using the property inspector (pages 31–34)

- Customized font combinations and settings (page 33)

- Automated the process of formatting text by creating and applying HTML styles (pages 36–40)

- Added special characters to the page (pages 40–41)

- Switched document views and edited the HTML in code view (pages 42–46)

- Added a date to the page and set it to update every time the page is saved (pages 49–50)

- Created and edited Flash text (pages 50–52)

# working with graphics

Although the Web is still primarily a text-based medium, graphics are key to capturing the attention of your audience and communicating your message effectively. In this lesson, you will create a Web page that incorporates graphics, text, and Flash. In the process, you will learn about different graphic file formats and how to control their appearances in an HTML document.

*In this lesson, you'll create a page like this one while you learn to incorporate graphics with text on your Web pages.*

Dreamweaver simplifies graphics management by allowing you to modify image properties quickly and by providing a quick way to change an image in an external image editor. One of the most powerful graphics features in Dreamweaver allows you to create catalogs of all the images used in your site or of images that you need to have accessible.

If you would like to view the final result of this lesson, open travel_log.html in the Completed folder within the Lesson_02_Graphics folder.

## WHAT YOU WILL LEARN

**In this lesson, you will:**

- Identify graphics formats and explore their differences
- Insert graphics into a page
- Modify the properties of your images
- Give your images names and <alt> tags
- Change the positioning of graphics on a page
- Align text with an image
- Wrap text around an image
- Use the Assets panel to manage graphics
- Insert buttons and animations from Macromedia Flash

## APPROXIMATE TIME

This lesson should take about one hour to complete.

## LESSON FILES

**Media Files:**

*Lesson_02_Graphics/Images/banner_head.gif*
*Lesson_02_Graphics/Images/diver.jpg*
*Lesson_02_Graphics/Images/fish.gif*

**Starting File:**

*Lesson_02_Graphics/Text/diving.txt*

**Completed Project:**

*Lesson_02_Graphics/Completed/
    travel_log.htm*

## PLACING GRAPHICS ON THE PAGE

The most common and widely supported graphic formats on the Web are GIF and JPEG. In general, use GIF if the artwork has large areas of solid colors and no blending of colors, and use JPEG for photographic images or images with a large tonal range. A picture of blue sky with clouds, for example, looks posterized when it is saved as a GIF image. All the different shades of blue are mapped to only a few colors. GIF images are saved, at maximum, in 8-bit color mode, which means that only 256 colors can be represented. Browsers display only 216 colors, which makes the problem even worse. JPEG saves the image in 24-bit mode, retaining all the colors and using a lossy form of compression in which redundant data is lost. The lower the quality of a JPEG, the more information is lost about the image through this discard of data. GIF files tend to load faster, have more optimization options, and support transparency and animation. If you are working with a graphic that can be saved as either GIF or JPEG, choose GIF whenever possible.

**Interlacing** is a method of defining the way the image is displayed in the browser. Interlacing displays every other pixel in every other line and then goes back and repeats the process, filling in areas that are not already displayed. Without interlacing, the graphic is "painted" on the screen line by line, starting at the top of the image. Interlacing adds slightly to the file size and download time, but it gives a visual clue that something is happening.

**NOTE** *A second way to provide a visual is to use a low source image—a lower quality version of the image that you can set to appear first. The higher-quality image will appear in its place when the download is complete.*

**1) Create a new file and save it as travel_log.html in the DW4_Intro/ Lesson_02_Graphics folder. Use Compass Extreme Adventures as the document title.**

In this step and the following step, you are specifying the basic document settings you learned in Lesson 1.

**2) In Modify › Page Properties, change the background color to #006699 and the default font color to #FFFFFF. Position the insertion point in the first line of the document.**

It is best to apply these general document settings before you begin laying out your pages. You can always modify them later, but it helps to see the document with the colors and settings it will be using.

### 3) Click the Image button in the Common Objects panel.

You are going to insert a graphic into the page. An alternative method is to choose Insert > Image.

IMAGE
BUTTON—

The Select Image Source dialog box opens.

### 4) Select Preview Options (Windows) or Show Preview (Macintosh) to see a thumbnail of the images you click.

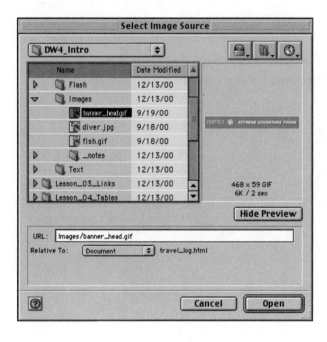

On the Macintosh, the button will change to Hide Preview. Images are displayed in the Select Image Source dialog box along with their dimensions, file size, and approximate download time.

**5) Locate the file Lesson_02_Graphics/Images/banner_head.gif. From the Relative To menu, choose Document.**

The document file name travel_log.html appears to the right of the Relative To menu.

Dreamweaver lets you choose how it references images: with document-relative or site-root-relative references. In **document-relative referencing**, Dreamweaver constructs the path to the image based on the relative location of the graphics file to your HTML document. **Site-root-relative referencing** constructs the path to the image based on the relative location of the graphics file to the site root directory.

Generally, you should use document-relative links and paths. If you have an extremely large site or plan to move pages frequently, you might want to use site-root-relative referencing.

Until you save your file, Dreamweaver has no way to make the reference, so it substitutes a path name based on the location of the image on your hard disk instead of a valid link. These paths will not work on a remote site. You should always save your document before you insert graphics. If you don't, Dreamweaver displays an alert box and then fixes the path when you do save the Dreamweaver file.

**6) Click Select (Windows) or Open (Macintosh).**

The image appears in the document window.

**TIP** *The property inspector for images features an Edit button in the bottom-right corner. This option provides a quick way to open and modify your images in an external image editor. To choose your preferred editor, choose Edit > Preferences and select File Types/Editors in the Category list of the Preferences dialog box. You can use this dialog box to assign different editors according to the file extensions.*

## RESIZING AND REFRESHING GRAPHICS

When you insert a graphic, the width and height of the image are added in the property inspector automatically, giving the browser the information it needs to define the layout of the page. This important information can make a difference in the speed of loading your graphics. You can change these numbers in Dreamweaver.

**1) In travel_log.html, click the banner_head.gif image to select it. In the property inspector, change the width to 30 pixels and the height to 200 pixels.**

You are using the width and height tags to create a special effect for this graphic without making the actual graphic larger or smaller. The file size of the selected image is displayed in the property inspector.

WIDTH AND HEIGHT

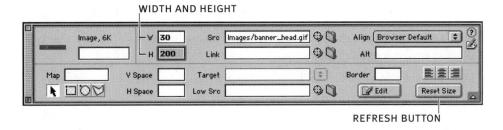

REFRESH BUTTON

**2) Click one of the selection handles—the black squares—on the border. Drag to resize the image and make it larger.**

The width and height specifications update automatically. Notice that the new dimensions you have set are displayed in bold. This formatting is a clue to let you know that the graphic has been resized. At times, you may resize a graphic accidentally, and the bold numbers indicate that change. You can also change the size by changing the numbers in the width and height text boxes.

**TIP** *Hold down the Shift key while you drag the image's handles to constrain the proportions of the image.*

Notice that when you scaled the image larger, the image quality diminished. When you resize a rasterized image (such as a GIF or a JPEG) the blocks of color that make up the image simply become larger, and thus, more visible as blocks. You could scale the image smaller, and it will look OK, but you won't have changed the file size, so the graphic will take just as long to download. When you adjust the size of an image within Dreamweaver, you are changing the size only at which it displays in the browser—not resizing the actual graphic itself. Always adjust the image size in your image-editing software (such as Macromedia Fireworks or Adobe Photoshop) to ensure that you have the smallest file size possible.

**3) In the property inspector, click Reset Size in the bottom-right corner.**

The image resets to the original size of the graphic. Notice that the width and height numbers revert to plain text, indicating that the image is set at the original size.

## POSITIONING GRAPHICS

When you place an image directly in the body of a document, you have a limited number of options for positioning it. The following exercise is a method of creating an alignment that uses <div> tags. These tags essentially are containers that specify the alignment of everything between the tags. You learn about other ways to align images later in this lesson and also in Lesson 4.

**1)  In travel_log.html, click the banner_head.gif image to select it. In the property inspector, click the Align Center button.**

If you don't see the Align Center button, click the expander arrow in the bottom-right corner. The image becomes centered on the page.

ALIGN CENTER BUTTON

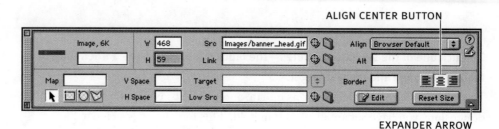

EXPANDER ARROW

**2)  Insert a paragraph break after the banner by clicking off of the image and pressing Return or Enter. Type _My Diving Travel Log_, and click the Align Left button in the property inspector to move the text to the left.**

The text does not have to be selected, but your insertion point should be on the same line. When you work with multiple elements, you must put them in separate paragraphs to give them different alignments. You cannot center part of a paragraph and left-align the rest. When you insert text directly below an image, for example, you need to use a regular paragraph break between the image and the text (Return on a Macintosh or Enter in Windows). If you use a single line break between them (by pressing Shift+Return or Shift+Enter), any alignment you apply affects both the image and the text, because they would be considered to be part of the same paragraph block.

## ADDING A BORDER AROUND AN IMAGE

At times, you need to set an image apart from the background to make it stand out. One way to create this effect is to place a border around the image.

**In travel_log.html, click the banner_head.gif image to select it. Then, in the Border text box of the property inspector, type *1*.**

Dreamweaver adds a 1-pixel border around the image.

You can set the width of the border to any number you want. The border color will be the same as the default text color that was specified in Page Properties dialog box. You can change the color of the border by putting the image between font-color tags.

> **NOTE** *When you start assigning links to images in Lesson 3, the border color will be the same as the default link color specified in Page Properties.*

## ASSIGNING NAMES AND *‹ALT›* TAGS TO IMAGES

Names and <alt> tags are important, although largely invisible, parts of your Web pages. It generally is good practice to assign names and <alt> tags, because they help both you and the users of your site. The functions of these elements are described in the following exercise.

**1) In the property inspector, type *banner* in the image-name text box for the banner_head.gif image.**

IMAGE-NAME TEXT BOX

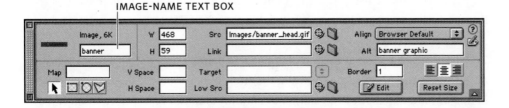

This name that you assign to the image is an internal name, used mainly for functions such as Behaviors (covered in Lesson 5). Although naming your images is not essential, doing so is good practice. You should keep image names short, enter them in lowercase, and avoid using spaces or special characters.

**2) Type *banner graphic* in the Alt text box.**

The Alt option lets you specify text that will be displayed if users have graphics disabled, if their browsers are not capable of displaying graphics, or if a particular image fails to load.

You must add <alt> tags to any graphics that are critical for site navigation. Adding <alt> tags to other images is also useful, because if users have graphics disabled or are using a text-only browser, they will be able to see some of the information they are missing. Additionally, people with vision disabilities use a reader that voices the <alt> tags along with the text on a Web page. Further, <alt> text is displayed briefly in Internet Explorer when the user moves the mouse pointer over the graphic.

## INSERTING AN IMAGE FROM THE ASSETS PANEL

You may find it difficult to manage all your images, especially if you are working on a large site. The Assets panel provides a way for you to keep track of those images. Before you begin the following exercise, make sure that the Assets panel is open. If not, choose Window > Assets.

**1) In the Assets panel, click the Images button, located at the top of the column of buttons on the left side of the panel.**

The other buttons represent different types of assets that may be available to your site, including colors, which you used in Lesson 1.

You can work with the Assets panel in two ways: view it with the Site list, which gives you a complete list of the images in your site; or view it with the Favorites list, to which you can add frequently-used images for easier reference.

**2) Click the Site button at the top of the Assets panel.**

All images within the site are shown in the site-assets window. The images appear in this window automatically, whether or not they are used in any document. It may take a few seconds for the panel to create a catalog of the image assets available for your site. If you haven't created a site cache for this site, the Assets panel prompts you to do so; the asset list cannot be created without a site cache.

If you add a new asset to your site, it might not appear in the Assets panel immediately. To update the panel to match all the images in your site, you need to refresh the site catalog. To do so, click the Refresh Site button in the bottom-right corner of the Assets panel.

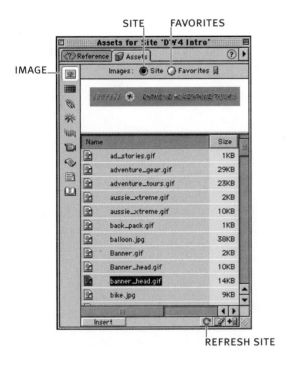

SITE    FAVORITES

IMAGE

REFRESH SITE

### 3) Drag the diver.jpg graphic from the Assets panel to the document and place it below the heading.

The image appears in the document window.

**TIP** *Alternatively, you can place the insertion point in the document, select the image in the Assets panel, and click the Insert button.*

### 4) In the image-name text box of the property inspector, type *diver*. In the Alt text box, type *diver pic.*

Giving names and <alt> tags to your images as you insert them will save you time and make it easier to work with them in code view later, if necessary.

## MANAGING IMAGES WITH THE FAVORITES LIST

Placing images that you use repeatedly in a Favorites list can be a time-saver. You can add any image contained within the site to your Favorites list. This list will be empty when you start using Dreamweaver. In the following exercise, you will add an image from the Site category to your Favorites list and then organize that list.

**1) In travel_log.html, select "fish" in the Site list and click the Add to Favorites button, located in the bottom-right corner.**

SITE    FAVORITES

ADD TO FAVORITES

A dialog box appears to let you know that the selected assets have been added to this site's Favorites list. Choose OK to acknowledge the message and close the dialog box. Graphics are listed in the Site list by their name only, and do not include the .gif or .jpg extensions.

**TIP** *You can use an alternative method to add an image to the Favorites list. First, in site view, select the image you want to use. From the drop-down menu in the top-right corner of the Assets panel, choose Add to Favorites. Yet another method is to make an image in your document window a favorite. To do this, Control-click (Macintosh) or right-click (Windows) the image and choose Add to Favorites from the context menu that appears. This context menu contains a wide variety of options.*

### 2) In the Assets panel, choose Images > Favorites.

The image is now listed in Favorites.

As you begin to manage your images through the Assets panel, you probably will need to remove as well as add images. When an image is selected in the Favorites list, the Add to Favorites button becomes the Remove from Favorites button. Clicking Remove from Favorites causes the selected image to disappear from the list.

### 3) Click the icon for New Favorites Folder at the bottom of the panel and type *Fish* in the folder-name text box.

You can organize your images in folders to make them easy to locate.

**TIP** *You can also use the drop-down menu from the arrow at the top right of the panel to select New Favorites Folder.*

SITE        FAVORITES

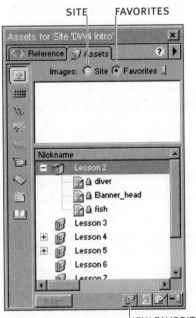

NEW FAVORITES FOLDER

### 4) Drag the fish.gif image into the Fish folder.

A small plus sign (Windows) or an arrow (Macintosh) appears to the left of the folder name, indicating that the folder contains an image. Click the plus sign or arrow to see the contents of the folder.

Images in Favorites are listed by their nicknames, which Dreamweaver assigns automatically based on the image's file names. You can change these nicknames— in the Favorites list only—by clicking the name, pausing, and clicking again. Don't

65

double-click. A border appears around the text box, and the name is highlighted. Start typing to replace the highlighted text.

> **NOTE** *If you need to delete a folder that you created in the Favorites list, select the folder and then click Remove from Favorites at the bottom of the Assets panel.*

## WRAPPING TEXT AROUND IMAGES

Layout options in HTML include wrapping text around images. The following exercise demonstrates how to create a text wrap. You can use the same procedure to align images with other elements, such as other images.

**1)  Select and copy the text from Lesson_02_Graphics/Text/diving.txt.**
This file contains the text you will wrap.

**2)  In travel_log.htm, paste the copied text to the right of the diver graphic. Select and left-align all the text.**
The text appears in the default position, with the first line of the text starting at the baseline of the image.

**3)  Select the diver graphic and choose Left from the Align drop-down menu in the property inspector.**

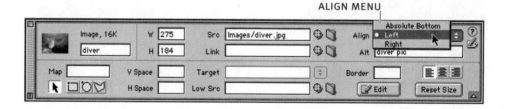

The image is aligned left. The text on the right wraps to the bottom of the diver graphic and then returns to the left margin of the window. By changing the Align attribute, you can wrap multiple lines of text around the image. When you choose Left or Right from the Align menu, Dreamweaver places an image-anchor symbol at the point where the image was inserted. If necessary, you can move this anchor to a new location. The anchor needs to be at the beginning of the text for the text wrap to work properly. This symbol indicates where the HTML tag for the image is in relation to the text. If you don't see the symbol, choose View > Visual Aids > Invisible Elements. A check next to this command indicates that the option is selected. The symbol will not be visible in the browser.

*The Align menu contains several options for images, including Top and Text Top. The list is confusing, but remember that text can wrap only on the left or the right side of an image, so the only options you can choose are Left and Right. The other options are for placement of a single line of text next to a graphic.*

### 4) Save the file and preview it in the browser.

Keep in mind that whenever you select an alignment option other than Browser Default, you are applying an alignment to an image. When this happens, the image is offset slightly from the original position. You cannot control or get rid of this offset. The amount of offset varies from browser to browser but usually is only a couple of pixels and not noticeable. The offset may be a problem, however, if you are trying to align images in tables. In that case, you need to use other methods to control the placement of your images.

## ADJUSTING THE SPACE AROUND AN IMAGE

When you wrap text around graphics, you'll probably want to adjust the space around the image as well. You can add vertical space (V Space) and horizontal space (H Space).

### 1) In travel_log.html, click the diver.jpg image to select it.

Right now, the text is very close to the edge of this graphic. The page would look better and the text would be easier to read if space appeared around the image.

### 2) In the property inspector, type *15* in the H Space text box.

V SPACE TEXT BOX

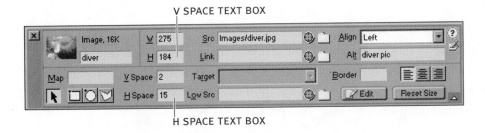

H SPACE TEXT BOX

This setting creates 15 pixels of space on the left and right sides of the image. You cannot add space on only one side.

### 3) Type *2* in the V Space text box.

This setting creates 2 pixels of space at the top and bottom of the image. You cannot add space on only one side.

## ALIGNING AN IMAGE RELATIVE TO A SINGLE LINE OF TEXT

Many times, you'll want to control the placement of an image in relation to a single line of text that appears near it. You can change the relative location of the image to the text by using alignment options. The seven options discussed in the following exercise work well for aligning a single line of text near a graphic.

**TIP** *These options don't work for wrapping multiple lines around a graphic. To wrap multiple lines, choose the Left or Right option, as you did in the preceding exercise.*

**1) From the Fish folder in the Assets panel's Favorites list, drag the fish image to a new line after the body text.**

The image appears in the document window.

**2) Type *fish* in the image-name text box and type *fish pic* in the Alt text box.**

Don't forget these important settings.

**3) Position the insertion point after the fish graphic and type *Check out some of the fish we saw.***

Initially, the text is aligned with the bottom of the graphic, and it is too close to the graphic.

**4) Select the fish graphic and add a 1-pixel border to it. In the property inspector, type *15* in the H Space text box.**

The graphic and text move apart, and a thin border appears around the image.

**5) From the Align drop-down menu, choose Middle.**

This option aligns the baseline of the text with the middle of the image. There are other alignment options to choose from, as well. Baseline aligns the bottom of the image with the baseline, or bottom line, on which the text sits. This option normally is the browser default. Bottom aligns the same way as Baseline.

Top aligns the image with the top of the tallest item in the line. That item may be text or a larger image. Text Top does what many people think Top should do, which is align the image with the top of the tallest text in the line. (This option usually, but not always, is the same as Top.)

Absolute Middle aligns the middle of the image with the middle of the text line or the largest item in the line, while Absolute Bottom aligns the bottom of the image with the lowest point of the text line.

### 6) Save the file and preview it in the browser.

You can also use these options to position images relative to other images; you're not limited to text.

## ADDING FLASH BUTTONS

You can easily achieve special effects by using Flash objects. Because Flash graphics are vector-based, their file sizes are very small, which helps them load quickly in the user's browser.

Flash buttons have several states, depending on the position of the mouse pointer and whether the mouse button has been clicked. The first state is the appearance of the button when the pointer is not on it. The second state is when the pointer is on the button but the mouse button has not been clicked. The third state is when the pointer is on the button and the mouse button has been clicked. You can create and maintain Flash buttons in Dreamweaver from a set of available button styles.

### 1) In travel_log.html, position the insertion point below the fish graphic in the center of the document window.

You'll insert a Flash button here to take the user back to the main page of the site.

### 2) In the Common Objects panel, click Flash Button.

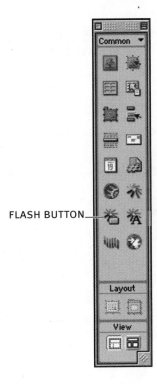

FLASH BUTTON

The Insert Flash Button dialog box opens.

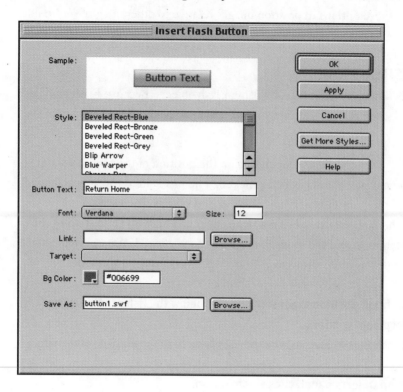

**3) In the Style list, select Beveled Rect-Blue. In the Button Text text box, type** *Return Home.* **Choose Verdana (or another font if Verdana is not available) from the Font menu. In the Size text box, type** *12.*

You can edit these settings later, if necessary. The next exercise shows you how.

**4) For Bg Color, click the color box. Then, using the eyedropper pointer, click anywhere in the background of the document window.**

The background-color code #006699 appears in the Bg Color text box.

**5) In the Save As text box, type** *home_button.swf* **and then click OK.**

The Insert Flash Button dialog box closes.

You should always name your Flash buttons. If you don't, Dreamweaver automatically assigns them a name.

**6) In the property inspector, click Play.**

The button is in its original state.

**7) In the document window, move the mouse pointer over the Return Home button. Then click the button.**

The button changes to its rollover state when the pointer is moved over it. The button changes to its clicked state when clicked.

**8) Save the file and preview it in the browser.**

The button changes states just as it did in Dreamweaver, depending on the pointer position and mouse click.

## MODIFYING FLASH BUTTONS

You can change many of the button attributes.

**1) In the document window, double-click the Flash button.**

The Insert Flash Button dialog box opens. If the dialog box does not open, click Stop in the property inspector and double-click the Flash button again.

**2) Set the options however you want.**

Change the font to Arial, for example.

**3) Click Apply to see the changes, and then click OK when you finish.**

You can add your own template buttons by using Flash to create them outside Dreamweaver.

## ADDING FLASH ANIMATIONS

You can add Flash animations to your document as easily as you can add an image, provided that the animation already exists. You can resize animations by dragging the handles. You cannot create animations directly within Dreamweaver.

**1) In travel_log.html, position the insertion point below the Flash button.**

If the insertion point is not centered, click Center in the property inspector.

The insertion point is centered on the page. The next object you add to the page will be centered.

### 2) In the Assets panel, click the Flash button in the left column.

The Flash assets appear in the panel. The Site and Favorites lists for Flash assets work the same way as they do for image assets. You can use the same techniques to manage and organize Flash files as you do to manage and organize images.

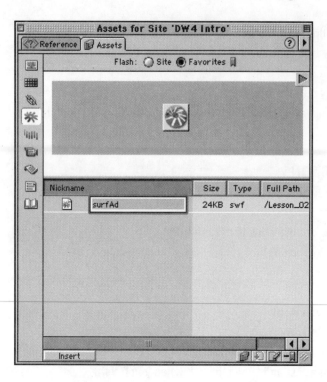

### 3) In the Favorites list, select surfAd, and then click Insert.

The Flash animation is placed on the page.

### 4) In the property inspector, choose Loop and Autoplay. Click Play to view the animation in Dreamweaver.

To view animation files in Dreamweaver, you must click Play. Click Stop when you are done testing.

### 5) Save the file and preview it in the browser.

Autoplay causes the Flash animation to begin playing as soon as the page is loaded into the browser. The animation plays repeatedly because the Loop property was set in Dreamweaver.

**TIP** *Always be sure to select a .swf file when you insert a Flash animation. Do not insert .fla or .swt files, because they do not show up in a browser.*

## WHAT YOU HAVE LEARNED

### In this lesson, you have:

- Placed JPEG and GIF images on the page (pages 56–58)

- Resized images and reset them to their original dimensions (pages 58–59)

- Used tags to align and position images (page 60)

- Added a border around an image (page 61)

- Assigned names and `<alt>` tags to images (pages 61–62)

- Used the Assets panel to manage images in the site (pages 62–65)

- Wrapped text around images (pages 66–67)

- Adjusted the space around images (page 67)

- Aligned images relative to text (pages 68–69)

- Added and modified Flash buttons (pages 69–71)

- Added Flash animations (pages 71–72)

# creating links

The power of HTML comes from its capability to connect regions of text and images with other documents. The browser may highlight these regions (usually, with color or underlines) to indicate that they are **hypertext links**—links that are not required to be sequential or linear. Hypertext links are often called hyperlinks or simply links. A link in HTML has two parts: the name of the file (or URL of the file) to which you want to link; and the text or graphic that serves as the clickable area on the page. When the user points to the clickable area and clicks it, the browser uses the path of the link to jump to the linked document. In some browsers, the path of the link is displayed in

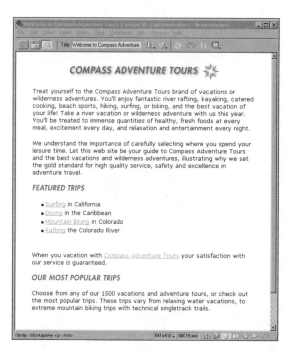

*In this lesson, you will create text and graphic links to pages within this site, as well as to another Web site.*

the status area of the browser window (bottom-left part of the window) when the pointer is positioned over the link.

In this lesson, you will create text and image links on a Web page, add clickable areas to an image to make it an image map, and link to named anchors within a page.

To see examples of the finished pages, open Lesson_03_Links/Completed/ welcome.htm for the text and graphic links, map.htm for the image map, and trips.htm for the named anchors.

## WHAT YOU WILL LEARN

**In this lesson, you will:**

- Specify link colors according to the link type

- Create text and graphic links

- Create e-mail links automatically and manually

- Use anchors to jump to different parts of the page

- Create image maps to provide multiple links in the same image

## APPROXIMATE TIME

This lesson should take about one hour to complete.

## LESSON FILES

**Media Files:**

*Lesson_03_Links/Images/aussie_xtreme.gif*

*Lesson_03_Links/Images/boy_surfer.jpg*

*Lesson_03_Links/Images/ compass_logo_gray.gif*

*Lesson_03_Links/Images/diver.jpg*

*Lesson_03_Links/Images/downhill.jpg*

*Lesson_03_Links/Images/featured.gif*

*Lesson_03_Links/Images/popular.gif*

*Lesson_03_Links/Images/tri_top.gif*

*Lesson_03_Links/Images/worldmap.gif*

**Starting Files:**

*Lesson_03_Links/welcome.htm*

*Lesson_03_Links/trips.htm*

*Lesson_03_Links/map.htm*

*Lesson_03_Links/biking.htm*

*Lesson_03_Links/diving.htm*

*Lesson_03_Links/rafting.htm*

*Lesson_03_Links/surfing.htm*

**Completed Project:**

*Lesson_03_Links/Completed/map.htm*

*Lesson_03_Links/Completed/trips.htm*

*Lesson_03_Links/Completed/welcome.htm*

## SPECIFYING LINK COLORS

You can choose to specify the default color of text links on your page in order to match the colors used most in your document. These colors should contrast with the background enough to read clearly. Browsers will display the colors you set for links unless the option to override a page's colors is checked in the user's browser preferences. You will use the same dialog box to choose these colors as you used when selecting the default text color in Lesson 1.

**1) ) Open the welcome.htm document, located in the Lesson_03_Links folder. Choose Modify › Page Properties to open the Page Properties dialog box, and then click the color box next to the link state you want to change.**

There are three link states. Links is the initial color a user sees before clicking the link. The normal default browser color for a link is blue. Visited Links is the color a link changes to when a user clicks the link. The normal default browser color for a visited link is purple. Active Links is the color to which a link turns if a user holds down the mouse button after clicking the link. The normal default browser color for an active link is red. Some pages use the same color for Active Links as they do for Links.

**2) Using the text boxes next to the color boxes, select the colors for your links by typing in *#996600* for the Links color, *#996600* for the Active Link color, and *#999966* for the Visited Links color.**

When you know the hexadecimal values of your colors, you can enter the numbers directly in these text boxes. Dreamweaver automatically fills in the color box with the matching color swatch. On the other hand, if you choose a color swatch from the color picker, Dreamweaver automatically fills in the text box with the hexadecimal value. You can click the color box to bring up the color picker, as you did in Lesson 1, and the hexadecimal value will be displayed at the top of the color picker as you roll over the color swatches.

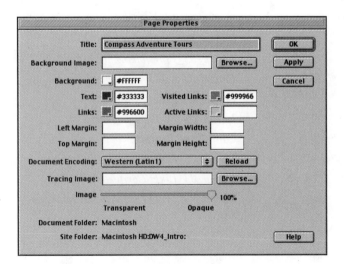

**3) Click OK to close the Page Properties dialog box, return to your document, and save the file.**

The default link colors for your page are now the colors you specified. You will see the colors after you begin to create links. Keep this document, welcome.htm, open. It contains all the text and graphics you will need to create links in the following exercises.

**NOTE** *You can override the page's default link color for individual links by placing the font-color tags inside the link tags. You may have to move the tags manually in code view as you did in Lesson 1.*

## INSERTING E-MAIL LINKS

Linking to an e-mail address makes it easy for your visitors to contact you from a Web page. You should always include some method that allows visitors to correspond or interact with someone in your organization.

**1) Click in the white space to the right of the graphic at the bottom of the page and press Return (Macintosh) or Enter (Windows) to place the insertion point in a blank line below the graphic.**

Contact information commonly appears at the bottom of a page, often near copyright information.

**2) Click the Insert E-Mail Link icon in the Common Objects panel, or choose Insert › E-Mail Link.**

The Insert E-Mail Link dialog box appears, displaying options for text and e-mail.

INSERT EMAIL LINK

77

**3) In the Text text box, type *Send us your questions!*. In the E-Mail text box, type your e-mail address. Click OK.**

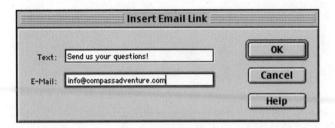

The text appears on the page as a link. The property inspector shows the e-mail address in the Link text box when you place the insertion point within the link.

**4) Select *Compass Adventure Tours* in the sentence that begins "When you vacation..."**

**5) In the Link text box of the property inspector, type *mailto:* followed by your e-mail address. Make sure that you type the colon and use no spaces.**

You have entered an e-mail link manually.

## CREATING HYPERTEXT LINKS

Hypertext links can take the user to another document within the current Web site or to a page on another Web site. They can direct the user to other HTML files, images and other media, and downloadable files. The following exercise shows you how to link to a document within the current site.

**1)  In the welcome.htm document window, select the word "Surfing" below "Featured Trips."**

You will create a link for this word.

**2)  In the property inspector, click the folder icon to the right of the Link text box.**

The Select File dialog box opens.

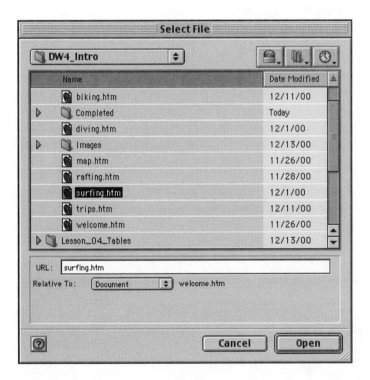

**3)  Select the surfing.htm file in the Lesson_03_Links folder and click Open (Macintosh) or Select (Windows).**

The file name surfing.htm appears in the Link text box, and the text you selected in the document is marked as a link. The link is underlined and appears in the color you chose for your links in the preceding exercise.

This link is an example of a document-relative path, which is the best option to use for local links in most Web sites. A **document-relative path** omits the part of the absolute URL that is the same for the current document and the linked document, leaving only the portion of the path that differs. A path to a file in the same folder, for example, would be expressed as myfile.htm.

**4) Repeat steps 1 through 3 to link the word "Diving" to diving.htm, the words "Mountain Biking" to biking.htm, and the word "Rafting" to rafting.htm.**

**TIP** *If you use the same links repetitively, you can save time by choosing recently used links from the drop-down menu to the right of the Link text box.*

**5) Save the file and preview it in the browser.**
All four links you created should take you to the corresponding pages. Always test your links!

## CREATING GRAPHIC LINKS

You can also use images to link to documents and sites other than your own. This exercise shows you how to create an external link. You can use the same techniques you used in the preceding exercise to link images to files on your site.

**1) In the welcome.htm document, click the graphic at the bottom of the page to select it and type *http://www.australia.com* in the property inspector's Link text box.**
You must type the complete URL.

This link is an absolute path. An **absolute path** provides the complete URL of the linked document. You must use an absolute path to link to a document that is located in a Web site other than your own.

**TIP** *If the URL is long or complex, you can go to that site in your browser, copy the URL, and then paste it into the Link text box.*

**2) Save the file and preview it in the browser.**

Notice that when you roll over the graphic at the bottom of the page, you see that it is linked. The link location appears in your browser's status bar.

**NOTE** *When you attach a link to an image, if you have not specified the image border in the property inspector, Dreamweaver applies a default border of 0 pixels. If you do define a border, the color will be the same as your page's default link color.*

## TARGETING LINKS

When you link to a page, the linked page usually replaces the current browser page. At times, however, you want to display the new browser page in a different location or window. If you link to a site outside your site, for example, you lead users out of your pages. If users haven't bookmarked your URL, they might not remember how to return to your site. When an outside link opens a new browser window, the original page remains in the first window.

**1) In the welcome.htm document, select the bottom graphic. From the property inspector's Target menu, choose _blank.**

In Dreamweaver, you change where the linked page is to be displayed by using the following targets:

_blank: Loads the linked document into a new, unnamed browser window.

_parent: Loads the linked document into the parent frameset or window of the frame that contains the link.

_self: Loads the linked document into the same frame or window as the link. This target is implied, so you usually don't have to specify it.

_top: Loads the linked document into the full browser window, thereby removing all frames.

Targets other than _blank work only when you create frames for your page (see Lesson 9).

**2) Save the file and preview it in the browser.**

When you click the bottom graphic, the linked page opens in a new browser window. You can close this file.

**TIP** *Use caution when opening new browser windows. New windows impose extra RAM requirements on the user's computer as each window is opened. Besides taxing a machine's memory resources, multiple windows may annoy or confuse your visitors.*

## INSERTING AND LINKING TO NAMED ANCHORS

When a document is long or has many sections, you may need to create a series of links that jump the user to specific places in the document. This technique eliminates the need for the user to scroll through the document. A **named anchor** marks the place in the page to which a link jumps. In this exercise, you insert a named anchor.

**1) Open trips.htm from the Lesson_03_Links folder. Choose Modify › Page Properties to open the Page Properties dialog box. Apply the same colors for links and visited links that you used for the welcome.htm document in this lesson's first exercise.**

Recall the links color's hexadecimal value was #996600 and the visited-links value was #999966. This file contains a large amount of text that requires the visitor to scroll to see the entire document.

**2) Position the insertion point before the heading "Hawaii – Multisport" at the bottom of the document. Choose Invisibles from the Objects panel's Options menu, and click Named Anchor to insert a named anchor.**

The Insert Named Anchor dialog box opens.

**TIP** *You can also insert a named anchor by choosing Insert > Invisible Tags > Named Anchor.*

**3) Type *hawaii* in the Anchor Name text box and click OK.**

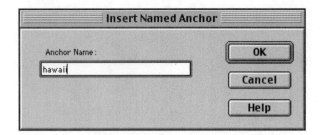

Don't use spaces, punctuation, or special characters (such as copyright symbols, number signs, etc.) in the name. Each anchor name must be unique. There should never be more than one anchor with the same name in the same document—if there is, the browser will not be able to jump the user to the correct anchor.

A yellow icon appears on the page to represent the anchor. This icon is an invisible element that will not appear in the browser.

## ▲ 🔖Alaska Vacations

**TIP** *If you can't see the named anchor icon, make sure that the Invisible Elements option is turned on by choosing View > Visual Aids > Invisible Elements. When you insert a named anchor, a dialog box opens to warn you if the Invisible Elements option is not turned on.*

### 4) Select the text "Hawaii – Multisport" at the top of the document.

This text will act as a navigational element by jumping the user to the corresponding section of the page. You will make this text a link that references the named anchor you created in the preceding steps.

### 5) In the Link text box of the property inspector, type #hawaii.

The number sign (#) is required to tell the browser that this link is internal (will remain on the original page). Make sure that the name you type after the number sign is exactly the same as the anchor name. You should follow the naming guidelines from Lesson 1 when you name your anchors, because they are case-sensitive. If you name an anchor top and then type *#Top* in the Link text box, your link might not work consistently in all browsers.

The text "Hawaii – Multisport" is now linked to the Hawaii section farther down on the page. Now you will repeat the process for "Alaska Vacation."

**6) Add another anchor before the "Alaska Vacation" heading and name the anchor *alaska*.**

You have created a second anchor.

**TIP** *If the anchor is inserted in the wrong place, you can drag it to a new position.*

**7) Select the words "Alaska Vacations" at the top of the document. Drag the Point to File icon (located next to the Link text box in the property inspector) to the Alaska anchor you just made. Release the mouse button when the pointer is directly over the anchor.**

NAMED ANCHOR

POINT TO
FILE ARROW    SELECTED LINK

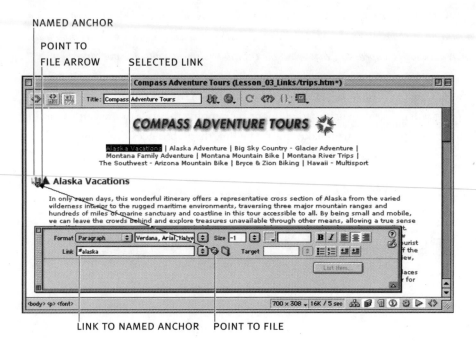

LINK TO NAMED ANCHOR    POINT TO FILE

The link is made. Using the Point to File icon to create links may help prevent typing errors.

**8) Insert anchors and links for the remaining navigational headings and the corresponding sections of the document.**

You can edit the names of any anchors you create by clicking the anchor. The property inspector will change to show that a named anchor is selected. You can change the name in the property inspector's Name text box.

### 9) Save the file and preview it in the browser.

The navigational terms at the top of the page will now link to their corresponding sections. You can close this file.

In the following exercise, you will continue to use named anchors and learn how to link to particular section in another document.

## CREATING IMAGE MAPS

You've experienced how easy it is to make an image link to a page. The user can click the image to go to that linked page. You can also divide the image into several links by using an image map to place individual hotspots or clickable areas on the image. These hotspots are not limited to rectangles; they can have other shapes. In the following exercise, you will add a rectangular hotspot, a circular hotspot, and a polygonal hotspot to an image.

### 1) Open map.htm from the Lesson_03_Links folder. Select the map graphic.

This large map graphic needs to be divided into three hotspots.

### 2) In the property inspector, type *worldmap* in the Map text box.

Don't use spaces or special characters in the name. You can have several image maps on a page, but each map must be uniquely named.

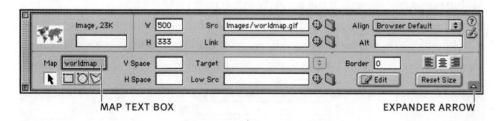

MAP TEXT BOX                    EXPANDER ARROW

**3) Select the rectangular hotspot tool below the map name in the property inspector. Click and drag around the words "Hawaiian Islands."**

A translucent blue-green area with handles appears around the text, and the property inspector displays hotspot properties. Dreamweaver automatically places a null link (#) in the property inspector's Link text box.

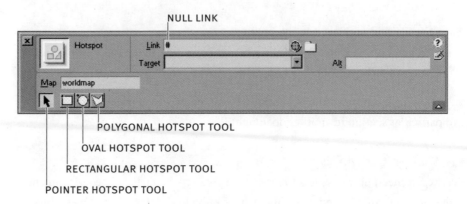

**4) Select the pointer hotspot tool below the Map name text box on the property inspector. Resize the hotspot you created in step 3 by dragging a handle until the hotspot encompasses the small dot representing the Hawaiian Islands.**

The hotspots you create are easy to edit; you can resize, move, or delete them at any time. To move the hotspot, position the pointer inside the hotspot and drag. To delete the hotspot, select it and press Delete (Mac) or Backspace (Windows).

**5) In the property inspector, type *Hawaiian Islands* in the Alt text box.**

This text serves the same purposes as <alt> text for images.

**6) Type *trips.htm#hawaii* in the property inspector's Link text box.**

In the preceding exercise, you created a named anchor in the Hawaii section of the trips.htm file. Now you are making this region of the image point directly to the Hawaii section, instead of linking to the top of the page.

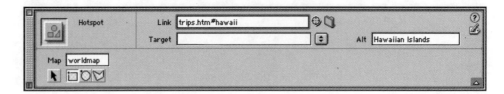

**7) In the property inspector, select the oval hotspot tool. Drag a circle around Australia, including the words "Australia & South Pacific."**

You have created a circular hotspot.

**8) In the property inspector's Alt text box, type *Australia* and, in the Link text box, replace the number sign (#) with *http://www.australia.com*. Then choose _blank from the Target pop-up menu to have the link open in a new browser window.**

You have directed the circular region to open the link in a new, unnamed browser window.

**9) In the property inspector, select the polygonal hotspot tool. Click at multiple points around North America.**

When you use the polygon tool, each click creates a point. A line connects each subsequent point to the preceding point. As you click, you'll see the translucent hotspot area begin to form. Continue clicking around North America until you have the shape you want.

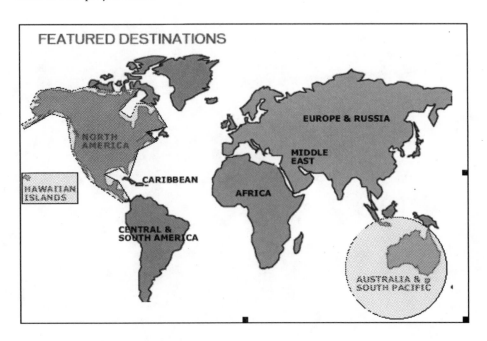

**10) In the Alt text box of the property inspector, type *North America*. In the Link text box, type *trips.htm*, or click the folder icon next to the text box to locate and select the trips.htm file.**

When you finish working with the image map, you can click another area of the image. Clicking outside the image map resets the property inspector to display image properties.

**11) Save the file and preview it in the browser.**

Test the links you have created.

NOTE *If you copy an image map and paste it into another document, Dreamweaver retains the links and hotspots. Since image map information is saved separately from image information, you can use an image map on a different image, if you like. However, if you want to copy both the image map and the image, you'll have to do so in two separate steps.*

## WHAT YOU HAVE LEARNED

**In this lesson, you have:**

- Specified the default colors of links, visited links, and active links to match the colors of graphics used in the page (pages 76–77)

- Created e-mail links automatically using the Objects panel and manually using the property inspector's link text box (pages 77–78)

- Created text and graphic links to pages within the site, as well as to other sites (pages 79–80)

- Targeted a link to open in a new window (pages 81–82)

- Inserted named anchors for each section of a document and linked the corresponding titles of those sections at the beginning of the document to each named anchor (pages 82–85)

- Created and edited image maps with multiple hotspots of different shapes and sizes (pages 85–88)

# ements of
# page design

## LESSON 4

Up to this point, you've had very little control of the design of your pages. You've wrapped text around a graphic and indented text on the page, but these options are limited and don't always provide the desired effect. Tables can provide more control of the placement of these elements. Tables in HTML were originally a means of presenting information in an organized manner; they contain rows and columns where you can place data in cells. Those cells allow you to design pages with a greater degree

*In this lesson's exercise, you will create tables to hold text and graphics. You will learn how to lay out pages like this one with consideration for the constraints of your users' viewable area.*

of control when you place text and graphics. Tables enable you to put the graphics in a location other than the next thing vertically on the page. You can use a cell to create a sidebar for your text, for example.

If you would like to view the final result of this lesson, open biking_table.htm in the Completed folder within the Lesson_04_Tables folder.

## WHAT YOU WILL LEARN

**In this lesson, you will:**

- Learn how to create tables to control the layout of your pages
- Modify the table properties, including border, background, spacing, color, alignment, and size
- Import tabular data from spreadsheets
- Modify a table by adjusting rows and columns
- Sort a table
- Export a table
- Determine the optimal size of your layout
- Import a tracing image

## APPROXIMATE TIME

This lesson should take about two hours to complete.

## LESSON FILES

**Media Files:**

*Lesson_04_Tables/Images/*

**Starting Files:**

*Lesson_04_Tables/Text/bikingtable.txt*

*Lesson_04_Tables/Text/mt_biking.txt*

*Lesson_04_Tables/Text/rafting_text.htm*

*Lesson_04_Tables/Text/
  student_table_project.txt*

**Completed Project:**

*Lesson_04_Tables/Completed/
  biking_table.htm*

*Lesson_04_Tables/Completed/
  destinations.htm*

*Lesson_04_Tables/Completed/layout.htm*

## CREATING A TABLE IN LAYOUT MODE

If you have ever had to hand-code an HTML table, you know how tedious the task can be. To simplify the building of a table, Dreamweaver 4 provides the option to create and edit tables in either layout view or standard view. In layout view, you see just the cells (boxes) that hold your content. In standard view, you see all the rows and columns of the table.

**1) Create a new document and save it as layout.htm. Title the document Rafting Tours.**

You will create a table in this document in the following steps.

**2) Choose View > Table View > Layout View or click Layout View in the Objects panel.**

LAYOUT VIEW

You have switched to layout view, in which you can easily place elements on the page. You may see an info box, Getting Started in Layout View, which briefly describes the main tools. Layout view works much like page-layout programs in which you draw boxes on the page and then fill the boxes with text or graphics. You can resize the boxes, and you can place the boxes anywhere on the page.

Likewise, when you are in layout view, you can add layout cells or a layout table to the page.

### 3) Click Draw Layout Cell in the Layout area of the Objects panel(s).

The pointer changes to a plus sign (+) when you move the pointer into the document window.

DRAW LAYOUT CELL

### 4) Place the pointer in the center of the page; then click and drag to draw the cell.

A layout table is drawn automatically to contain the cell. The layout table is drawn as wide as the document window, but you can resize the table to any size you need. The cell is outlined in blue to distinguish it from the table, which appears in green. When you move the pointer over the border of the cell, it turns red to indicate which cell you are over.

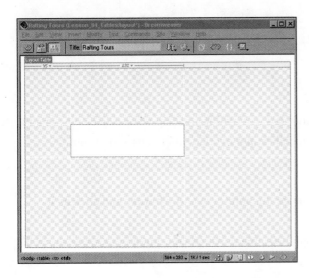

93

**5) Use the Image Favorites Assets panel to insert into this cell the compass_tours_logo2 graphic from the Lesson 4 folder.**

You have inserted an image, as you did in Lesson 2. The cell expands to fit the graphic if it was smaller than the size of the graphic. The new size is displayed in parentheses at the top of the window.

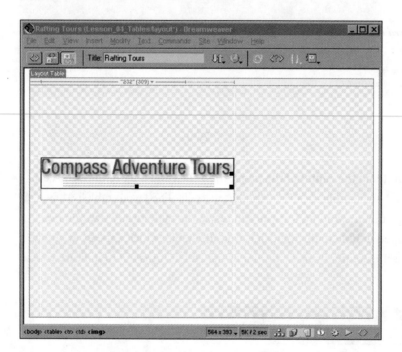

## MODIFYING TABLE LAYOUT

As you design your pages in layout view, you will want to move or resize cells, or add new cells to add content. A layout cell cannot overlap other cells and cannot be moved outside the layout table.

**1) In the layout.htm document, move the pointer over the border and click as it turns red to select the cell.**

The cell border turns blue and handles appear, which you can drag to resize the cell.

**TIP** *You can also Ctrl-click (Windows) or Command-click (Macintosh) within a cell to display the resize handles.*

**2) Drag the cell border to resize the cell, fitting it closely around the graphic.**

In the table tab, the size listed in the parentheses replaces the old size display.

**3) Drag the border of the cell to move it to the top and center of the page.**

If you moved the cell to the right or left to center it, notice that the column numbers in the surrounding layout table change to display the new size.

**NOTE** *Sometimes, the old and new numbers remain on-screen, showing conflicting widths for the same column. If this happens, you need to choose Make Cell Widths Consistent from the column-header menu. The column-header menu is a drop-down menu that you can access from the arrow next to the number displaying the width of the column. If only one number is displayed, this option is grayed out.*

**4) Use the arrow keys to move the cell to the left.**

The arrow keys move the cell one pixel at a time. Hold down the Shift key to move the cell 10 pixels at a time. Leave some space in the column between this cell and the side of the table—approximately 30 pixels.

**5) Below the top cell, draw three more cells side by side, with a little space between them. Make the last cell the largest.**

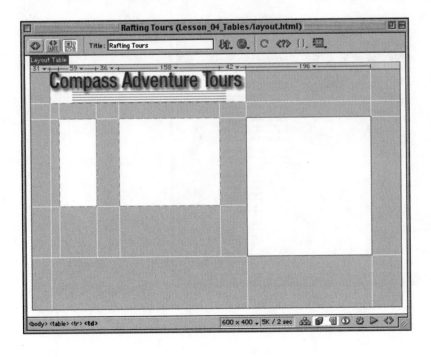

95

When you draw a cell on the page, white guides appear to help you place other cells that you want to align with the first cell. Use the horizontal guides to align the tops of the cells.

**TIP** *To draw multiple cells without clicking Draw Layout Cell more than once, hold down Ctrl (Windows) or Command (Macintosh) as you draw the first cell. You can continue to draw new cells until you release the modifier key.*

**6)  Insert the rafting_tours graphic into the first cell; then insert the rafting graphic into the second cell. Both graphics are located in the Lesson_04_Tables/ Images folder.**

If the graphics are too large, the cell sizes will enlarge horizontally or vertically as necessary to fit the graphics. If the graphics are too small, you should resize the cells to fit closely around the graphics, as you did with the Compass Adventure Tours image.

**7)  Open the rafting_text.htm file in the Lesson_04_Tables/Text folder and copy all the text. Paste the text into the third cell of the table.**

You will adjust the size of this cell later in this lesson.

**8)  Add another cell below the rafting graphic and type the caption *Rafting the Rockies*.**

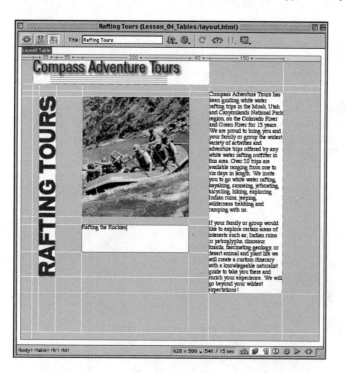

You will adjust the formatting of this cell in the following exercise.

## CELL FORMATTING

You can change several options for each cell. You can add background colors to each cell or to the entire table.

You can also control the alignment of objects within each cell of a table horizontally and vertically. The default HTML setting for horizontal alignment in a cell is left. The default HTML setting for vertical alignment in a cell is center. When you draw a cell in layout view, Dreamweaver changes the vertical alignment to top, but you can change that option easily.

**1) In the layout.htm document, select the cell in which you just added the caption for the rafting picture. Click the Bg color box in the property inspector, and use the eyedropper to select the yellow color in the raft.**

The color of the cell changes to the selected color. To change the background color of the entire table, select the table by clicking the Layout Table tab or any of the gray areas. Click the Bg color box and choose a color for the table.

**2) Choose Center from the Horz drop-down menu in the property inspector.**

This step changes the alignment of the text in the cell to center.

**3) Change the Vert setting to Middle.**

This step centers the text vertically in the cell.

## LAYOUT WIDTH AND SPACER IMAGES

In layout view, you can control the width of tables in two ways: by setting a fixed width, which is the default; or by using Autostretch, which causes the cells to change width depending on the width of the browser. In this exercise, you will apply Autostretch and learn about spacer images.

**1) In the layout.htm document, select the main text cell. Click Autostretch in the property inspector, or click the column header's drop-down menu and choose Make Column Autostretch.**

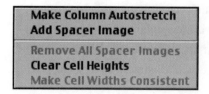

This menu is contextual—it will change based on the properties of the column.

The Choose Spacer Image dialog box appears if a spacer image is not associated with your site.

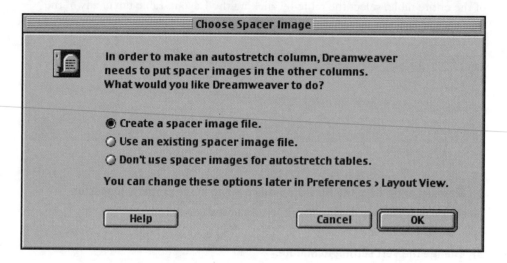

If the dialog box appears, choose the Use an existing spacer image file button, and locate spacer.gif in the Lesson_04_Tables/Images folder. The spacer-file location is saved in your preferences. Choose Edit > Preferences > Layout View to change or remove the spacer image.

**NOTE** *The dialog box includes an option to create a spacer-image file. If you are working on a site for which there is not an existing spacer image that you have created, you should choose this option and click OK to navigate to the directory where you want Dreamweaver to save the spacer image. The Images folder is the best place.*

The Autostretch column is displayed in the table tab as a wavy line. Dreamweaver inserts spacer images to control the layout of the fixed-width columns when you select Autostretch. A spacer image controls the spacing in the layout but is not visible in the browser window.

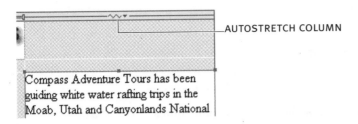

AUTOSTRETCH COLUMN

Compass Adventure Tours has been guiding white water rafting trips in the Moab, Utah and Canyonlands National

### 2) View the page in the browser and change the width of the browser.

Notice that the column stretches as you change the width. When you select a column to autostretch, you cause all cells in that column to autostretch. Use the white guides on the page to determine whether another cell is within the column you've selected.

If you choose not to use spacer images, columns change size or even disappear if they do not hold content. You can insert and remove spacer images yourself or let Dreamweaver add them automatically when it creates an Autostretch column. To insert and remove these images yourself, choose one of the following options from the column-header menu:

Add Spacer Image: The spacer image is inserted into the column. You will not see the spacer image, but the column might shift slightly.

Remove Spacer Image: The spacer image is removed, and the column might shift.

Remove All Spacer Images: Your whole layout might shift slightly—or dramatically, depending on your content. If you do not have content in some columns, they might disappear.

The column-header menu is contextual and will change depending on which column you select. All three options above will not be available in all columns.

You've completed a page by using layout view. Next, you'll work in standard view to create tables.

## CREATING A TABLE IN STANDARD VIEW

Although layout view is the easiest way to design your pages, you will often need to view your page in standard view, which shows you the HTML table structure. You can create tables yourself in this view or view the table Dreamweaver created when you drew a table in layout view.

If the information you want to present is structured in rows and columns, using a standard table is easier than drawing the rows and columns yourself. Often, you will have more control of your table in standard view.

**1) Open a new document. Name the file biking_table.htm and title the page *Montana Mountain Biking*.**

You'll use this document in the following exercises to learn more about creating tables and working with their contents.

**2) Click Standard View in the View area of the Objects panel.**

STANDARD VIEW

When you create tables in this view, you'll see the table borders and all the cells of the table. The layout icons in the Objects panel should be grayed out.

**3) Open the mt_biking.txt file. Copy the "Montana Mountain Biking" header and the first paragraph and paste them in your page. Change the header to heading 3 style.**

Your table will follow this text.

**4) Place the insertion point in a line after the text and choose Insert › Table or click Table in the Objects panel.**

The Insert Table dialog box opens.

The Insert Table dialog box contains a number of options. The Rows and Columns text boxes set the number of table rows and columns, while the Border field defines the width of the table border.

The Width field defines the width of the table in pixels or as a percentage of the browser window. Tables specified in pixels are better for precise layout of text and images. Tables specified in percentages are a good choice when the proportions of the columns are more important than their actual widths.

Cell Padding sets the amount of spacing between the cell content and the cell walls. If you leave this option blank, cell padding defaults to 1 pixel. If you don't want cell padding, be sure to type *0* in the text box.

Cell Spacing sets the amount of spacing between table cells, not including the border. If you leave this option blank, cell spacing defaults to 1 pixel. If you don't want cell spacing, be sure to type *0* in the text box.

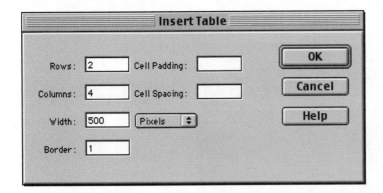

**5) Type *2* for Rows and *4* for Columns. Change the width to 500 pixels, set the border to 1, and leave the Cell Padding and Cell Spacing text boxes blank. Then click OK to close the dialog box.**

The table appears on your page with a gray border, showing the two rows and four columns.

**6)  Type *Ride Name* in the first cell of the first row; then press Tab to move to the next cell. Type the word *type* and press Tab again; type *Location* and press Tab; and type *Rating*.**

You can use both Tab and the arrow keys to move between cells. Tab is the quickest method, and if you move to a cell that already has content in it, that content is selected when you use Tab.

**7)  Click after the table; then press Enter (Windows) or Return (Macintosh).**

The insertion point is in a new paragraph.

You could continue to enter the remaining text for the table. In the next exercise, however, you will use another method to fill the table.

## IMPORTING DATA FROM SPREADSHEETS

If you have text in a spreadsheet or even in a Microsoft Word table, inserting it into Dreamweaver is easy. You need to save or export the text from Microsoft Word as a tab- or comma-delimited file in order to make it compatible with Dreamweaver. You can also use tab- or comma-delimited files that have been exported from other programs such as Microsoft Excel. In this exercise, the text file has already been exported for you.

**1)  In the biking_table.htm document, choose Insert > Tabular Data or click Tabular Data in the Objects panel.**

The Insert Tabular Data dialog box opens.

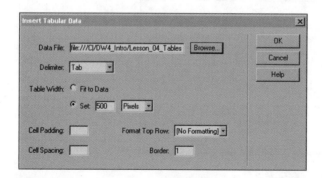

**2)  Click Browse and choose bikingtable.txt in the Lesson_04_Tables/Text folder. Then choose Tab from the Delimiter menu. For Table Width, choose Set, type *500* in the text box, and choose Pixels from the drop-down menu. Leave both Cell Padding and Cell Spacing blank. Format Top Row should be set to (No Formatting) by default, and Border should be 1.**

The data is imported, and a table is built for you with the settings you chose.

## COPYING AND PASTING TABLE CELLS

You now have two tables—the first table contains titles for each column, and the second table contains the data. Now you want to combine the two tables. You can copy and paste multiple table cells at the same time, preserving the cell's formatting, or you can copy and paste only the contents of the cell.

Cells can be pasted at an insertion point or in place of a selection in an existing table. If you want to paste multiple table cells, the contents of the Clipboard must be compatible with the structure of the table or with the selection in the table into which the cells will be pasted.

**1) In the biking_table.htm document, select all the cells in the second table by clicking the top-left cell and dragging across the cells to the bottom-right cell.**

The selected cells are displayed with black borders.

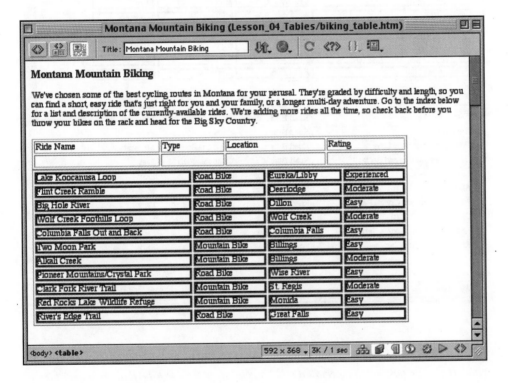

**2) Choose Edit > Copy or press Ctrl+C (Windows) or Command+C (Macintosh).**

To be cut or copied, the selected cells must form a rectangle.

**3) Click the first cell of the second row in the top table.**

This cell is where the copied cells will be pasted.

103

**4) Choose Edit > Paste or press Ctrl+V (Windows) or Command+V (Macintosh).**

All the cells from the second table are inserted into the first table.

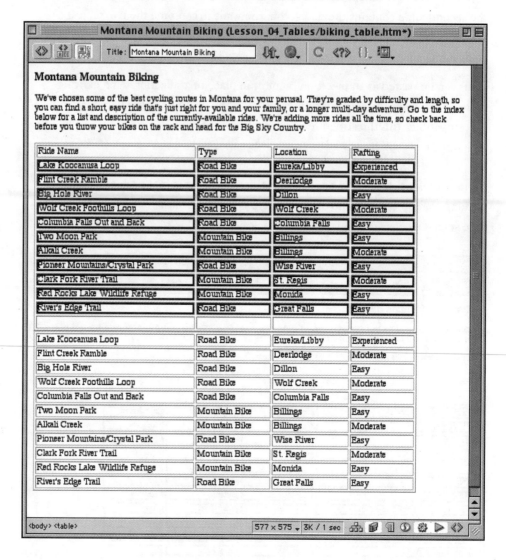

**NOTE** *If you are pasting entire rows or columns, the rows or columns are added to the table. If you are pasting an individual cell, the contents of the selected cell are replaced if the clipboard contents are compatible with the selected cell. If you are pasting outside a table, the rows, columns, or cells are used to define a new table.*

*If you need to remove the contents of cells but leave the cells themselves intact, select one or more cells but not an entire row or column. Then choose Edit > Clear or press Delete. If you need to remove an entire row, drag across all the cells in the row to select it and press Delete. The row and all its contents will be deleted.*

## SELECTING A TABLE

Now that all the content from the second table is in the first table, you no longer need the second table. To delete it, you need to select the table first. Dreamweaver provides several methods for selecting a table. You will find that some methods are easier to use than others, depending on the complexity of the table structure.

**1)  In the biking_table.htm document, select the second table by positioning the pointer anywhere inside the table and selecting the `<table>` tag in the tag selector on the bottom-left corner of the document window. Alternatively, you can click inside the table, and then choose Modify >Table > Select Table.**

**TIP**  *You can also select a table by clicking the top-left corner of the table (Windows) or anywhere on the right or bottom edge. The pointer turns to a cross (Windows) or a hand (Macintosh) when you are close to the edge. Wait until the pointer changes before you click.*

Selection handles appear around the table when it is selected. When the table is selected, you cannot see the black borders around any of the cells; you see only one black border around the entire table.

**2)  With the table selected, press Delete to remove the second table.**

The second table is gone.

## SELECTING AND MODIFYING TABLE ELEMENTS

You can easily select a row, a column, or all the cells in the table. You selected contiguous cells (cells that touch one another) earlier in this lesson. You can also select noncontiguous cells in a table and modify the properties of those cells. You cannot copy or paste noncontiguous cells. The following steps demonstrate various selection methods.

**1) In the biking_table.htm document, select the noncontiguous cells in the top row of the remaining table by holding down Ctrl (Windows) or Command (Macintosh) and clicking the first cell, which contains the text "Ride Name." Continue to hold down the Ctrl or Command key and click the cell containing the text "Location."**

Both noncontiguous cells are selected, as shown by the black borders around the individual cells.

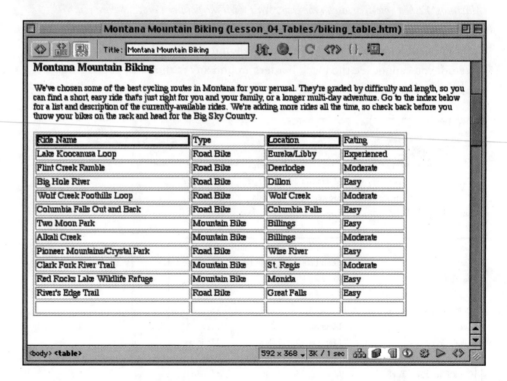

**2) Change the background color of the selected cells to #FFCC66 using the property inspector.**

You can change the background color of single cells, multiple cells, or the entire table, depending on what you have selected. In this step, you change multiple cells at the same time.

### 3) Select the Type and Rating cells and change their background color to #CC9966.

You can also apply a background image to single cells, multiple cells, or entire tables. The background-image option is also available in the property inspector, right above the background-color option.

### 4) Select the Flint Creek Ramble row and position the pointer at the left end of the row, just on the table border. Click when the selection arrow appears; then change the background color to #6699CC.

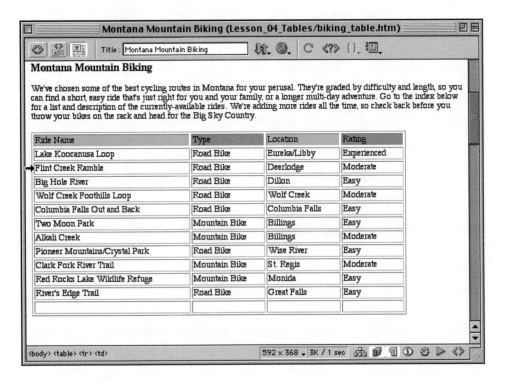

This selection arrow is a quick way to select a single row or column in a table. All cells in the table are selected and show black borders.

**5) Continue to change the color of other rows in the table to match the example.**

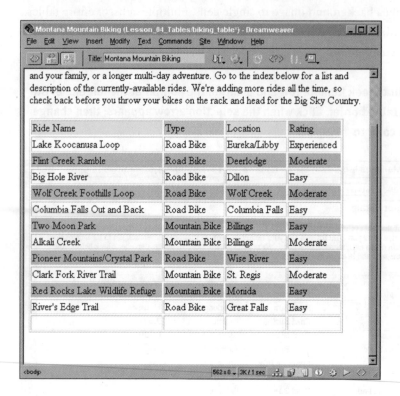

The rows now alternate between white and blue.

**6) Select the Location column by positioning the pointer at the top of the column. Click when the selection arrow appears.**

You have selected the entire column.

**7) In the property inspector, change the horizontal alignment to Center. Leave the vertical alignment as Default.**

In standard view, the default setting for horizontal alignment does the same thing the left setting does: It aligns the contents of the selected cells to the left. The default setting for vertical alignment does the same thing as the middle setting: It aligns the contents of the selected cells to the middle.

**8)  Select the Rating column by clicking the top cell; then hold down the Shift key and click the bottom cell.**

The entire column is selected.

**9)  In the property inspector, change the horizontal alignment to Right.**

The property inspector contains a number of row and column options. Horz sets the horizontal alignment of the cell's contents to the browser default (usually, left for regular cells and center for header cells) or to left, right, or center. Vert sets the vertical alignment of the cell's contents to the browser's default (usually, middle) or to top, middle, bottom, or baseline.

W and H set the width and height of selected cells in pixels. To use percentages, follow the value with a percent (%) sign.

No Wrap prevents word wrapping, so that cells expand in width to accommodate all data. Normally, cells expand horizontally to accommodate the longest word and then expand vertically.

Header formats each cell as a table header. The contents of table header cells are bold and centered by default.

The Bg text field (top) sets the background image for the cells. The Bg color box and text field (bottom) sets the background color for the cells. Background color appears inside the cells only—that is, it does not flow over cell spacing or table borders. If your cell spacing and cell padding are not set to 0, gaps may appear between the colored areas even if the border is set to 0. And finally, Brdr sets the border color for the cells. The border color will only display if the border value is greater than zero.

## SORTING A TABLE

You can perform a simple table sort by sorting on the contents of a single column. You can also perform a more complicated sort by sorting on the contents of two columns. You cannot sort tables that contain merged cells. The following exercise demonstrates sorting.

**1) In the biking_table.htm document, select the table and choose Commands ›
Sort Table.**

The Sort Table dialog box opens.

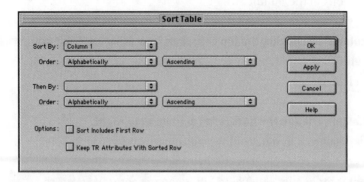

All the default settings will work for this exercise. The first row in the table contains
the column headers; you don't want to sort them. (Note that not including the first
row is the default option, because the checkbox is initially unchecked.)

**2) In the Sort By drop-down menu, select the first column to sort. Then, in the Order
drop-down menu, select Alphabetically.**

The Order menu specifies whether you want to sort the column alphabetically or
numerically. This option is important when the contents of a column are numerical.
An alphabetical sort applied to a list of one- and two-digit numbers results in an
alphanumeric sort (such as 1, 10, 2, 20, 3, 30) rather than a straight numeric sort
(such as 1, 2, 3, 10, 20, 30). Choose Ascending (A to Z, or low to high) or Descending
for the sort order.

**3) Leave the Then By drop-down blank. In the Order drop-down menu to the right,
select Alphabetically.**

Then By lets you choose to perform a secondary sort on a different column. The sort
methods in the menu are the same as the methods that are available in Sort By.

**4) For this exercise, leave the Sort Includes First Row option unchecked.**

Choose this option to include the first row in the sort. If the first row is a heading that
shouldn't be moved (as it is in this exercise), leave this checkbox unchecked.

**5) For this exercise, leave the Keep TR Attributes with Sorted Row box unchecked.**

If you changed any attributes for a row, you can retain that attribute in the row by
choosing this option. Suppose that you sort a table with a color in the first row. After

sorting, the data in the first row moves to the second row. If Keep TR Attributes with Sort Row is selected, the color moves with the data to the second row. If this option is not selected, the color remains in the first row.

### 6) Click Apply or OK.

Your table is sorted alphabetically by the first column, but the row headers remain in the first row.

## RESIZING A TABLE

After you create a table, you may find that it is too large or too small, or you may need to add columns and rows. You can adjust these table properties easily.

**1) In the biking_table.htm document, move the pointer over the vertical table border on the right side of the table. When the pointer changes to a two-headed arrow, drag the column border slightly to the right.**

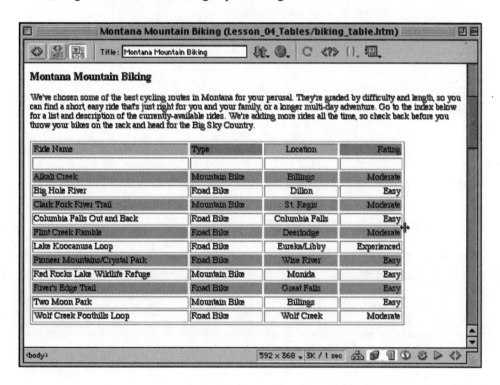

You have enlarged the table. You can see the new width by selecting the table and looking at the number in the Width text box in the property inspector. Whenever you drag table borders in this way, Dreamweaver automatically assigns and updates widths. Sometimes this width may not be what you want. In that case, click the Clear Column Widths and Clear Row Heights buttons in the property inspector.

**2) Click the last row of the table, and choose Modify › Table › Insert Rows or Columns to insert one row below the current row. You can also right-click (Windows) or Control-click (Macintosh) the row above and choose Table › Insert Rows or Columns from the context menu.**

The Insert Rows or Columns dialog box appears. This dialog box allows you to specify whether to insert before or after the current row. When you choose Rows, type *1* in the Number of Rows text box. When you use this dialog box, you have more control of where the new rows or columns are placed, and you can insert any number of rows or columns.

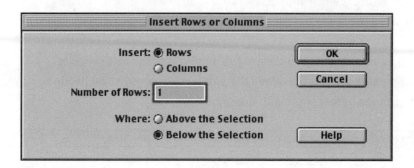

**TIP** *You can also click the last cell of the last row and press Tab to insert another row at the bottom of the table. If you choose Modify > Table > Insert Row, the new row is inserted above the current row by default.*

**3) In the left cell of the row you just inserted, click and drag to the right to select all the cells in the row. Click the Merge Cells button in the property inspector. You can also choose Modify ›Table › Merge Cells.**

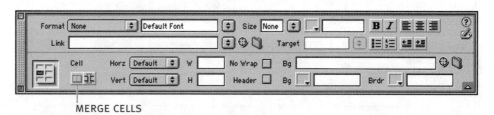

MERGE CELLS

The four cells now form one long cell that spans four columns. The attributes of the first cell, such as color and alignment, are applied to the merged cell.

**NOTE** *You can split cells in the same manner by clicking the Split Cell button in the property inspector or by choosing Modify > Table > Split Cell. This method returns the number of cells to the original number if you merged them, or it can split a cell into any number of rows or columns.*

### 4) In the cell you just merged, type © 2000, Compass Adventure Travel.

Merging cells gives you many more options for layout. You can merge any number of cells as long as they make up a rectangular selection.

**NOTE** *If you need to delete a row, click the row and then choose Modify > Table > Delete Row. You can also right-click (Windows) or Control-click (Macintosh) in the table and choose Table > Delete Row from the context menu.*

## EXPORTING A TABLE

The table you create in HTML has all the tags required to display the table in a browser. If you need to extract the table information to place in a database, a spreadsheet, or a word-processing or page-layout application, you can't just copy and paste the text. All you'll get is the text with no row and column formatting. But you can export the table and save the file as a tab-delimited file that most applications can read.

### 1) In the biking_table.htm document, select the table. You can be in layout view or standard view.

You will export this table from Dreamweaver into a new file.

### 2) Choose File > Export > Export Table.

The Export Table dialog box opens.

### 3) From the Delimiter drop-down menu, choose a delimiter value for the table data.

Your choices are Tab, Space, Comma, Semicolon, and Colon. Tab is the default. If you are not sure which option to use, choose Tab.

Most applications can read both comma- and tab-delimited tables.

**4) From the Line Breaks drop-down menu, choose line breaks for the operating system for which you are exporting the file: Windows, Macintosh, or UNIX.**

Line breaks are the characters inserted at the end of each line. You dealt with them in Lesson 1 when you imported text.

**5) Click Export. In the dialog box that opens, type the name of your file. The file you are creating is an ASCII text file. You should add the .txt extension to the file name.**

The entire table is exported to the file.

## DESIGNING FOR COMPUTER SCREENS

In the print world, a designer creates pages to be viewed in final form at a fixed size. The paper stock, printing quality, and size are all controlled. A Web designer, on the other hand, has to account for a greater number of possibilities. You have to consider not only the variety of browsers users might have, but also the size and resolution of their monitors. The kinds of screens on which users are viewing Web pages have increased and will continue to do so. It is now possible to view Web pages on a cell phone or PDA, such as the Palm Pilot.

If you have only text on a page, the text reflows within the page, based on the size of the browser window. As a Web designer, you then have no control of the look of the page. The user can maximize the window, making long, hard-to-read lines. If you want to control the flow of the text on the page, you can place your text within a table so that you can limit line length for text in a cell.

When you design with tables with a fixed table width, you may want to design to the lowest common denominator of monitor resolution your audience will be using. If you think most of your users have 640×480 resolution, you should use that size. Remember that the browser takes up some room to the left and right of the screen, even if the user maximizes the window. There is no set rule for the amount of room a browser uses, so you should allow for the browser. For 13-inch monitors, for example, make the maximum table size 600 pixels. To determine the maximum table size, refer to the following chart.

| RESOLUTION | DEVICE |
|------------|--------|
| 160×160 | Palm-type device |
| 240×320 | Pocket PC |
| 544×372 | Web TV |
| 640×240 | Windows CE |
| 640×480 | 13-inch monitor |
| 800×600 | 15- to 17-inch monitor |
| 1024×768 | 17- to 19-inch monitor |
| 1200×1024 | 21-inch monitor |

## USING A TRACING IMAGE

Many times, you will be given pages that someone else has designed in a graphics program such as Macromedia FreeHand, Adobe Photoshop, or QuarkXPress. If you can convert the page to a JPEG, GIF, or PNG graphic, you can import that image into Dreamweaver and use it as a guide, or **tracing image**, to re-create the HTML page.

The tracing image is visible only inside Dreamweaver. It is not embedded in the HTML code and will not be displayed in the browser. While you're using a tracing image, the background color or background image of your page is hidden, but it displays in the browser.

**1)  Create a new document and save it as destinations.htm in the Lesson_04_Tables folder. Title the page Featured Destinations.**

You'll insert a tracing image into this document in this exercise.

**2)  Choose View > Tracing Image > Load.**

The Select Image Source dialog box opens.

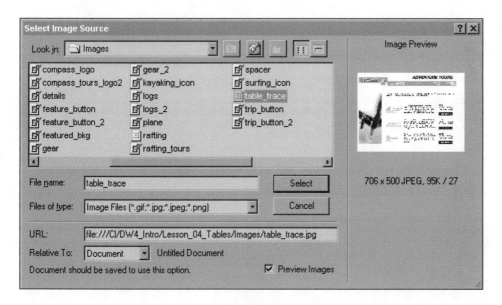

**3)  Choose the file table_trace.jpg, located in Lesson_04_Tables/Images; then click Select.**

The Page Properties dialog box opens.

**4) To see your image on the page, click Apply. Drag the Image Transparency slider to the left to lighten the image. Click Apply to see the change. Then click OK.**

You want to be able to see the image but not be distracted by it.

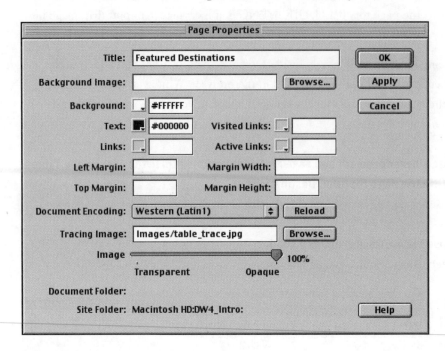

**NOTE** *You can change the position of a tracing image, align it to a selected object, or hide the image by choosing View > Tracing Image.*

**5) Choose View > Tracing Image > Adjust Position. To specify the position of the tracing image precisely, type coordinate values.**

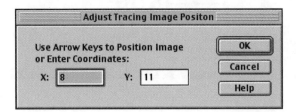

You can also move the tracing image one pixel at a time by using the arrow keys while the Adjust Position dialog box is open. To move the image five pixels at a time, press Shift and an arrow key. Dreamweaver simulates the margin created by the browser between the edge of the browser window and the items in the page.

**TIP** *You can get rid of this margin by entering 0 in all four margin text boxes in the Page Properties dialog box; but this may not work on older browsers.*

This margin may vary depending on the browser, but it is approximately 7 pixels. When you move the tracing image into the margin space, the coordinate values will appear to be negative numbers.

**NOTE** *Choosing View > Tracing Image > Reset Position returns the tracing image to the top-left corner of the document window with margin space (0,0). Choosing View > Tracing Image > Align with Selection aligns the tracing image with the selected element. The top-left corner of the tracing image is aligned with the top-left corner of the selected element*

## WHAT YOU HAVE LEARNED

**In this lesson, you have:**

- Used tables to lay out your pages (in layout view) (pages 92–99)

- Created a standard table (in standard view) (pages 100–104)

- Imported tabular data from an external document as a Dreamweaver table (page 102)

- Modified the table properties, including border, background, spacing, color, alignment, and size (pages 105–109)

- Sorted the information in a table (pages 109–111)

- Modified a table by adding and merging rows and columns to adjust the layout (pages 111–113)

- Exported a Dreamweaver table to an ASCII text file that other applications can read (pages 113–114)

- Learned how the variety of page sizes and screen resolutions can affect how you determine your page layout (page 114)

- Imported a tracing image that you can use as a guide for your layouts (pages 115–116)

# adding user interactivity

In this lesson, you will use behaviors to create rollovers, new browser windows, and working navigation bars. A **behavior** combines a user event (such as moving the pointer over a graphic button) with an action or series of actions that take place as result of that event. Behaviors are prewritten JavaScript codes that you can easily incorporate into your page. You can use behaviors to add interactivity to your pages, enabling your users to change or control the information they see.

You can specify more than one event to trigger a behavior and more than one action for each event. Dreamweaver includes several predefined behavior actions. If you are proficient with JavaScript, you can add your own behaviors. You can also download

*In this project, you will create rollovers with images that are already on the page and learn how to make more than one image on the page change at the same time.*

new behaviors from the Dreamweaver Exchange Web site by choosing Help ›
Dreamweaver Exchange. If you have an Internet connection, your primary browser
will open, and you will be taken directly to the Web site.

To see examples of the finished pages, open Lesson_05_Behaviors/Completed/
rollem.htm for the basic rollover; Lesson_05_Behaviors/Completed/disjointed.htm for
the multiple rollovers, pop-up message, and status-bar message; Lesson_05_Behaviors/
Completed/Check_browser/check_static.htm for the browser redirect; Lesson_05_
Behaviors/Completed/lake_tahoe.htm for the new browser window; and Lesson_05_
Behaviors/Nav_bar/nav.html for the nav bar.

## WHAT YOU WILL LEARN

**In this lesson, you will:**

- Create rollovers
- Add user interactivity to your pages by using behaviors
- Add multiple behaviors to one user action
- Create a status-bar message
- Redirect users, based on the browser version
- Open new browser windows and control their placement
- Create a navigation bar

## APPROXIMATE TIME

This lesson should take about two hours to complete.

## LESSON FILES

**Media Files:**

*Lesson_05_Behaviors/Check_browser/
    Images/…(all files)*

*Lesson_05_Behaviors/Disjointed/…(all files)*

*Lesson_05_Behaviors/Images/…(all files)*

*Lesson_05_Behaviors/Nav_bar/Images/…
    (all files)*

*Lesson_05_Behaviors/Rollovers/…(all files)*

**Starting Files:**

*Lesson_05_Behaviors/Check_browser/…
    (all files)*

*Lesson_05_Behaviors/disjointed.htm*

*Lesson_05_Behaviors/lake_tahoe.htm*

*Lesson_05_Behaviors/lingo.htm*

*Lesson_05_Behaviors/Nav_bar/…(all files)*

*Lesson_05_Behaviors/Text/…(all files)*

**Completed Project:**

*Lesson_05_Behaviors/Completed/…(all files)*

## USING INSERT ROLLOVER IMAGE

The most common use of JavaScript on Web pages is to create a **rollover**—an image that changes when the user moves the pointer over an image. You can create rollovers in Dreamweaver without ever looking at the HTML or JavaScript code. A rollover is a simple behavior that is included in the Common Objects panel. When you use this method, Dreamweaver creates the behavior behind the scenes. When the rollover image is selected, the resulting behavior will appear in the Behaviors panel, which you'll use in the next exercise.

**1) Create a new document and save it as rollem.htm in the Lesson_05_Behaviors folder. Title the page Learning Rollovers.**

In the following steps, you will create a rollover on this page.

**2) Place the mouse pointer at the top of the page. In the Objects panel, click the Insert Rollover Image button. Alternatively, you can choose Insert > Interactive Images > Rollover Image.**

The Insert Rollover Image dialog box opens.

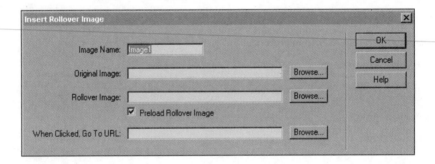

Dreamweaver steps you through the process of creating rollovers in this dialog box. If you haven't initially placed your images on the page, you might prefer this method, because it enables you to insert an image and a rollover specify image at the same time. In the following exercise, you will define rollover states for images that have already been placed on the page.

**3) In the Image Name text box, type *off* for the graphic name.**

The dialog box provides a text box where you can name the image so that you won't forget. If you don't name your rollover images, Dreamweaver assigns generic names automatically in numeric order: Image1, Image2, etc... When naming your images, don't use spaces or any special characters.

**4) Click the Browse button next to the Original Image text box and find off1.jpg in the Rollovers folder.**

This image will appear on the page before the user rolls over it.

**5) Click the Browse button next to the Rollover Image text box and find the rollover image off2.jpg.**

This image will replace the first one when the user rolls over it.

**TIP** *When creating your graphics, make each image the same size. If you don't, the second rollover image will be resized to the size of the first image. Resizing distorts the second image.*

**6) Click the Browse button next to the When Clicked, Go To URL text box and find the file lake_tahoe.htm in the Lesson_05_Behaviors folder. Then click OK.**

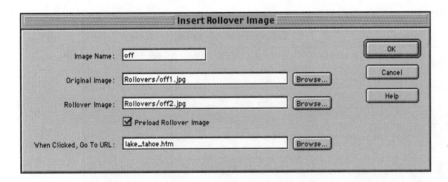

The rollover now links to the file you chose. The URL you chose in the When Clicked, Go To URL text box now appears in the Link text box on the property inspector when the image is selected.

**NOTE** *If you leave the text box blank, Dreamweaver fills it with a number sign (#),   ·
which creates a null link, in the Link text box of the property inspector. The number sign tells the browser to display the pointing-hand pointer when the user rolls over the graphic. You can replace the number sign with a link value, but do not leave the Link text box in the property inspector empty, because doing so will remove the JavaScript.*

**7) Save your file and test it in the browser.**

You can close this file.

**TIP** *When creating your graphics, make the buttons as small as possible. Remember that with rollovers, you are displaying not one but two images for the same button. Although you can use the Choosing the Preload Rollover Image option to speed up the user's experience, it's still wise to keep your buttons small.*

121

## ADDING BEHAVIORS

This exercise demonstrates defining rollovers for graphics that have already been placed on the page. The result is the same as the last lesson—an image will swap to show a different image when the user rolls over it. In this exercise, however, you are defining rollovers for images that are already on the page, and you are using a different method to do so. You will now insert the behavior for the rollover using the behaviors panel. When you create your own Web pages, if you have already placed your original images on a page, you should use this method. If you haven't, you should use the method from the previous exercise to set both the original image and the rollover image in one step.

**1) Open the disjointed.htm file in the Lesson_05_Behaviors folder.**

The file contains a table with some graphics already placed for you.

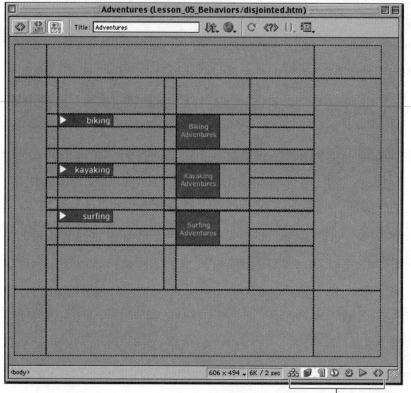

MINI-LAUNCHER

**2) In the property inspector, name all the images.**

A good method is to name the images to match their functions. You could use "biking" for the Biking image with the white arrow, "bikingad" for the Biking Adventures image, "kayaking" for the Kayaking image with the white arrow, and so on.

122

**3)  Select the Biking image (with the white arrow) and click the Behaviors button in the mini-launcher at the bottom of the document window. Alternatively, you can choose Window > Behaviors.**

The Behaviors panel opens. The title bar of the panel shows you have an image selected by displaying Behaviors – <img> Actions.

**4)  In the Behaviors panel, click the plus-sign (+) button and choose Swap Image from the Actions drop-down menu.**

The Swap Image dialog box opens.

An **action** is what happens as a result of user interaction. When you select an action, Dreamweaver adds that action to the list in the Behaviors panel. The Actions drop-down menu displays or disables actions depending on what element you have selected in the document window.

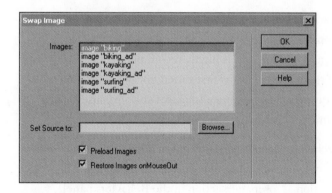

**NOTE**  *Dreamweaver also adds an appropriate event (or events) for that action automatically. The* **event** *is what happens to cause the action to occur. An event could be the user's rolling over an image or clicking a button, for example. For rollovers, Dreamweaver uses onMouseOver events by default. You will learn to change the events later in this lesson.*

**5) In the Images list, select the biking image.**

The image will be listed as "biking." This is the image you selected in the document window and are adding an action for in the Behaviors panel. By selecting the image in the list, you are designating that, when the user rolls over it, the image it will be replaced with is the rollover image. You will choose the rollover image in the next step. If you were to choose a different image from this list, that image would be replaced with the rollover image when the user rolls over the biking image.

**NOTE** *If you don't name your images, they all appear as unnamed (img) in this dialog box. This is why it is so important to name your images properly; it is very hard to work with behaviors if the images are not clearly and logically named.*

**6) Click the Browse button next to the Set Source To text box. Find bike_f2.gif in the Disjointed folder to use for the rollover image.**

All the rollover graphics you will use for this exercise are in the Disjointed folder, and the names of the rollover-image files have the suffix _f2.

Set Source To defines what the rollover image will be. This is the same as choosing the rollover in the previous exercise.

**7) Click Select (Windows) or Open (Macintosh) to pick the image and return to the Swap Image dialog box.**

An asterisk appears at the end of the image name in the Images list to indicate that an alternative image has been assigned to it for the rollover.

**8) Make sure that the Preload Images and Restore Images onMouseOut checkboxes are checked. Then click OK.**

The preload option is checked by default and is highly recommended. Loading the images along with the rest of the page when it is first called up by the browser will make your rollovers happen quickly. This setting eliminates any lag caused when the download occurs at the time the user rolls over the image.

The restore option is also checked by default and is recommended. This option makes your images revert to the original images when the user rolls off them. You will notice that Dreamweaver lists this option as a separate action in the Behaviors panel.

**9) Repeat steps 3 through 8 for the Kayaking and Surfing buttons.**

If you ever need to delete a behavior, you can select the object that contains the behavior, select (in the Behaviors panel) the action you want to delete, and then click the minus-sign button (–), or you can press Delete (Macintosh) or Backspace (Windows).

**10) Save your file and test the rollovers in your browser.**

The images change when you roll over them.

The next exercise demonstrates assigning two swap images to the same user event.

## SWAPPING MULTIPLE IMAGES WITH ONE EVENT

You can also have several images swap from their original images to their rollover images at the same time as a result of the same event. For example, you might want two images to swap out, each from their original image to the rollover image, when the user rolls over one button.

In this exercise, you will make the Biking Adventures graphic swap from the original image to the rollover image as the user rolls over the Biking button. At the same time, the Biking button will change from its original image to the rollover you defined in the previous exercise. For this additional rollover to occur using the same event, you will edit the existing Swap Image action and add the swap image to it in the following steps.

**1) In the disjointed.htm document, select the Biking button and double-click the existing Swap Image action in the Behaviors panel.**

Make sure that you double-click the Swap Image action, not the Swap Image Restore action.

The Swap Image dialog box opens.

**2)  In the Swap Image dialog box, select the image named bike_ad. Click the Browse button to find the image to swap for the bike_ad image. Choose the bike_ad_f2.gif file in the Disjointed folder.**

Look at the Images list in the Swap Image dialog box. Images with an asterisk at the end of the name have been assigned a rollover image. Checking this list is a quick way to verify which images will swap from their original images to rollover images.

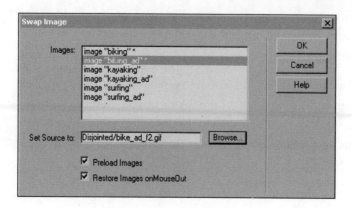

**3)  Click OK to close the Swap Image dialog box. Then repeat the same process for all the buttons, with their respective images.**

Swapping multiple images can be useful for giving the user additional information, but keep in mind that too many extra image swaps on one action can slow the browser.

**4)  Save your file again and test it in the browser.**

When you move your pointer over each button, the button image should change, and the corresponding Biking Adventures image should also change. When you move away from the button, both the button and the Biking Adventures graphic should return to the original images.

## EDITING ACTIONS AND EVENTS

You can edit actions and events in several ways: You can change the event to which an action corresponds, you can attach several actions to a single event, or you can change the order in which those actions occur. For example, Swap Image is the action, and OnMouseOver is the event that corresponds to the rollover behavior. In this exercise, you will add an action for a Popup Message and select a corresponding event.

126

**1) In the disjointed.htm document, select the Biking button. Click the plus-sign (+) button in the Behaviors panel and choose Popup Message from the Actions drop-down menu.**

The Popup Message dialog box opens, displaying a text box where you can type your message.

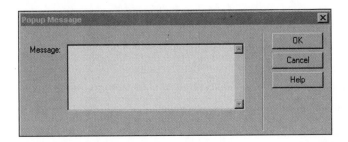

**2) Type *Learn about exciting bike adventures here!* in the Message text box and click OK.**

The Popup Message action and the corresponding event appear in the Behaviors panel.

**3) Select the event in the Behaviors panel, and then choose (onMouseOver) from the Events drop-down menu to the right of the event.**

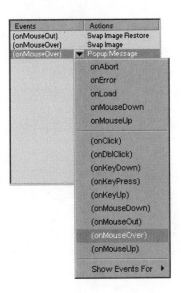

The events in the drop-down menu might change, depending on the action and the browser type you choose. The Events menu appears only when you select an action and event combination in the list. You can choose what browser type to display events for by making a choice from the Show Events For menu at the bottom of the Events menu.

127

**NOTE** *The Events pop-up menu is divided into two sections. In the top portion, Dreamweaver displays events that can be attached to objects directly. The bottom section shows, in parentheses, events that need an anchor placed around the object. If you insert a Rollover Image (either by choosing Insert > Interactive Images > Rollover Image or by choosing Insert Rollover Image from the Objects panel), as you did in the first exercise of this lesson, Dreamweaver adds the anchor for you by inserting a number sign (#) into the Link text box of the property inspector. If you are not using a rollover, you need to add a null link, using a number sign or a working link in the property inspector, yourself.*

**4) Click the up- or down-arrow button in the Behaviors panel to change the order in which the actions are executed.**

The browser will perform the actions in the order in which they appear in this list. The up arrow moves the action up in the list; the down arrow moves the action down in the list.

**5) Save and preview the page in the browser.**

Leave this file open to use in the next exercise.

## CREATING A STATUS-BAR MESSAGE

A status-bar message can give users extra information about where links will lead them. This message, which appears in the status bar at the bottom of the browser window, replaces the default display of the URL or path to the linked page.

**1) In the disjointed.htm document, select the Biking button. Click the plus-sign (+) button in the Behaviors panel and choose Set Text > Set Text of Status Bar from the Actions drop-down menu.**

The Set Text of Status Bar dialog box opens, displaying a text box in which you can type your message.

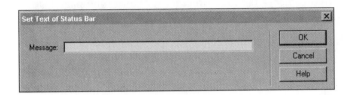

**2) Type *Biking Adventures* and click OK.**

**TIP** *If you use status-bar messages, a concise description of the linked material will help your users navigate your pages.*

**3) Save the file and test it in the browser.**
When you move your pointer over the Biking button, you will see the message you created displayed in the status bar at the bottom of the browser window.

You can close the file. In the next exercise, you will use behaviors to check what browser your user has.

## CHECKING THE BROWSER

Not all browsers support dynamic HTML (DHTML), which defines layers and animations. With the Check Browser action, you can detect users' browsers and redirect users to another page if your page contains features that won't display correctly in their browsers. If, for example, your page contains layers (covered in Lesson 10) or animations (covered in Lesson 14), you could create a static page without the layers or animations and then redirect users with 4.0 browsers to the animation page. Users with older browsers or with JavaScript turned off would remain on the static page.

This exercise uses a page built with tables and a similar page built with layers. You will add a Check Browser behavior and redirect the users with 4.0 browsers to the page that uses layers.

**1) Open the check_static.htm file in the Lesson_05_Behaviors/Check_browser folder.**
This file was created with tables and thus will display properly in most browsers.

**2) Select the <body> tag by clicking <body> in the tag selector (in the bottom-left corner of the document window).**

You are attaching the action to the <body> tag to redirect a user before the page loads. You should see <body> displayed in the title bar of the Behaviors panel, indicating that the <body> tag is selected.

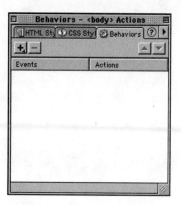

**3) Click the plus-sign (+) button in the Behaviors panel and choose Check Browser from the Actions drop-down menu.**

The Check Browser dialog box opens.

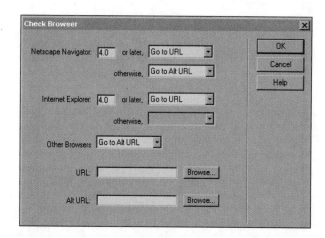

**4) For both Netscape 4.0 and Explorer 4.0 or later, choose Go to URL from the appropriate drop-down menu. For both Netscape and Explorer earlier versions, choose Stay on This Page from the appropriate drop-down menu next to Otherwise. For Other Browsers, choose Stay on This Page.**

When you use the Check Browser behavior, you need to redirect the users who have the latest browsers to another page. If you tried to use this behavior to redirect users with older browsers to another page, it would not work for anyone who is using a

130

browser that does not support Javascript or who simply turned off JavaScript. If you want to redirect only those users who have older browsers, you need to use a metatag refresh instead. (Using metatags to redirect the user depending upon the version of their browser is beyond the scope of this book.)

**NOTE** *To redirect all users to a different page, regardless of their browser version, use a metatag refresh by choosing Insert > Head Tags > Refresh, or you can click the Insert Refresh button in the Head category of the Objects panel. In the Go To URL text field of the dialog box, type the URL you want users redirected to. If you want users to remain on the page for a certain length of time before the browser loads the page you are redirecting them to, type the time, in seconds, into the Delay text field. The Refresh This Document option will reload the page in the browser.*

**5) Click the Browse button next to the URL text box and locate the check_layers.htm file in the Lesson_04_Behaviors/Check_browser folder.**

This file is the page to which users of the latest browsers will be redirected.

**6) Click OK to insert the JavaScript into your page.**

The onLoad event appears with the corresponding Check Browser action in the Behaviors panel.

**7) Save the file and test the page in your browser.**

If you have a 4.0 or later browser, you will be taken to the page with layers; otherwise, you will remain on the static page. You can close this file.

**TIP** *Many Web designers test their pages in multiple versions of Netscape and Explorer. It is a good idea to have multiple versions on your computer for this reason. You also want to check your pages in both Macintosh and Windows. More information on using Dreamweaver to test your site can be found in Lesson 15.*

## OPENING A NEW BROWSER WINDOW

This exercise demonstrates how to open a new browser window when the page loads, for displaying an ad page or other information. You could open a browser window by using a target window, but this method lets you control the size and attributes of the new browser window.

**TIP** *Although the Open Browser window option is easy to add, think it through before using it on a Web page. Make sure that the extra window is necessary. Users might get irritated if new windows continually pop up as they browse your Web site.*

**1) Open the lake_tahoe.htm file in the Lesson_05_Behaviors folder. Click the** <body> **tag in the tag selector.**

Because you want another page to load when this page opens, you use the <body> tag to trigger the behavior.

**2) Click the plus-sign (+) button in the Behaviors panel to add a new behavior and select Open Browser Window in the list.**

The Open Browser Window dialog box opens.

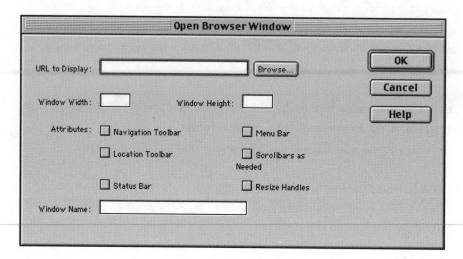

**3) Click the Browse button and locate the lingo.htm file.**

This file is the page that will load in the new window.

**4) Type** *275* **for the window width and** *600* **for the window height, and then choose any of the other attribute options you want (see the description that follows). Then click OK.**

The width and height are chosen based on the size of the content in the new window. If you are simply displaying a banner ad, you should set the size of the new window to the width and height of the image; if the content has more elements, you should adjust the size the window accordingly. The new window's attribute options are as follows:

The Navigation Toolbar is a row of browser buttons that includes Back, Forward, Home, and Reload. Check this box for this exercise.

The row of browser options that includes the location field is the Location Toolbar. Check this box for this exercise.

A Status Bar consists of the area at the bottom of the browser window in which messages (such as the load time remaining and the URLs associated with links) appear. Check this box for this exercise.

The area of the browser window (Windows) or desktop (Macintosh) where menus such as File, Edit, View, Go, and Help appear is the Menu Bar. You should set this option if you want users to be able to navigate from the new window. If you do not set this option, users can only close or minimize the window (Windows) or close the window or quit the application (Macintosh) from the new window. Check this box for this exercise.

Scrollbars as Needed specifies that scroll bars should appear if the content extends beyond the visible area. If you do not set this option, scroll bars do not appear. If the Resize Handles option is also turned off, users have no way of seeing content that extends beyond the original size of the window. If this is the case, you need to make sure the window is sized appropriately for the content of the page. If the window is too small or too large and has no scroll bars, it will be very frustrating for users. Check this box for this exercise.

Resize Handles specifies that users should be able to resize the window, either by dragging the bottom-right corner of the window or by clicking the Maximize button (Windows) or size box (Macintosh) in the top-right corner. If you do not set this option, the resize controls are unavailable, and the user cannot drag the bottom-right corner of the window. Check this box for this exercise.

Window Name indicates the name of the new window. You should name the new window if you want to target it with links or control it with JavaScript.

### 5) Save your file and test your page in the browser.
A new window with cycling definitions opens when you load the page.

## ADJUSTING PLACEMENT OF THE NEW WINDOW

When you tested the Lake Tahoe cycling page, the lingo.html page opened in a new browser window, but you had no control of the exact placement of the window. You can add some parameters to the JavaScript code to place the window exactly where you want it. You can position the page against the top and left part of the screen, but be careful not to position the window too far down or too far to the right; users who have smaller monitors might not be able to see your window.

**1) In the lake_tahoe.htm document, switch to code view by choosing Window › Code Inspector or clicking the Show Code View button in the toolbar.**

Look for the <body> tag. You'll see some code like this:

```
onLoad="MM_openBrWindow('lingo.htm','lingo','toolbar=yes,location=yes,
status=yes,menubar=yes,scrollbars=yes,resizable=yes,width=275,height=600')"
```

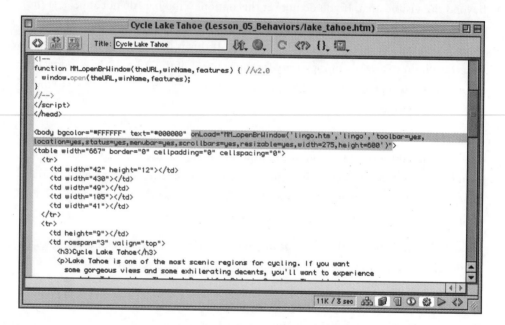

**2) After the height parameter, type the following code:** screenX=0,screenY=0, top=0,left=0.

The screenX and screenY parameters are for Netscape 4.0 and later; they position the window at the top and left side of the screen. The top and left parameters are for Internet Explorer 4.0 and later; they do the same thing as screenX and screenY. Using a parameter of 0 will place the new window at those coordinates—in the top-left corner of the screen.

**TIP** *Make sure to place the code before the single quote.*

The resulting code should look like this:

```
onLoad="MM_openBrWindow('lingo.htm','lingo','toolbar=yes,location=yes,
status=yes,menubar=yes,scrollbars=yes,resizable=yes,width=275,height=600,
screenX=0,screenY=0,top=0,left=0')"
```

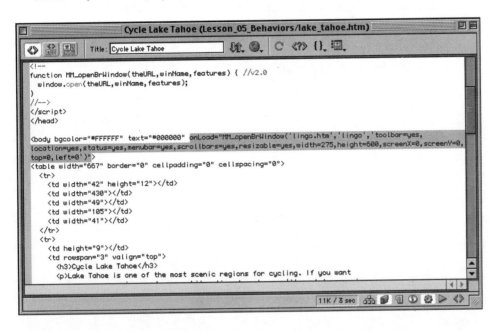

### 3) Save your page and test it in the browser.

The new window displays at the top and left side of your screen.

### 4) Change all four parameters to 20; notice the difference when you view the page in the browser.

The new window displays in a different position.

## ADDING A NAVIGATION BAR

A **navigation bar** is a set of images used to link to pages in your site. Navigation bars are similar to simple rollovers, but you can add up to four states for each image, based on user interaction. The first state of an image, Up Image, in a navigation bar appears when the page first loads. The second state of an image, Over Image, is displayed when the user rolls over the image. (These states are the same two that occur in a simple rollover.) When the user clicks an image, a third state, Down Image, is displayed. The fourth state of an image, Over While Down Image, is displayed when the user rolls over an image after the image has been clicked.

135

The navigation bar adds effective user feedback. You can make the third image look like a "clicked" button, indicating that it has been selected. Users can understand what pages they are looking at based on the selected button. When the user is on the home page, for example, the Home Page button looks like the clicked button, and all other buttons are in their normal state. When the user clicks another button, the user goes to that page; that page's button is in the clicked state, and the Home Page button returns to normal. On each visited page, the appropriate button appears to be clicked, and the others are back to their normal state.

To use navigation bars without frames, you can create them on one page and then copy them to the other pages in your site. Then you need to modify the behaviors for each button on all the other pages. Examples of a navigation bar on several pages (not in frames) are included in the Nav_Bar_Example folder. Another way to implement a navigation bar is to use frames (covered in Lesson 9), with the navigation buttons in one of the frames.

In this next exercise, you will create a navigation bar (not using frames). The completed page will look like the following figure.

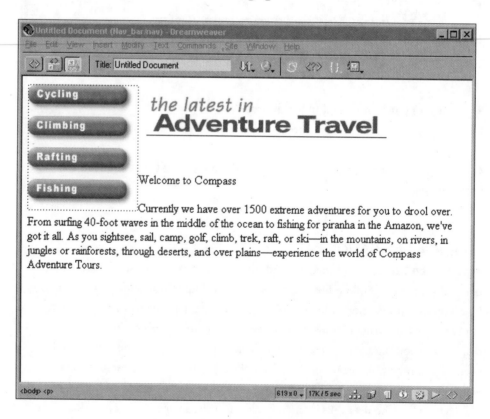

**1) Create a new page. Save it as nav.htm in the Nav_bar folder, inside the Lesson_05_Behaviors folder, and title the page Compass Adventure Travels.**

You have saved the page into the folder in which the files you will link to are located.

**2) Insert the latest.gif graphic from the Images folder inside the Nav_Bar folder in the Lesson_05_Behaviors folder.**

In the following step, you will place the text for this introductory page below the image you just inserted on the page.

**3) Copy the text from the welcome.txt file in the Nav_bar/Text folder and paste it below the image.**

In the following steps, you will place the navigation bar to the left of the image and text that you have inserted into the page.

**4) Place the insertion point before the latest.gif graphic. Choose Insert › Interactive Images › Navigation Bar.**

The Insert Navigation Bar dialog box opens.

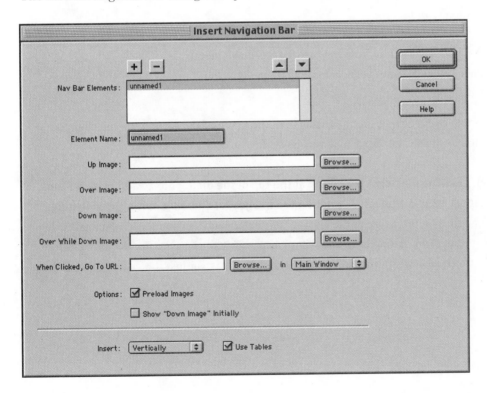

**5)  In the Element Name text box, type** *cycling* **as the name of the first image in the navigation bar.**

The graphics you need are in the Lesson_05_Behaviors/Nav_bar/Images folder.

**6)  Click the Browse button next to the Up Image text box and locate the cycling.gif file. Click the Browse button next to the Over Image text box and locate the cycling_f2.gif file. Click the Browse button next to the Down Image text box and locate the cycling_f3.gif file. Click the Browse button next to the Over While Down Image text box and locate the cycling_f4.gif file.**

These different image states will display according to the user actions. The image you chose for the Over Image option will display in the browser when the viewer rolls over the image you chose for the Up Image option. The Up Image is the first state, and the original image the user will see.

**7)  Click the Browse button next to the When Clicked, Go To URL text box, and then choose the cycling.htm file in the Nav_bar folder.**

The file named in When Clicked, Go To URL is the link to which the user will be directed.

**8)  Choose Vertically from the Insert drop-down menu.**

This option inserts a vertical table that contains your buttons when you exit the dialog box.

As you make changes in the dialog box, the name of the element being changed appears in the Nav Bar Elements list at the top of the dialog box.

**9)  Click the plus-sign (+) button at the top of the dialog box to add more buttons. Repeat steps 5 through 7, entering the images for climbing, rafting, and fishing.**

The files to link to are in the Lesson_05_Behaviors/Nav_bar folder: cycling.htm, climbing.htm, rafting.htm, and fishing.htm. You can click the up- and down-arrow buttons, located above the Nav Bar Elements list, to adjust the order of the buttons.

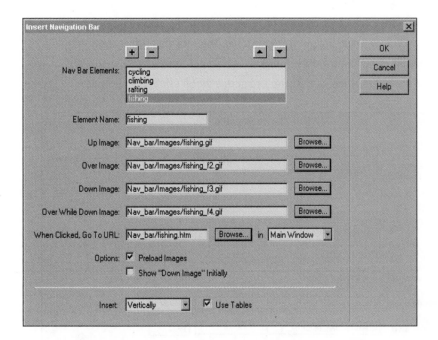

**10) Click OK when you finish.**

The table with all your buttons ready to go is placed in the document.

**11) Select the table and choose Align Left in the property inspector.**

The table will appear to the left.

**12) Copy the table and paste it into the four documents (cycling.htm, climbing.htm, rafting.htm, and fishing.htm) to the left of the content table on each page.**

The table with all your buttons is now in each document.

**13) In cycling.htm, choose Modify › Navigation Bar to open the Modify Navigation Bar dialog box. Select cycling in the Nav Bar Elements list, and then check the Show "Down Image" Initially checkbox at the bottom of the dialog box.**

The Modify Navigation Bar dialog box is the almost exactly the same as the Insert Navigation Bar dialog box in which you created the navigation bar several steps earlier. The only differences are that the Modify Navigation Bar dialog box does not provide the option to choose whether the navigation bar is inserted horizontally or vertically, nor does it provide the option to use tables when inserting the navigation bar.

Repeat this step for each of the remaining files—climbing, rafting, and fishing—checking the Show "Down Image" Initially checkbox for the corresponding navigation-bar element. The Down Image is the image state that is displayed in the clicked state. It indicates that the image has been clicked.

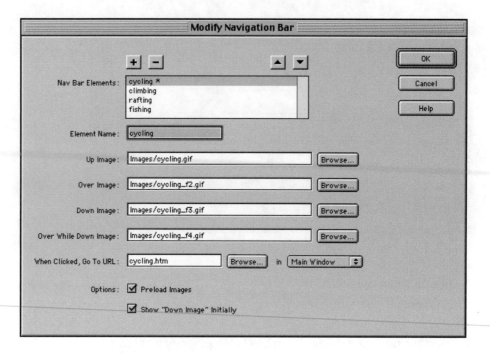

**14) Save all your files and test them in the browser.**

You will be able to navigate to all four pages from each one. The button for each page will appear in the down-image state when you are on that page.

## WHAT YOU HAVE LEARNED

**In this lesson, you have:**

- Created basic rollovers (pages 120–125)

- Learned how to make multiple images on the page change when the user rolls over them by adding multiple behaviors to one user action (pages 125–126)

- Learned how to edit the behaviors by choosing different events and adding actions while creating a pop-up message. (pages 126–128)

- Created a status-bar message to give your viewers more information about a link when they roll over it (pages 128–129)

- Used the Check Browser behavior to redirect users to different pages based on the browser version they are using (pages 129–131)

- Used a behavior to make a new browser window open when the page loads and controlled its placement by modifying the HTML in code view (pages 131–135)

- Created a navigation bar with multiple rollover states for a set of pages and modified the buttons for each of those pages (pages 135–140)

# managing
# your site

The Site window provides extensive management options for your Web site. You can use it to manage both your local and remote sites. You can view your site as a list of files, or as a site map that displays a graphical representation of your Web site's hierarchy. Site maintenance, including adding and deleting files and folders, is best done in the Site window, because Dreamweaver can keep track of your site and update your files accordingly.

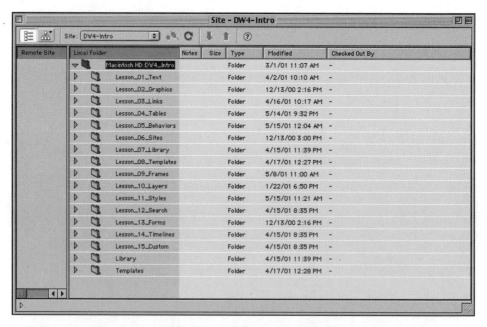

*In this lesson, you'll be working with the Site window to manage files and connect to a remote site.*

## WHAT YOU WILL LEARN

**In this lesson, you will:**

- Learn about the purposes and uses of the Site window

- Perform site-management functions within the Site window

- Customize the Site window

- Create a site map and use it to manage your files

- Understand the difference between a local site and a remote site

- Set up a connection to a remote site

- Copy files to and from a remote site

## APPROXIMATE TIME

This lesson should take about one hour to complete.

## LESSON FILES

**Media Files:**

*Lesson_06_Sites/Biking_Images/…(all files)*

*Lesson_06_Sites/Images/…(all files)*

**Starting Files:**

*Lesson_06_Sites/…(all files)*

**Completed Project:**

*None*

## USING THE SITE WINDOW

The Site window displays the file and folder structure of your site. You can add, delete, rename, and move files and folders here. By doing file maintenance within the Site window, you are assured that the paths that direct Dreamweaver and the browser to links, images, and other elements will stay correct, because Dreamweaver will be able to track your changes and update your files based on those changes. Conversely, if you make file or folder changes in Windows Explorer (Windows) or Finder (Macintosh), Dreamweaver doesn't recognize the changes and cannot keep the paths correct.

**1) Choose Site > Open Site to open the Site window. Select your site, DW4 Intro, in the list.**

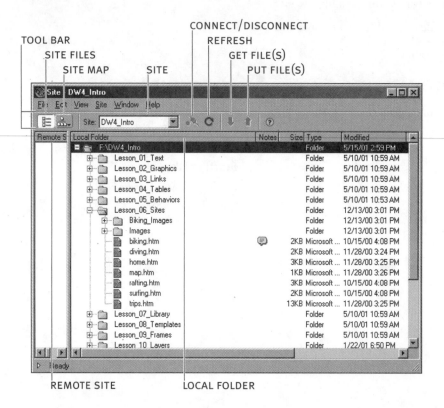

The Site window opens showing only your local files. The default settings place your local files in the right pane of the Site window (the Local Folder pane). When you connect to the remote site, the remote files appear in the left pane (the Remote Site pane).

The Site window's options are as follows:

Connect/Disconnect connects to or disconnects from the remote site. By default, Dreamweaver disconnects the remote site if it has been idle for more than 30 minutes. Choose Edit > Preferences to change the time limit.

Refresh does what you would expect: It refreshes the local and remote directory lists.

Get File(s) copies the selected files from the remote site to your local site, overwriting any existing local copies. The files remain available on the remote site for other team members to get or check out. Put File(s) copies the selected files from the local site to the remote site without changing the file's checked-in or checked-out status.

Check Out File(s) transfers a copy of the file from the remote server to your local site, overwriting any existing copies. The file is marked as checked out on the server. The check-out feature makes collaborating on a Web site easier. You can check in and check out files on the remote server; then others can see when you're working on a file and know not to edit that file at the same time. This option is not available if file check-in and check-out is turned off for this site. Alternatively, Check In File(s) transfers a copy of the local file to the remote server and makes the file available for editing by others. The local file becomes read-only. This option is not available if file check-in and check-out is turned off for this site. If Enable File Check-In and Check-Out is turned off in the Site Definition dialog box, getting a file transfers a copy of the file with both read and write privileges.

## ADDING NEW FILES OR FOLDERS TO A SITE

You can add new pages and folders to your site directly from the Site window.

### 1) In the Local Folder pane of the Site window, right-click (Windows) or Control-click (Macintosh) inside the Lesson_06_Sites folder.

A context menu opens, displaying a variety of options relative to the selected file or to the entire site if no file is selected.

**2) Choose New File.**

A new, unnamed document is added to the Lesson_06_Sites folder. The name field is highlighted, indicating that you need to type a name for this document.

**3) Type *kayaking.htm* and press Enter (Windows) or Return (Macintosh) to name the new file.**

Don't forget the .htm extension for the file name. When you add a file in the Site window, you need to type the complete file name. When you save a file in Dreamweaver, the extension is added for you.

**NOTE** *To add a new folder instead, choose New Folder from the context menu, and then type the folder name.*

## CREATING A SITE MAP

A **site map** gives you a visual representation of your site and all its linked pages. You can save the site map as a graphic to be used in documentation. To create a site map, first define your home page.

**1) In the Local Folder pane of the Site window, select Lesson_06_Sites/home.htm. Choose Site › Set As Home Page (Windows) or Site › Site Map View › Set As Home Page (Macintosh). Alternatively, right-click (Windows) or Control-click (Macintosh) the file and choose Set As Home Page from the context menu.**

You will not see the result of this command until you create the site map. Now that you have defined the home page, you can create the site map.

**2) Click the Site Map button on the Site window tool bar or choose Window › Site Map.**

The site map is a graphical representation of your entire site, with the home page displayed at the top level (also known as the **root level**). A connecting line with an arrowhead shows a link from one page to another. Pages containing links are displayed with a plus or minus sign. Clicking the plus sign displays the linked pages. If a link displays in red type, the link is broken. External links, such as e-mail links and URLs, are blue and display a small globe.

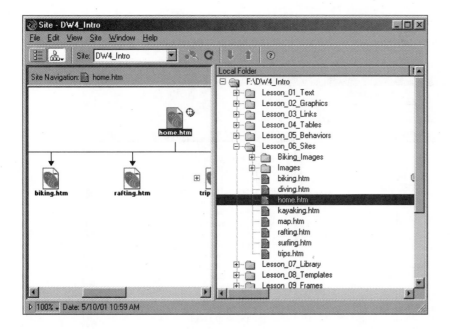

By default, Dreamweaver displays the site map horizontally. If the home page has many links, there might not be enough room on the site map to show all the pages. You can change the number of columns and the column width to make the site map fit a single page for printing. You can also switch the layout to a vertical format.

**3) In the Site window, choose View › Layout (Windows) or Site › Site Map View › Layout (Macintosh).**

The Site Definition dialog box opens, displaying the Site Map Layout options.

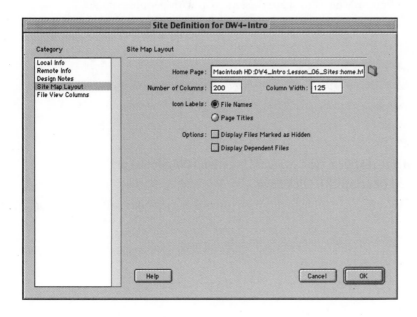

**4) In the Number of Columns text box, type *1* and click OK.**

The site map is regenerated to show all the linked pages in a single column.

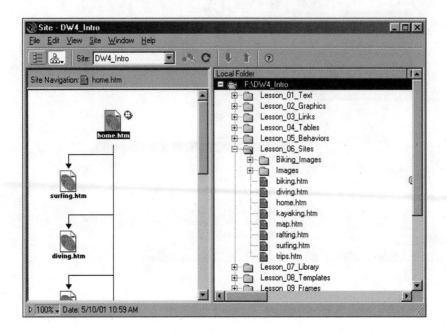

**5) Choose File > Save Site Map (Windows) or Site > Site Map View > Save Site Map > Save Site Map As JPEG (Macintosh).**

The Save Site Map dialog box opens so that you can save the site map as a graphic. On Windows computers, the site-map graphic is saved as a BMP or PNG file. On Macintosh computers, you can choose whether to save the graphic in PICT or JPEG format. At times, you may need to share the site map with people outside Dreamweaver. The option to save the site map as a graphic makes it easier to show to other users.

**TIP** *If Save Site Map is grayed out, go back to the Site window and click the empty white space of the site-map pane to make sure it is active. Then go back and choose the Save Site Map command again.*

**6) In the File Name text box, type *compass_site.bmp* (Windows) or *compass_site.jpg* (Macintosh). Click Save.**

The site map is saved as a graphic that can be printed or viewed in an image editor.

## VIEWING A SUBSET OF THE ENTIRE SITE

As your site becomes larger and more complex, the site map might become too big to see in the Site window. You can refine the view to show just a selected page and its links.

### 1) In the Site window, select the map.htm page in the site map.

You might need to scroll to see this page.

### 2) Choose View > View as Root (Windows) or Site > Site Map View > View as Root (Macintosh).

The site map changes to show the map.htm page as the root (the top level) and its links (the second level). Below the site-map icon, notice a gray bar displaying site navigation. For this exercise, you should see home.htm > map.htm.

SITE NAVIGATION

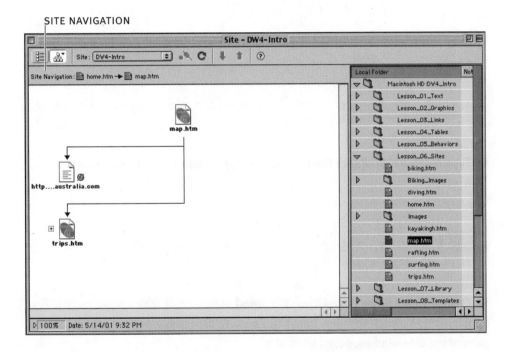

### 3) Click the Dreamweaver icon to the left of home.htm, the home page for this site.

The site root is returned to your home page.

## MODIFYING PAGES FROM THE SITE WINDOW

As you view pages in the site map and move the pointer over the pages, you'll see information about each page in the status area (bottom-left corner) of the Site window. One piece of information is the title of the page. If you forgot to title the page or want to change the title, you can do so in the Site window.

### 1) In the site map, place the pointer over biking.htm.

The status area shows that the document is untitled. Make sure that you roll over the file name, not the file icon. The title won't appear in the status area unless the pointer is over a file name.

### 2) Choose View › Show Page Titles (Windows) or Site › Site Map › Show Page Titles (Macintosh) to see page titles instead of file names in the site map.

The list is regenerated to display the files by title.

### 3) Click the page title "Untitled Document" to select it. Pause, and then click the title again.

A rectangle is placed around the title to indicate that it can be edited. Don't double-click; you don't want to open the file. You just need to select the title so you can edit it.

### 4) Type *Mountain Biking* as the new title and press Enter (Windows) or Return (Macintosh).

The site map shows the new title.

**NOTE** *You can also open a page for editing from either the site map or the site files list by double-clicking the file in either the site-map pane or the Local Folder pane.*

### 5) Choose View › Show Page Titles (Windows) or Site › Site Map › Show Page Titles (Macintosh) to switch the view from titles back to file names. In the Local Folder pane of the Site window, select trips.htm.

The file name is highlighted.

**NOTE** *When you need to change the name of one of your files, you should change the name in the Site window to preserve the link information maintained by Dreamweaver. If you change the file name of either a HTML file or graphics file outside Dreamweaver, Dreamweaver has no way to track your changes. If you make the change within the Site window, Dreamweaver updates all pages that link to the file or contain the graphic.*

### 6) Click the file name.

A rectangle appears around the name, indicating that it can be edited.

### 7) Change the file name to na_trips.htm and press Enter (Windows) or Return (Macintosh).

The Update Files dialog box opens, listing all the files affected by this name change.

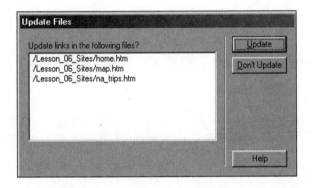

### 8) Click Update to update the files with the new file path.

The site map and files list now show the new file names.

**NOTE** *Dreamweaver opens each file in the list, makes the change, and then closes the file. If a file in the list is open, Dreamweaver makes the change but does not save or close the file.*

### 9) In the Local Folder pane of the Site window, open the Biking_Images folder in Lesson_06_Sites.

Only one image, downhill.jpg, is in the folder. If a file or folder is not in its proper place, you can move the file or folder to its correct location. Making this change in the Site window ensures that all the link information remains correct and intact.

### 10) Drag the downhill.jpg image's icon to the Images folder, located just below the Biking Images folder.

Any files that use this image will be affected by the move; you will need to fix the path to the image. The Update Files dialog box opens, asking whether affected files should be updated.

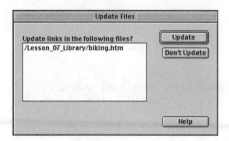

### 11) Click Update to keep the link to this graphic correct.

The graphic moves to the Images folder, and any references to it in the HTML files are still working.

## CUSTOMIZING THE SITE WINDOW

The information displayed in the Site window might not provide all the information you want. Dreamweaver offers you the option of customizing the Site window to your liking. You can reorder existing information, show or hide columns, or even add your own columns.

### 1) In the Site window, choose View > File View Columns (Windows) or Site > Site Files View > File View Columns (Macintosh).

The Site Definition dialog box opens, displaying the File View Columns list.

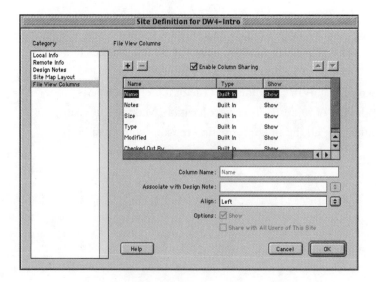

**2) Select Size in the File View Columns list and click the down-arrow button in the top-right corner of the dialog box.**

Size moves down in the list.

**3) Select Modified in the list and uncheck the Options Show checkbox.**

Hide appears in the Show column.

**4) Click the plus-sign (+) button above the Name column. In the Column Name text box, type *Priority* and click OK.**

A new column called Priority is added to the bottom of the list; the columns of the Site window change to reflect your choices. Notice that the modification date no longer appears.

**TIP** *You can use the scroll bar at the bottom of the pane to see all the columns.*

You can close the site window.

## CONNECTING TO A REMOTE SITE

In Lesson 1, you created a local site—that is, a folder on your hard drive to store all the folders and files needed for your site. You've been working in the local site, developing pages and testing links. For visitors to see your Web pages, however, you need to copy them to a remote site. Typically, the remote site is on a server specified by your Web administrator or client, but it could also be on a local network.

**1) Choose Site > Define Sites.**

The Define Sites dialog box opens.

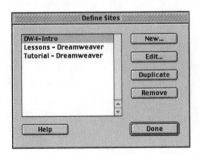

## 2) Select your site, DW4 Intro, in the list and click Edit.

The Site Definition dialog box opens.

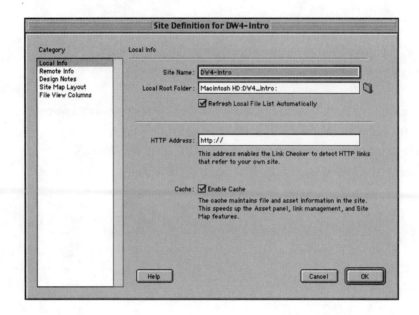

## 3) In the Category list, select Remote Info.

The Remote Info section of the Define Sites dialog box is where you will enter information to tell Dreamweaver which remote site to connect to and the attributes of that remote site.

## 4) From the Access drop-down menu, choose Local/Network.

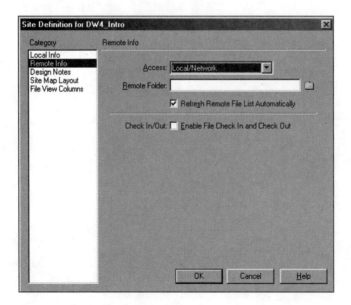

In the following steps, you will create a folder to simulate a remote FTP (File Transfer Protocol) site on your desktop. This procedure will enable you to experiment with the Get and Put functions without the possibility of corrupting an actual remote site.

**NOTE** *FTP access is a common method of getting files from or putting files on a remote site. Because you may not have access to a remote FTP site while you complete this lesson, the following information is presented as reference material only. Consult your network administrator to set these options correctly. The following list of options is available by choosing FTP from the Access drop-down menu in the Site Definition dialog box.*

*FTP Host: The host name of your Web server (such as ftp://mysite.com).*

*Host Directory: The directory on the remote site where documents visible to the public are stored (also known as the site root).*

*Login and Password: Your login name and password on the server. If you deselect the Save checkbox, you'll be prompted for a password when you connect to the remote site.*

*Use Passive FTP: May be used when you have a firewall between your computer and the server.*

*Use Firewall (in Preferences): Used if you are connecting to the remote server from behind a firewall.*

### 5) Click the folder icon to the right of the Remote Folder text box to specify the remote folder.

The Choose Remote Folder dialog box opens.

### 6) Choose Desktop and click the Create New Folder icon (Windows) or New (Macintosh). Type *MyRemote* for the folder name and select it.

For Windows: Select the MyRemote folder and click Open. Then click Select to use the MyRemote folder as your remote folder.

For the Macintosh: Select the MyRemote folder and click Choose.

This folder will act as a stand-in for a remote server and will be a mirror of the root folder of your site, which you defined in Lesson 1.

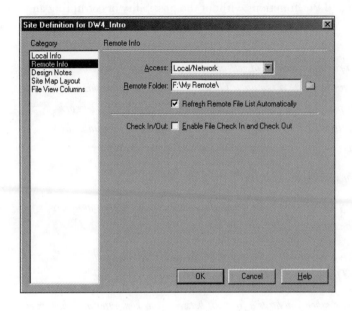

**7) Click OK to save your site information and click Done to close the Define Sites dialog box.**

You can always edit your site information later by choosing Site > Define Sites to open the Define Sites dialog box, and then selecting the site that you want to change.

## UPLOADING FILES

If you've selected FTP or Local/Network access to connect to your remote site, you can use Dreamweaver to check which are the newest files on your local site. This way, you can update only files that have changed.

**1) Open the DW4-Intro Site window by choosing Site > Open Site > DW4-Intro. Click the Site Files button on the Site window tool bar.**

At the top of the window, you will see a Connect icon, which logs you on to a specified remote server. For this exercise, you've defined a local folder, so the Connect button is not active.

**2) In the Local Folder pane, select the top-level folder.**

This folder is your root folder.

**3) Choose Edit > Select Newer Local (Windows) or Site > Site Files View > Select Newer Local (Macintosh).**

Dreamweaver compares the modification dates of all local files with the corresponding file information in the remote site and selects only the newest local files.

**4) Click the Put File(s) button on the Site window tool bar to upload only the selected files to the server.**

The Dependent Files dialog box opens. Your choices are Yes, No, and Cancel. Yes sends the images on the selected page, along with the HTML page, to the server. No sends only the HTML page. If you have changed only the HTML page and the images are already on the server, you have no reason to send the images again, so you would click No. If you have modified an image or added an image to the page, you should click Yes.

**NOTE** *The Dependent Files dialog box also contains the Don't Ask Me Again checkbox. If this option has been checked previously, you will not see the Dependent Files dialog box.*

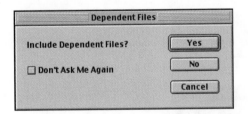

**5) Click Yes if you see the dialog box.**

All the files in the local folder are copied to the remote site in the Site window.

This option could take a long time to execute, depending on the size of your site, so be prepared to wait. If you have changed only a few files, you might find it quicker to select the updated files and upload them manually.

When the upload has finished, you will see a list of files in the remote-site pane that mirrors the list in the Local Folder pane.

## CHECKING IN AND CHECKING OUT

If you are working on a team, the check-in and check-out options can make collaborating on a Web site much easier. When these features are activated, if a team member checks out a file to edit it, Dreamweaver locks that file on the remote server. Everyone else on the team would be able to download the file with only read-only privileges until the file gets checked back in. As long as the entire team enables check-in/check-out and uses the Site window, these features let your group know when someone else is working on a specific file, preventing accidental overwriting of material or duplicate efforts.

### 1) Choose Site › Define Sites.

The Define Sites dialog box opens.

### 2) Select the DW4 Intro site in the list and click Edit.

The Site Definition dialog box opens.

### 3) Select Remote Info in the Category list.

The remote-site information is displayed.

### 4) Check the Enable File Check In and Check Out checkbox.

One additional checkbox and two additional text boxes appear. Files become checked out automatically as you open them if Check Out Files When Opening is checked. You must be connected to the site for this feature to function properly. If you are not connected, Dreamweaver attempts to connect to the remote site automatically.

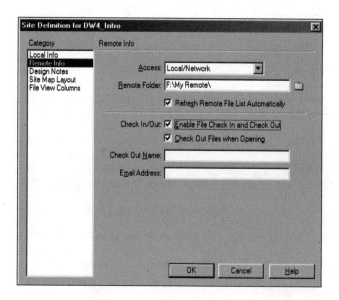

The text boxes are Check Out Name and Email Address.

**5) Type a check-out name and your e-mail address in the appropriate text boxes. Click OK in the Site Definition dialog box and click Done in the Define Sites dialog box.**

Your check-out name is only for group reference; it can be your full name or simply a user name. This name will be displayed in the Checked Out By column of the site window when you check out a file. Your e-mail address is available to allow team members to contact you with questions.

**6) In the Site window, select the home.htm page in the Local Folder pane and click the Check In icon at the top of the window. Do the same for the map.htm page.**

Dreamweaver uploads the selected files to the remote site. In the Local Folder pane of the site window, the files are marked with a small lock to let you know that the files have been checked in and will need to be checked out for you to edit them locally.

**TIP** *If you disable Enable File Check In and Check Out, you still see the small lock. To unlock a file, select it by clicking the file once and choose Site > Unlock (Macintosh) File > Turn Off Read Only (Windows).*

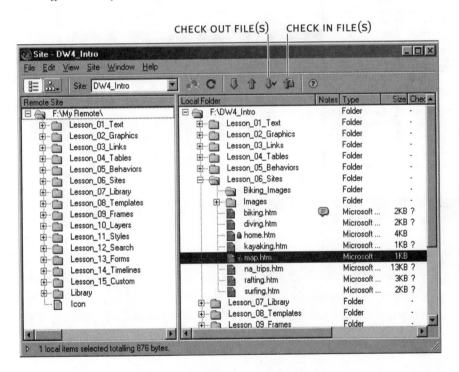

When you are working with a group of people and using the check-in/check-out feature, everyone should use the Check In File(s) and Check Out File(s) icons to upload and download files instead of the Get File(s) and Put File(s) icons.

**7) In the Site window, select the map.htm page in the local panel. Click the Check Out icon at the top of the window.**

To ensure that you will be working with the most recent version, the file is downloaded to your local site. The file is marked in both the local and remote panes with a small green check, indicating the file's checked-out status. The Checked Out By columns in both the local and remote panes show your check-out name in the form of a clickable link to your e-mail address. Files checked out by other members of your team are displayed with a red check, indicating that you will be unable to overwrite them.

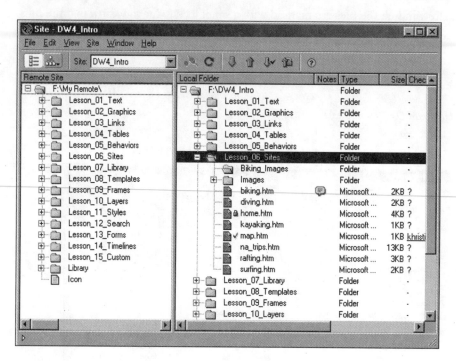

**NOTE** *For the check-in/check-out feature to work properly, everyone on your team should be using Dreamweaver. This feature is not recognized by other FTP programs. Those programs will be able to overwrite files, negating the purpose of checking files in and out.*

## USING DESIGN NOTES

Design notes are useful for keeping track of information related to your files. These notes are for your information only; they are hidden text files that cannot be accessed or displayed in browsers by the users of your site. You can share the information with your co-workers easily by uploading design notes to the remote server. These notes can be used with all files on your site, including HTML and image files.

**1) In the Site window, select the biking.htm file. Double-click the yellow text bubble in the Notes column, located to the right of the file name.**

The Design Notes dialog box appears. The Basic Info tab displays information about the file to which the note is attached and the path of that file in the site. You can change the status of the file by making a choice from the Status drop-down menu.

DATE

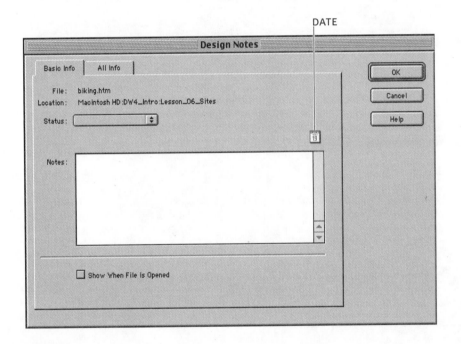

**NOTE** *The Design Notes option in the Category column of the Site Definition dialog box allows you to turn design notes on or off. By default, both the Maintain Design Notes and the Upload Design Notes for Sharing checkboxes are checked. Dreamweaver automatically uploads or downloads the design notes for any file you get, put, check in, or check out from the remote server when the Upload Design Notes for Sharing checkbox is checked.*

## 2) Click the date icon above the Notes text box.

The date is inserted into the first line of the Notes text box. Use this area to enter any important information about your files.

A checkbox at the bottom of this window allows you have this note displayed when the file is opened.

## 3) Click OK.

The note is closed with the information you added. The Design Notes icons remain in the Notes columns to indicate that a note is attached to the file.

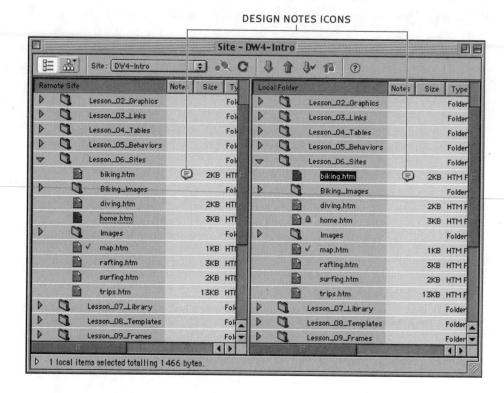

## 4) Select the rafting.htm page and choose File > Design Notes.

The Design Notes dialog box appears. You can use this method to attach a design note to a file when it is selected in the Site window or when the file is open in the document window.

**TIP** *You can also attach a design note from the Site window by double-clicking the Notes column for the selected file.*

## 5) In the Status drop-down menu, change the status to revision 1 and click OK.

The Design Notes dialog box closes.

## WHAT YOU HAVE LEARNED

**In this lesson, you have:**

- Performed site-management functions within the Site window, including creating new files, renaming files, and moving files (pages 144–146)

- Created a site map, viewed it horizontally and vertically, used it to manage your files, and learned how to save the site map as an image (pages 146–152)

- Used the Update Files dialog box to ensure that your paths and links stay correct when you moved files (page 151)

- Customized the Site window and edited the columns (pages 152–153)

- Learned the difference between a local site and a remote site, how to use Local/Network and FTP to connect to servers, as well as how to define and edit both kinds of site (pages 153–155)

- Set up a connection to a local/network folder as your remote site (page 154)

- Copied files to and from a remote site using the Select Newer Local command to save time (pages 156–157)

- Attached a design note to a file, edited design notes, and learned to use them to share information with team members and keep track of file status and versions (pages 158–162)

# using libraries

Dreamweaver lets you store often-used content as library items. There may be elements you want to repeat throughout your site. These elements may include navigation tools, copyright information, headers and footers, or other elements that need to appear on multiple pages. Creating library items for these elements will allow you to quickly and easily insert this content into many documents. If you need to change information, such as copyright dates that may appear on a large number of pages throughout your site, library items will make it possible for you to edit the content and, with a single command, update all documents that reference it. Without a library item, you would

*In this project, you will add a library item like the one at the bottom of this page. After you modify the library item, you will use the update feature to quickly and efficiently make the same changes to all pages containing that item.*

have to open each page and modify the information. On a small site, this may not be difficult; however, on a very large site, it would be time-consuming and increase the probability of errors. Library items provide a way for you to maintain consistency and automate the process of updating your site.

To see examples of the finished pages, open biking.htm, cycling_intro.htm, and road.htm from the Lesson_07_Library/Completed folder.

## WHAT YOU WILL LEARN

**In this lesson, you will:**

- Learn when and why to use library items
- Create and insert a library item
- Recreate a library item
- Edit an existing library item
- Update all references to a library item
- Detach a library item
- Create and modify a library item containing behaviors

## APPROXIMATE TIME

This lesson should take about one hour to complete.

## LESSON FILES

**Media Files:**

*Lesson_07_Library/Images/bike_ad.gif*

*Lesson_07_Library/Images/bike_ad_f2.gif*

*Lesson_07_Library/Images/bike_overlook.jpg*

*Lesson_07_Library/Images/compass.gif*

*Lesson_07_Library/Images/
compass_logo_gray.gif*

*Lesson_07_Library/Images/kayak_ad_f2.gif*

**Starting Files:**

*Lesson_07_Library/biking.htm*

*Lesson_07_Library/cycling_intro.htm*

*Lesson_07_Library/road.htm*

**Completed Project:**

*Lesson_07_Library/Completed/biking.htm*

*Lesson_07_Library/Completed/
cycling_intro.htm*

*Lesson_07_Library/Completed/road.htm*

## CREATING A LIBRARY ITEM

When you create a library item, Dreamweaver creates a folder named Library at the top level of your local root folder and stores each library item there. This folder and the library files it contains are only stored locally; they do not need to be uploaded to a server.

**NOTE** *Dreamweaver saves each library item with an .lbi file extension.*

You create a library item by selecting elements in a document and adding them to the library. When you do this, Dreamweaver converts the selection into a locked area of code linked to the library item. The following exercise demonstrates this process.

### 1) Open Lesson_07_Library/biking.htm.

Library items can only include content that appears between the <BODY> and </BODY> tags. They can include any document elements, such as text, tables, forms, images, Java applets, plug-ins, or ActiveX elements.

**NOTE** *Cascading style sheet (CSS) references (for example, <SPAN CLASS="green"> green text </SPAN>) are preserved in library items, but the style will not appear when the item is inserted in a document unless the style sheet containing that style is linked to the document. The Library panel offers a visual reminder of this fact (in addition to a warning message) by displaying the text as it would appear if the style sheet were omitted. The best way to make sure style sheet information is included is to use a kind of CSS called external style sheets. CSS are covered in Lesson 11.*

### 2) Select the copyright text, the e-mail address text, the modification date, and the horizontal rule.

The text and horizontal rule are highlighted.

The copyright, e-mail address, and modification date are standard information that might be used on all pages of a site. Libraries can be very useful for this type of information. Dreamweaver stores only a reference to linked items, such as images or other pages, which must remain at their original locations for the library item to work correctly.

**3) Choose Window > Library to open the Library panel.**

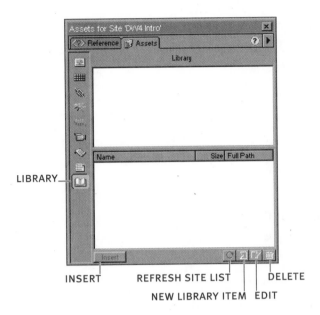

LIBRARY

INSERT    REFRESH SITE LIST    DELETE
NEW LIBRARY ITEM    EDIT

The Library category of the Assets panel opens. This is where you will manage all of your library items.

**4) Drag the selected objects from the document window to the lower half of the Library panel. Alternatively, you can click the new library item button at the bottom of the Library category of the Assets panel or choose Modify > Library > Add Object to Library.**

A new "Untitled" icon appears and is highlighted on the Library panel. A preview of the library item appears at the top of the panel.

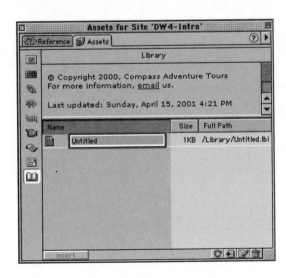

**5) Type *footer* for the new library item, and then press Enter (Windows) or Return (Macintosh).**

The footer library item is now added to the Library panel. You should give your library items descriptive names—the names are for your reference only and will not be displayed to the user in a browser window.

When you deselect the text in the biking.htm document window, it has a pale yellow background. The yellow background indicates the text is linked to a library item and is not directly editable. This block of text is now considered one item, so clicking any part of it will select the entire library item. Leave open the biking.htm document for the next exercise.

## PLACING A LIBRARY ITEM ON A PAGE

Placing a library item in a document inserts the contents of the file and creates a reference to the external file. When you insert a library item, the actual HTML is inserted, which means the content appears even if the file is viewed locally. Dreamweaver inserts comments around the item to show the name of the library file and reference the original item. The reference to the external library item file makes it possible to update the content on an entire site all at once by simply changing the library item.

**1) Open cycling_intro.htm and place the insertion point on a blank line at the bottom of the document.**

You will place the library item you created in the previous exercise into this document in the following steps.

**NOTE** *If the Library panel is not visible, choose Window > Library. You can also click Show Assets on the mini-launcher located at the bottom-right corner of the document window bar, and then click Library.*

**2) Drag the footer file icon from the Library panel to the document window. Alternatively, you can select the footer library item, and then click Insert at the bottom left of the panel.**

The text and rule are added to the document; footer is shown with a yellow background. While library items are highlighted with yellow by default, the color can be changed or turned off completely in the Preferences dialog box. This item cannot be modified directly on the page. You will modify library items in the next exercise.

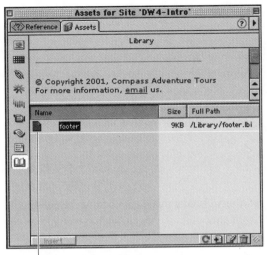

FOOTER FILE ICON

With the library items selected in the document window, you can use the property inspector to view the source path and perform maintenance functions on the library items.

The property inspector has several options to choose from. Src displays the file name and location of the source file for the library item. You can open the library item for editing with the Open option. You must save the file to keep the changes you make.

Detach from Original breaks the link between the selected library item and its source file. The content of the library item becomes editable within the document, but it can no longer be updated by the library update functions.

Recreate overwrites the original library item with the current selection. Use this option to create library items again if the library file isn't present, the item's name has been changed, or if the item has been edited.

You can save and close the biking.htm document.

### 3) Open road.htm and place the insertion point on a blank line at the bottom of the document.

You will place a copy of the library item with copyright information on this page so it is editable in the document.

**4) Hold down Control (Windows) or Option (Macintosh) and drag footer from the Library panel to the document.**

The library content is copied into the document but is not linked to the library, so there is no yellow highlighting. The elements can be modified directly on the page since they are not connected to a library item.

You can save and close the road.htm document. Save the cycling_intro.htm document, but leave it open for the next exercise.

## RECREATING A LIBRARY ITEM

If a library item is accidentally deleted from the Library category of the Assets panel and you still have a page showing the library item, you can recreate it.

**1) In the cycling_intro.htm document, select the library item at the top of the page by clicking once in the area that is shown with a yellow highlight.**

The entire item is selected and grayed out to show that it cannot be edited within the document. Although this element was marked as a library item in the document window, it does not appear in the Library category of the Assets panel.

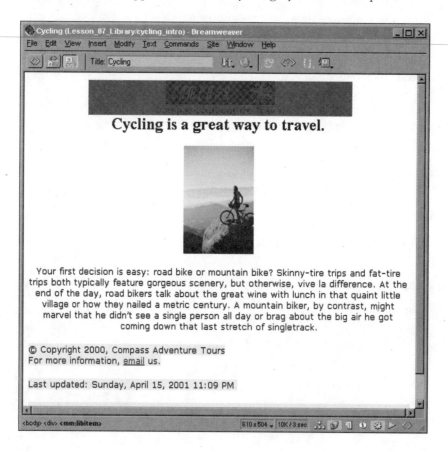

**2) Click Recreate on the property inspector.**

The library item file is recreated with the item name used on this page; it will now show up titled as "logo" in the Library category of the Assets panel.

You can close the cycling_intro.htm document.

## MODIFYING A LIBRARY ITEM

When you edit a library item, you need to edit the item's file in the Library folder. Editing a library item changes the library item only. When you finish editing, Dreamweaver prompts you to update all the pages in the site that use the item, letting you choose whether to make these changes throughout the entire site. Dreamweaver accomplishes the update by searching for comments that reference the library file you just edited, and then replacing the old HTML with your new HTML. If you remove the library comments, the HTML is no longer associated with the library item and cannot be changed by updating the library item.

**NOTE** *Any modifications to the library item must be made through the Assets panel. If you want to edit the content directly in a document, you must first break the link to the library item. To do this, use the Detach from Original button on the property inspector, or hold down Control (Windows) or Option (Macintosh) when inserting the item.*

**1) Double-click footer on the Library category of the Assets panel.**

Alternatively, you can select footer on the Library panel and click Edit on the panel. You can also select the library item on a page and click Open in the property inspector.

**NOTE** *If the Library category of the Assets panel is not open, choose Window > Library.*

Dreamweaver opens the footer library item for editing. Notice that the background of this page is gray. When library items are inserted on a page, they take on the properties of that document; text and link colors will be changed according to the default colors set for the document (unless you have specified the font color in the library item).

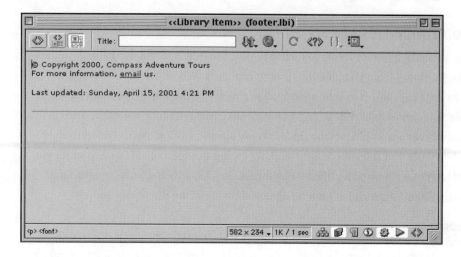

**2) In the document window, select the horizontal rule and move it above the copyright line. Save the document.**

The Update Library Items dialog box opens.

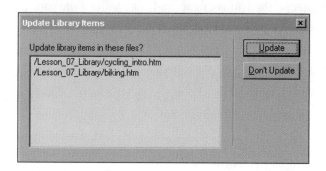

**3) Click Update to update all the documents in your site that use the footer library item.**

The Update Pages dialog box shows which pages have been updated with your changes.

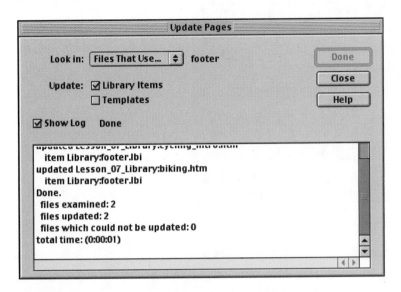

**NOTE** *If you have a large site, you might prefer to wait to update your site with all your changes at once. In that case, click the Don't Update button when you save the library item. The documents that use that library item will not change until you update the item.*

**4) Click Close to close the Update Pages dialog box.**

The horizontal rule should be in its new location in both biking.htm and cycling_intro.htm.

## UPDATING LIBRARY REFERENCES

If you choose not to update your pages at the time you edit a library item, but decide do so later, Dreamweaver lets you do all the updating with a single command.

**1) Open the footer library item from the Library panel. Change the copyright date to 2001 and save the document. In the Update Library Items dialog box, click Don't Update.**

Neither biking.htm nor cycling_intro.htm will show the new copyright date yet.

173

### 2) From the menu bar, choose Modify > Library > Update Pages.

The Update Pages dialog box opens.

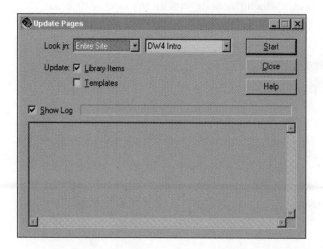

### 3) In the Look In drop-down menu, choose Entire Site.

The menu to the right will display the current site, DW4 Intro. You are choosing to update all files in your site that use the footer library item.

### 4) In the Update checkboxes, check the Library Items box and uncheck the Templates box. Check the Show Log box and click Start.

The Update Pages dialog box shows which files were updated.

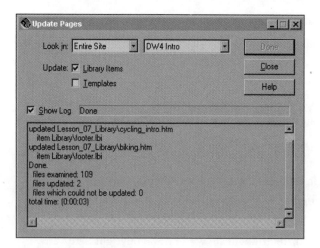

### 5) Click Close to close the dialog box.

The new copyright date appears in both biking.htm and cycling_intro.htm.

## CREATING A LIBRARY ITEM CONTAINING BEHAVIORS

Library items must be contained within the <BODY> of the document and cannot contain or reference any items outside of the <BODY> (unless the items referenced are in the containing HTML file). For this reason, JavaScript cannot be used in library items if the script requires code between the <HEAD> and </HEAD> tags of the document, because those tags are located before the <BODY> tag. There is one exception however: because behaviors are predefined JavaScripts for which Dreamweaver will insert the corresponding JavaScript functions into the <HEAD>, you can use Dreamweaver's behaviors in library items, even though the necessary JavaScript requires code to be placed between the <HEAD> and </HEAD> tags of the document. Although the code that is required in the <HEAD> is not included in the library item, Dreamweaver will automatically place the code into the <HEAD> whenever the library item is placed into a document.

**1) Open road.htm and select the table at the top of the document.**

This table contains a rollover that was created using Dreamweaver's Insert Rollover function. Insert Rollover and other behaviors were covered in Lesson 5.

**2) Click the new library item button at the bottom of the Library panel. Type *header* for the new library item name and press Enter (Windows) or Return (Macintosh).**

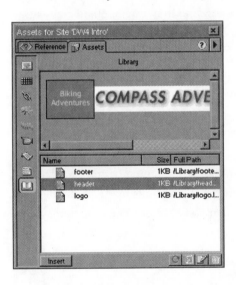

The library item contains certain portions of the code necessary for the behavior, including the event handler, as well as the action to call when the event occurs. It does not contain any of the functions that are required to be placed between the <HEAD> and </HEAD> tags of the document.

**3) Insert this new library item at the top of the page in the biking.htm document.**

The JavaScript functions that are required for the rollover in this library item are automatically inserted between the <HEAD> and </HEAD> tags of the document. While these functions are not included in the library item, they are inserted because Dreamweaver recognizes certain portions of the code in the library item as behaviors and automatically inserts the required code into the <HEAD>.

**NOTE** *If you write your own JavaScript that uses functions between the <HEAD> and </HEAD> tags of the document, you can use the Call JavaScript behavior (available at the top of the Events menu on the Behaviors panel) to execute the code. A behavior must be used in a library item in order for Dreamweaver to insert the corresponding functions.*

You can close the biking.htm document. Leave the road.htm document open for the next exercise.

## MODIFYING A LIBRARY ITEM CONTAINING BEHAVIORS

Library items that contain behaviors require a more complex editing process than items that do not contain behaviors. The options on the behaviors panel are grayed out while you are editing a library item, so you can't modify a behavior from the library panel. You must first detach the item from a page in order to make your changes. You can then delete the original item and create a new one from the modified elements. The following steps demonstrate how to edit these kinds of library items.

**1) In the road.htm document, select the header library item at the top of the document.**

You created a library item from this table in the previous exercise.

**2) Make a note of the name of the library item, and then click Detach from Original in the property inspector.**

The name of this library item is header. It is important to remember the exact name so that when you make this table a library item again, any links to the library item in the rest of your site will remain correct. Now that you have detached the item, you can edit the rollover.

**3)  Select road.htm and choose Window › Behaviors to open the Behaviors panel.**

This rollover uses the wrong graphic when it swaps. In the following steps, you'll change the graphic from a kayaking image to a biking image.

**4)  Double-click the existing Swap Image action in the list of attached behaviors on the Behaviors panel.**

**TIP**  *Make sure you double-click the Swap Image action, not the Swap Image Restore action.*

The Swap Image dialog box opens.

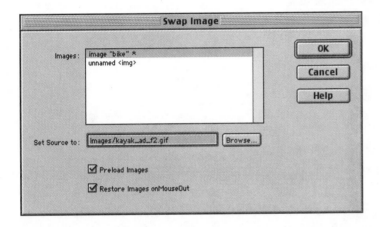

**5)  In the Swap Image dialog box, click Browse to find bike_ad_f2.gif and choose the image by clicking Open (Macintosh) or Select (Windows). Click OK to close the Swap Image dialog box.**

The Swap Image dialog box closes, and the rollover now uses the correct image.

**6)  Select the original library item, header, in the Library panel. Click the delete button at the bottom of the panel.**

The original library item is now deleted. Because it is not possible to edit behaviors directly in a library element, you have to delete the original item and replace it with a corrected version.

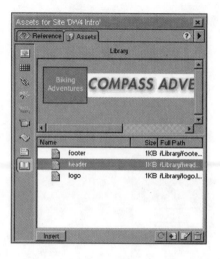

**7) Select the table at the top of the document.**

You will use this table to replace the original library item.

**8) Click the new library item button at the bottom of the Library panel and name the library item exactly as the original was named.**

The modified elements are now stored in the Library folder.

**9) Choose Modify › Library › Update Pages. In the Look In drop-down menu, choose Entire Site. In Update checkboxes, check the Library Items box and uncheck the Templates box. Check the Show Log box and click Start.**

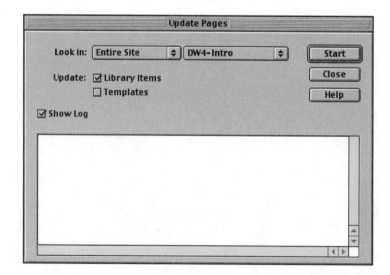

The pages in the rest of the site that once used the original header library item are now updated with the new version.

**10) Click Close to close the dialog box. Save the road.htm document and test your pages in the browser.**

Both road.htm and biking.htm will now use the correct rollover image.

## WHAT YOU HAVE LEARNED

### In this lesson, you have:

- Learned how to use library items for elements that need to be repeated on many pages within a site (pages 164–170)

- Created a library item, inserted it on a page with a link to the library item, and inserted it on another page without a link to the library item (pages 166–169)

- Used the property inspector to recreate a library item that was missing from the Library panel (pages 170–171)

- Edited an existing library item from the library panel and applied the changes to all pages in the site that used that item (pages 171–173)

- Updated all references to a library item at a later time (pages 173–174)

- Created and modified a library item containing rollovers in order to include behaviors in a library item and changed those behaviors when needed (pages 175–178)

# using templates

## LESSON 8

If you have a large site or multiple pages that share a common design, you can create a template to speed up the production process. With a template, you can change or update the look of your site, changing multiple pages within a few minutes. Templates are useful when you have a team working together to build an area of the site. The Web designer can create a template, inserting placeholders for the parts of the page that can be edited. The overall design of the page remains locked. For example, say you have an online catalog of your products and you want all the pages to look the

*In this lesson, you will create a template from an existing page, build other pages using that template, and modify the pages by editing the template.*

same except for the product picture, description, and price. If you create a template, you can have your team build the pages, and each page will look the same.

The advantages of templates are best seen in two situations: when you have a set of pages with an identical design and layout, or when a designer creates the look of the pages but content editors add the content to the pages. If you simply want pages with the same headers and footers but different layouts in between, use libraries (covered in Lesson 7).

## WHAT YOU WILL LEARN

**In this lesson, you will:**

- Create a template
- Add editable areas to the template
- Remove editable areas from the template
- Change the template highlight colors
- Build multiple pages based on the template
- Update a site by changing the template

## APPROXIMATE TIME

This lesson should take about one hour to complete.

## LESSON FILES

**Media Files:**

*Lesson_08_Templates/Images/…(all files)*

**Starting Files:**

*Lesson_08_Templates/gear.htm*

*Lesson_08_Templates/Text/catalog.txt*

**Completed Project:**

*Lesson_08_Templates/Completed/gear.htm*

*Lesson_08_Templates/Completed/pack.htm*

*Lesson_08_Templates/Completed/rope.htm*

*Lesson_08_Templates/Completed/vest.htm*

## CREATING TEMPLATES

You can build a template from scratch, or you can take an existing HTML page and save it as a template. In this exercise, you are creating a Web page for an online catalog for the Compass site. You will start with a page that has already been created using the Layout view. You will then save the file as a template and create other pages from it in the following exercises.

### 1) Open gear.htm in the Lesson_08_Templates folder.

For the areas that are to change from page to page, the content has been replaced with a descriptive placeholder.

Next you will save this page as a template you can use to build other pages.

### 2) Choose File › Save as Template.

The Save as Template dialog box opens. Dreamweaver automatically names the template "gear"—the name of your file.

**NOTE** *If you want to change the name of the template, type the new name in the Save As text field. The template name is only for your reference.*

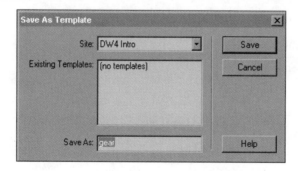

### 3) Click Save to close the dialog box.

Your template has been added to your site and saved with an extension of .dwt in the Templates folder. Dreamweaver adds the Templates folder at the root level if one doesn't already exist. Leave this file open to use in the next exercise.

The Assets panel opens to the Templates category. The template you just created—gear—appears in the Templates list. The file you are working with changes to gear.dwt, and the top of the document window will display <<Template>> (gear.dwt).

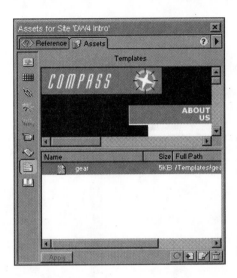

**NOTE** *Instead of creating a page and saving it as a template as you just did, you can also create a new template by choosing Window > Templates. The Assets panel opens, with the Templates category selected. Click the New Template button at the bottom of the Assets panel. A new, untitled template is added to the list of templates in the panel. While the template is still selected, enter a name for the template.*

## ADDING EDITABLE AREAS OF A TEMPLATE

As a rule, all areas of a template are locked. If you want to be able to change information on each page that uses the template, you need to create "editable" areas or regions. Everything not explicitly defined as editable is locked. You can make changes to both the editable and locked areas of a template, but on a page built from a template, you can change only the editable regions.

**1) Click in the cell for the product title (directly below the previous and next buttons) to position the insertion point. Use the tag selector at the bottom of the document window to select the cell.**

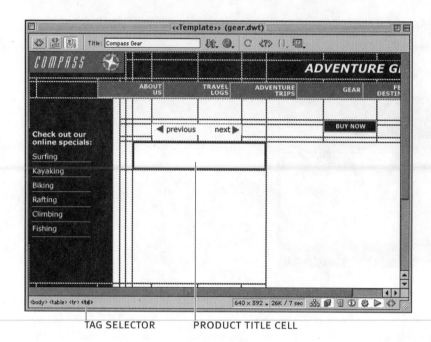

TAG SELECTOR          PRODUCT TITLE CELL

This section of the page needs to be editable so you can change the content in subsequent pages.

**NOTE** *If the file <<Template>> (gear.dwt) is not already open, choose Window > Templates. The Assets panel opens to the Templates category. The template you just created, gear, appears in the list. In the Assets panel, double-click the name of the template to open it. Alternatively, you can select the name in the list and click Edit at the bottom of the Assets panel.*

**2) Choose Modify › Templates › New Editable Region.**
The New Editable Region dialog box opens.

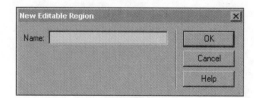

### 3) Type *title* for the region name and click OK.

Don't use any special characters for region names. Make each name unique—you can't have the same region name in the same template.

Since you selected the table cell when you defined the editable region, the region name appears on the top left corner of the cell.

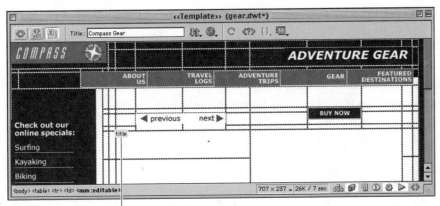

REGION NAME

### 4) Click inside the cell for the product picture (directly below the product title cell you just defined as editable) in order to position the insertion point. Don't select the cell. Choose Modify > Templates > New Editable Region and name the region *picture*.

Because the insertion point was within the cell when you defined the editable region, you'll see the region name at the top left of the cell, and the region name will be placed in braces within the cell. When you apply the template to a document, you will need to select the braces and name, and then replace them with text, images, or other content.

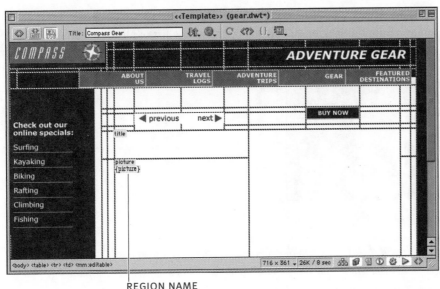

REGION NAME

185

**NOTE** *With this method, anything in the cell before or after the insertion point will be uneditable.*

**5)  Using the tag selector as you did with the first cell, select the cell for product description. Choose Modify › Templates › New Editable Region and name the region description.**

If you do not see the region names, choose View > Visual Aids > Invisible Elements.

The Next, Previous, and Buy Now buttons on the page also need to be editable.

**6)  Select the Next button and choose Modify › Templates › New Editable Region, naming the region *next*. Do the same for the Previous button, naming the region *previous*, and for the Buy Now button, naming the region *buy*.**

Anything that will need to change, including links, needs to be in an editable region.

**7)  Save the file.**

The region names appear highlighted within the cells to help you identify the areas you've designated as editable.

Leave this file open to use in the next exercise.

## REMOVING EDITABLE REGIONS

You have designated certain areas of the template as editable. You can also set them back to being locked. In locked areas, elements cannot be changed directly on a page that has been created from the template. These elements must be edited in the template itself.

**1)  In gear.dwt, choose Modify › Templates › Remove Editable Region.**

The Remove Editable Region dialog box opens with a list of all the editable regions in the gear template.

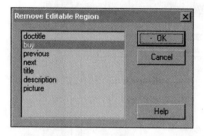

**NOTE** *If gear.dwt is not open, double-click the gear template in the Templates category of the Assets panel. You can use the Assets panel to move, rename, and delete template files. Use caution when deleting template files, as they are not as easily recreated as library items.*

**2) Select buy from the list and click OK.**

That portion of the template is now locked and cannot be changed in files that use the template.

Any pages that modified the previously editable region are changed when you update the pages after saving the template. The changes are deleted, and that area reverts to the template's content.

## CHANGING TEMPLATE HIGHLIGHT COLORS

You can change both the color of the highlighted regions and the color of the locked areas. You may need to change the highlight colors to be sure they will show up against the background color of your pages.

**1) Choose Edit › Preferences and select the Highlighting category.**

There are four types of items that Dreamweaver highlights: editable regions in templates, locked regions in templates, library items, and third-party tags.

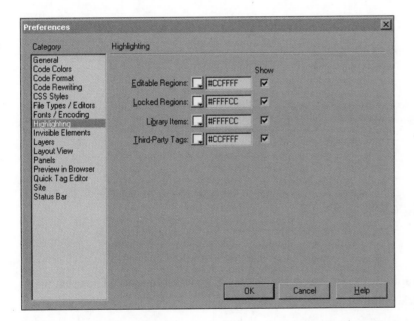

**2) Click the Editable Regions color box to open the color picker and select a highlight color, or enter the hexadecimal value for the highlight color in the text field. Do the same for the Locked Regions color box.**

The editable region color appears in the template itself and in documents based on the template; the locked region color appears only in documents based on the template. The default colors are light blue (#CCFFFF) for editable regions and pale yellow (#FFFFCC) for locked regions.

**3) Click Show to enable or disable the display of these colors in the document window and click OK.**

These highlight colors will only show in the document window if the option to view Invisible Elements is enabled. If invisible elements, such as the highlighting on template regions, do not appear in the document window, choose View > Visual Aids > Invisible Elements.

You can close the gear.dwt file.

## BUILDING PAGES BASED ON A TEMPLATE

After you create the template, you can begin creating pages based on the template. The only portions of the page you can change will be those parts you defined as editable in the template. In this exercise, you will create several pages based on the gear template. The graphics you need for building the pages are located in the Lesson 8 folder in the Favorites Assets panel (using the Favorites Assets panel to insert images was covered in Lesson 2).

**1) Choose File › New From Template.**

The Select Template dialog box opens. A list of all the templates you've created for the site appears.

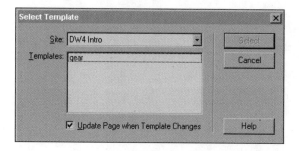

**2) Choose gear from the list. Leave the Update Page when Template Changes checkbox checked and click Select.**

A new page is created from the template. Although this document has a title already, it still needs to be saved.

**3) Save the file as pack.htm in the Lesson_08_Templates folder.**

You'll see the highlight color (the default color is pale yellow) of the locked regions on the page, around the edges of the document window. You can also see the template name at the top right of the document window.

The pointer will change when you roll over or try to click any of the locked regions. This indicates that those areas are not editable.

**4) Click the Image category on the Assets panel and choose Favorites. Open the Lesson 8 folder in the Favorites list and locate the pack_title and back_pack images. Add the pack_title image to the title region and the back_pack image to the picture region. These images are located in the Images folder inside Lesson_08_Templates.**

**NOTE** *To add the images from the Assets panel, select the image in the panel and click the insert button, or drag the image from the panel to the appropriate region.*

If the insertion point was within the cell when you defined the editable region, the region name will be repeated in braces within the cell. You should delete the title and braces before placing the images so the text does not remain on the page.

**5) Open the catalog.txt file from Lesson_08_Templates/Text and select the text for Day Pack. Copy the text and paste it within the description region of your pack.htm file.**

The text appears within an outlined border. The border color is the color of the editable regions. A tab at the upper-left corner of the region displays the name of the region.

**6) Format the first four paragraphs as a bulleted list. Bold the price and align it to the right.**

Your page should now look like the example here.

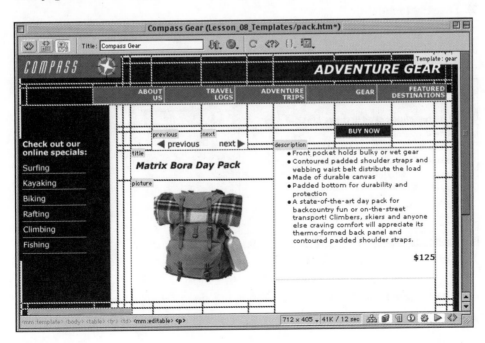

You can save and close the pack.htm file.

**7) Repeat steps 1 through 6 to create rope.htm and vest.htm. Use the text from the the catalog.txt file in the Text folder and the images from the Images folder.**

You have now created three pages from the template. You can close both the rope.htm and the vest.htm files.

## MODIFYING A TEMPLATE

You've seen how easy it is to build pages using a template—you just add the content that changes without worrying about creating the rest of the page or changing the design. The real time savings comes when you need to make changes to all the pages that were built using the template. Without a template, you'd have to edit each page. With a template, you simply edit the template to update all the pages built with the template.

**1) In the Templates category of the Assets panel, double-click the gear template that you've been using.**

The template opens.

**2) Select the Travel Logs navigation button and link it to the travel_log.htm page you created in Lesson 2 by clicking the folder icon next to the link text field in the property inspector and browsing to find the file in the Lesson_02_Graphics folder.**

The Travel Logs navigation button is now a link to travel_log.htm.

**3) Save the template.**

The Update Template Files dialog box opens, displaying a list of all files built from this template.

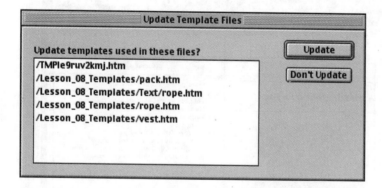

**4) Click Update to modify all the pages with the change you just made.**

*If you wish, you can update the pages later by choosing Don't Update, then at a later time choosing Modify > Templates > Update Pages.*

The pack.htm document you created from the template earlier will be updated with the link.

The ability to update all pages associated with a template can be very useful. For example, if you have a navigation section of the page with graphics for links you can set those graphics and their links in the template. If the links change, you simply change the template, and all pages designed with the template are updated.

**NOTE** *You can detach a page from a template by choosing Modify > Templates > Detach From Template. A detached page is completely editable, but it will no longer be updated if the template is changed.*

### 5) Open the pack.htm file and view it in the browser.

The link to the Travel Logs page should work on this page, as well as on the other two pages, rope.htm and vest.htm, that you built from the template.

## WHAT YOU HAVE LEARNED

### In this lesson, you have:

- Created a template from an existing page by saving the page as a template (pages 182–183)
- Added editable areas to the template in order to allow changes to be made on pages built from that template (pages 183–186)
- Removed editable areas from the template in order to prevent changes from being made on pages built from that template (pages 186–187)
- Changed the template highlight colors for both editable and locked regions (pages 187–188)
- Built multiple pages based on the template in order to create pages with the same layout (pages 188–189)
- Used the Assets panel to manage your templates (pages 189–191)
- Made changes to the template and updated multiple pages within the site to reflect those changes (pages 190–191)

# creating frames

## LESSON 9

Frames work by splitting the browser window into rectangular areas that contain independent HTML content. Each frame is a separate HTML file. Frames are commonly used to define navigation and content areas for a page. Typically, the navigation area remains constant, and the content area changes each time a navigation link is clicked. The use of frames can be extremely helpful to a user for navigation through a site. Frames can also make a site easier to modify, because there is only one navigation page to update. On the other hand, frames can degrade a Web site if they are poorly implemented: They may confuse and disorient users if they do not provide a clear site structure, or they may make the content difficult to view if they are not properly sized and formatted.

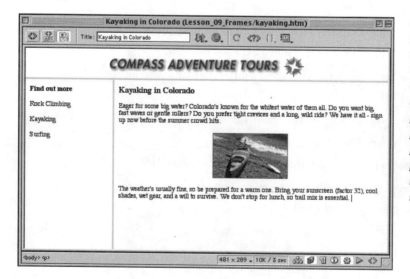

*In this lesson, you will work in the page shown here, and in others, to create and change the properties of framesets and frames, resize frames, and use links to control their contents.*

When a user views a Web page that has been created with two frames, the browser is actually using three separate files to display the page: the frameset file and the two files containing the content that appears inside each of the two frames. A frameset is an HTML file that is invisible to the user and which defines the structure of a Web page with frames. A frameset stores information about the size and location of each frame, along with the names of the files that supply the content for each of the frames. Frames have borders that can be turned off so the frames are not readily apparent to the user, or they can be turned on to clearly split the window into different panes.

In this lesson, you will work with frames to create a Web page containing a navigation area and a content area. You will develop a set of pages that will all appear in the content frame when the user selects a link from the navigation frame, and you will learn how to target links to different frames. You will also learn how to include content for browsers that do not support frames.

## WHAT YOU WILL LEARN

**In this lesson, you will:**

- Create a frameset
- Save a frameset
- Create frames and nested frames
- Resize frames
- Change frameset and frame properties
- Create documents within frames
- Target frame content
- Create NoFrames content

## APPROXIMATE TIME

This lesson should take about two hours to complete.

## LESSON FILES

**Media Files:**
*Lesson_09_Frames/Images/…(all files)*

**Starting Files:**
*Lesson_09_Frames/Text/calif_surf.txt*
*Lesson_09_Frames/Text/colo_kayak.txt*
*Lesson_09_Frames/Text/wyo_climb.txt*

**Completed Project:**
*Lesson_09_Frames/Completed/climbing.htm*
*Lesson_09_Frames/Completed/frameset.htm*
*Lesson_09_Frames/Completed/kayaking.htm*
*Lesson_09_Frames/Completed/nav.htm*
*Lesson_09_Frames/Completed/surfing.htm*

## CREATING A FRAMESET

A frameset defines the overall look of the framed page—the number of frame areas on the page, the size of each frame, and the border attributes. In the first part of this lesson, you will create a Web page consisting of two frames. The left frame will hold navigation elements that remain constant. The right frame will display pages whose content is relative to the links clicked in the navigation frame.

There are two ways to create a frameset in Dreamweaver: You can manually insert the frames, or you can choose from several predefined framesets. If you choose a predefined frameset, the frameset and frames are automatically set up for you. It is a quick way to create a layout using frames because most of the work is done for you. You just need to name the individual pages.

In this exercise, you will use a predefined frameset to make a Web page that uses frames.

### 1) Create a new file, but do not save it.

You must insert frames into the document in order for this page to become a frameset.

### 2) Choose View > Visual Aids > Frame Borders.

A thick border will appear around the page edges in the document window.

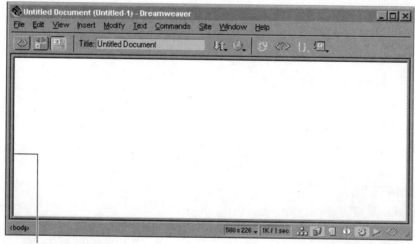

FRAME BORDER

**3) Click the Insert Top Frame icon from the Frames category of the Objects panel.**

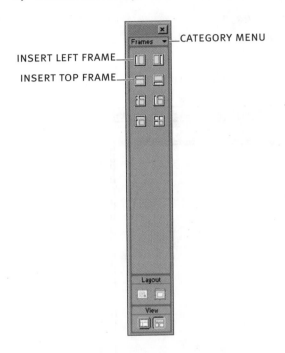

CATEGORY MENU

INSERT LEFT FRAME

INSERT TOP FRAME

**TIP** *If the Frames category on the Objects panel is not visible, click the down-arrow at the top of the panel and choose Frames from the list.*

The page is divided into two frames: a short frame on the top and a taller frame on the bottom. A thin gray line marks the division.

**NOTE** *To insert frames manually, drag the border surrounding the page into the document window. The document will become split horizontally (if you drag from the top or bottom of the border) or vertically (if you drag from the left or right sides of the border). If you drag the border from the corner, the document will become divided into four frames. You can also choose Modify > Frameset > Split Frame Left, Right, Up, or Down.*

**4) Click to place the insertion point in the bottom frame. Click the Insert Left Frame icon from the Frames category of the Objects panel.**

This creates another frameset inside the bottom frame. This second frameset is called a **nested frameset** because it is inside another frame. The single bottom frame has now been divided into two frames: a narrow frame on the left and a wider frame on the right. Several of Dreamweaver's predefined framesets use nested framesets. You can use combinations of these predefined framesets as you have done in this exercise to come up with any frame layout you want.

Your page should now look similar to the example shown here.

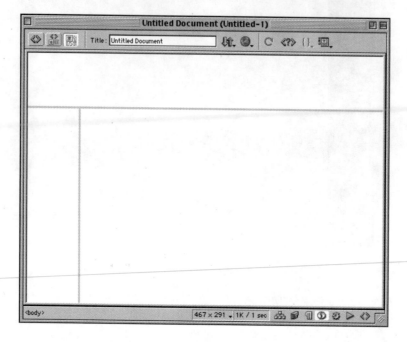

Leave this file open to use in the next exercise.

## SAVING A FRAMESET

When you have the page set with the number of frames you want, you need to save the frameset. The frameset and the files for each frame need to be saved before you can preview the page in a browser. If you attempt to preview the page in the browser prior to saving, Dreamweaver displays a message stating that all documents need to to be saved in order to preview. The frameset file is the one you reference when linking to this Web page. You can save each file individually, or you can save all open files at once. In this exercise, you will save only the frameset.

**1) In the document window, click the border between the frames in the document window to select the frameset.**

**TIP** *You can also select the frameset by choosing Window > Frames and then clicking the outermost border enclosing the frames in the Frames panel. The Frames panel shows you a simplified version of the structure of frames in the document.*

In the document window, all frame borders within the frameset are outlined by a dotted line, and the tag selector at the bottom of the window displays <frameset>. The document's title bar shows "Untitled Document (UntitledFrameset-1)," and the property inspector shows the frameset properties.

**NOTE** *If only one frame is selected, only that frame border will appear in the document window with a dotted line. In documents that have nested framesets, only the frames in the selected frameset display with a dotted line.*

In the Frames panel, framesets are displayed with a thick border, and frames are displayed with a thin border.

FRAMESET BORDER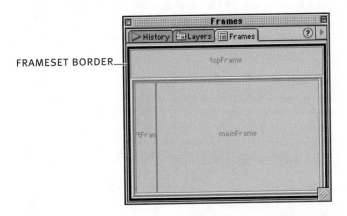

**2) Choose File › Save Frameset and save the file as frameset.htm in the Lesson_09_Frames folder.**

The document's title bar shows the file name and location are Lesson_09_Frames/frameset.htm.

**NOTE** *The default, temporary name given to the frameset is UntitledFrameset-1.htm.*

**3) With the frameset still selected, type *Compass USA Adventures* for the page title.**

If you don't have the frameset selected when you title the page, you are titling one of the pages in the frameset—not the frameset file. The document title bar displays the selected page title and the file name. If you have the frameset selected, the document title bar displays the frameset title and file name. Refer to the Frames panel to check what is selected; this will help ensure you are working within the frame or frameset that you intend to edit.

Leave this file open to use in the next exercise.

## RESIZING FRAMES IN A FRAMESET

You can use the property inspector to specify the size of your frames, or you can simply drag the borders in the document window to perform the same task. In addition to specifying a size in the property inspector, you can also determine how browsers will allocate space to frames when there is not enough room to display all frames at full size.

**1)  In the document window, position the pointer over the horizontal border between the top and bottom frames. When the pointer changes to a double arrow, click the border once to select the frameset.**

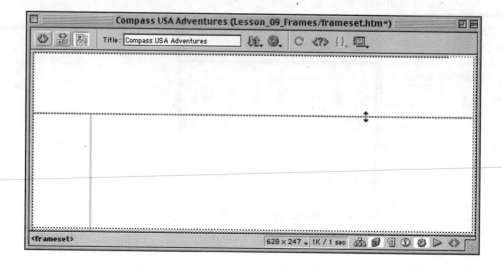

The frame borders in the document window will become dotted. The tag selector will display <frameset>, and the Frames panel will show the outermost frameset border selected.

The property inspector shows the Frameset properties. The property inspector will change depending on whether you have selected a frameset or a frame. In order to change the size of the frames, you will need to make sure you have selected the frameset.

**NOTE** *Click the expander arrow on the property inspector to view all Frameset properties if they are not visible.*

**2) Drag the border between the top and bottom frames until the top frame is approximately 50 pixels high.**

Use the Row Value in the property inspector to check the height, or you can type *50* in the Row Value text field to get the exact height. Make sure Pixels is selected from the Unit drop-down menu.

**3) With the outer frameset still selected, click the tab to the left of the bottom row in the property inspector to select the bottom frame of the frameset. Next to the Row Value text field, select Relative from the Unit drop-down menu.**

This will allow the bottom row to expand or contract depending on how large the user's browser is and how much space is left after the top row has been allocated the 50 pixels that were assigned to it. By default, Dreamweaver will automatically place a 1 in the Row Value text field. If you view the HTML code for the frameset size, you will see: frameset rows="50,*". The 1 in the Row Value text field *in conjunction with* the Relative unit chosen from the menu is the same as the asterisk (*) in the code; it represents a size that is relative or proportional to the other rows in the frameset.

**4) In the Frames panel, click the nested frameset, represented by the thick inner border around the two columns in the bottom row, to select it. In the visual representation of the frame in the property inspector, click the tab above the left column to select the left frame.**

The left column in the property inspector darkens to indicate it has been selected. Use these tabs to select the columns or rows in a frameset.

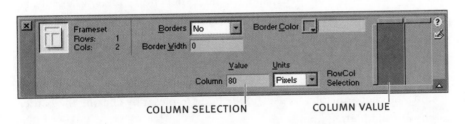

COLUMN SELECTION          COLUMN VALUE

**5) In the Column Value text field of the property inspector, type *155* and select Pixels from the Unit drop-down menu.**

The left frame's width is adjusted to 155 pixels.

*Pixels: This option sets the absolute size of the selected column or row to the number of pixels that you enter. It is the best option for any frame that needs to have a set size. If other columns or rows are defined by a different Unit option, those other columns or rows are allocated space only after rows or columns specified in pixels are their full size.*

*Percent: This option specifies a percentage that the current column or row should take up in its frameset. Columns or rows specified with units set to Percent are allocated space after columns or rows with units set to Pixels and before columns or rows with units set to Relative.*

*Relative: This option specifies that the current column or row will be allocated space using the current proportions relative to the other columns and rows. Columns or rows with units set to Relative are allocated space after columns or rows with units set to Pixels and Percent, but they take up all remaining space. If you set the bottom or the right frame to relative, the frame size changes to fill the remaining width or height of the browser window.*

*Note that setting all the values to pixels is counter-productive; if you do this, the columns and rows will be treated as percentage-based.*

**6) In the property inspector, click the tab above the right column to select the right frame of the nested frameset. Next to the Column Value text field, select Relative from the Unit drop-down menu.**

This will allow the right column to expand or contract depending on how large the users browser is and how much space remains after the left column has been allocated the 155 pixels assigned to it.

**7) Save the frameset by choosing File › Save Frameset.**

If this command is not available, first select the outer frameset by clicking the border between the top and bottom frames.

Leave this file open to use in the next exercise.

## SPECIFYING FRAME PROPERTIES

When you create a frameset, get in the habit of naming each frame. The name you assign to a frame does not name the file that appears in the frame—it just identifies the framed area of the document for your reference. Naming your frames is important when you create links to display pages within a framed area. In the previous exercise, you used the predefined top and left framesets. Each frame in the frameset has already been given a default name. In this exercise, you will change the name to reflect the future content of the frame.

**1) Select the top frame by choosing Window > Frames and clicking inside the top frame in the Frames panel. Alternatively, you can Alt+click (Windows) or Shift+Option+click (Macintosh) in the top frame in the document window to select the frame.**

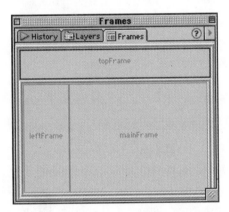

The Frames panel shows a dark border around the top frame with the name topFrame shown in the center. The property inspector displays frame properties for topFrame.

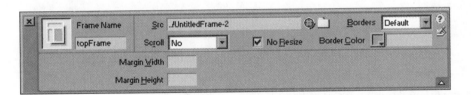

**2) In the Frame Name text field in the property inspector, type *logo*. Press Enter (Windows) or Return (Macintosh), or click in the document window to apply the name.**
The Frames panel displays "logo" in the top frame. You can always refer to the Frames panel for the name of a particular frame.

### 3) Make sure to select No in the Scroll drop-down menu and check the No Resize box.

The scroll option defines when scroll bars appear and applies to both vertical and horizontal scroll bars. The Auto setting will display scroll bars whenever there is not enough room in the frame to display the content of the page. The Default option is the browser default setting, which is usually Auto. Be careful how you set this option—if it is set to No and the frame is not large enough to display all the contents, the user will be unable to scroll to see the rest of the content; if it is set to Yes and the contents fit within the frame, scroll bars that are grayed out will still take up space on the page, even though it isn't possible to scroll.

No Resize locks the size of the frame when viewed in the browser. If this option is unchecked, users will be able to drag the frame borders in their browser window. Regardless of whether this option is checked or unchecked, it will not affect your ability to resize frames within Dreamweaver.

### 4) Select the bottom-left frame and name it nav. Set scroll to No and check No Resize.

The Frames panel displays the name "nav" in the bottom-left frame.

Notice that the Borders drop-down menu has Default selected. The predefined framesets that you used to create the page layout are automatically set to have no frame borders. When the Default setting is selected for the Borders option of an individual frame, that frame uses the setting of the parent frameset. If another setting (Yes or No) is selected, then the frame will override the setting of the parent frameset.

### 5) Select the bottom-right frame and name it content. Set scroll to Auto and check No Resize.

The Frames panel displays the name "content" in the bottom right frame.

Notice that the text fields for Margin Width and Margin Height are blank. This is the default for the predefined framesets you used to layout your page. Margin Width sets the left and right margins of the frame in pixels. Margin Height sets the top and bottom margins of the frame in pixels. Leaving them blank will use the browser default, which may vary in size depending on the browser version and type.

### 6) Save the frameset.

When you change Frame properties, you are really modifying the frameset. Frame and frameset properties are both defined within the frameset.

Leave this file open to use in the next exercise.

## CREATING AND EDITING FRAMES CONTENT

Remember that the content of a frame is an HTML page. You can create the page separately or within the constraints of the frame. Using the frame to help you design the page is always a good idea. That way, you don't create a page that is too wide or too narrow for the frame. Your users will find the pages difficult to view if they have to scroll in multiple directions to see all the content.

In this exercise, you will add content to each page in the frameset.

### 1) Place the insertion point in the logo frame (the top frame).

The document title bar shows this is an untitled, unsaved document.

### 2) Choose File › Save Frame and save the file as logo.htm in the Lesson_09_Frames folder and title it Compass Logo.

The document title bar changes to reflect the title and file name for the document in this frame. The title is actually unneccessary because the browser will use the title of the frameset in the browser window. But it is good practice to always title your documents; if this page is opened in a window by itself for any reason, it will contain a title.

### 3) Insert the compass_logo_gray.gif from the Lesson_09_Frames/Images folder and center it.

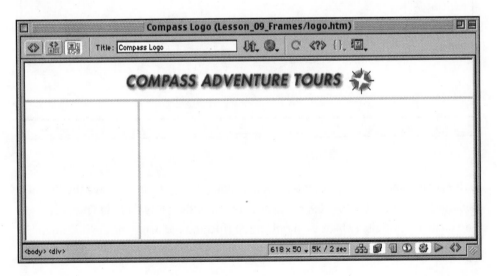

Save this document again. As you edit your pages, remember to save often. When you use the Save command, you are only saving the currently selected file. This does not save the frameset; you must do this separately. If you want to save a file located

203

in another frame, just click inside its frame in the document window and then save. Refer to the Frames panel to check which frame you are saving.

**4) Place the insertion point in the nav frame (the bottom left frame). Save the file as nav.htm in the Lesson_09_Frames folder and title it Compass Navigation.**

The document title bar changes to reflect the title and file name for the document in this frame.

**5) In the nav.htm document, type *Find out more* and format the text on this line as a heading 4. Below this line, type *Rock Climbing*, *Kayaking*, and *Surfing*, each on a separate line. Format these lines as paragraphs and save the file.**

This will be your navigation frame. It will contain links to various pages that will appear in the content frame to the right. These will be the links you target to open files in the content frame.

Your nav frame should now look like the example shown here.

**6) Place the insertion point in the content frame (the right frame). Save the file as kayaking.htm in the Lesson_09_Frames folder and title it Kayaking in Colorado.**

The document title bar changes to reflect the title and file name for the document in this frame.

**7) In the kayaking.htm document, type *Kayaking in Colorado* and press Enter (Windows) or Return (Macintosh). Format this text as a heading 3. Copy the text from Lesson_09_Frames/Text/colo_kayak.txt and paste it below the heading.**

This is the content page that will correspond with a Kayaking link you will create on the nav bar.

204

**8) Use the Assets panel to place the kayaking image (from the Favorites Lesson 9 folder) between the two paragraphs and center the image. Save the file.**

**NOTE** *In the Assets panel, the image is called kayaking; you can drag the image from the list into the document window. You can also use the Insert Image icon on the Objects panel to browse the Lesson_09_Frames/Images folder for kayaking.jpg.*

Your content frame should now look like the example shown here.

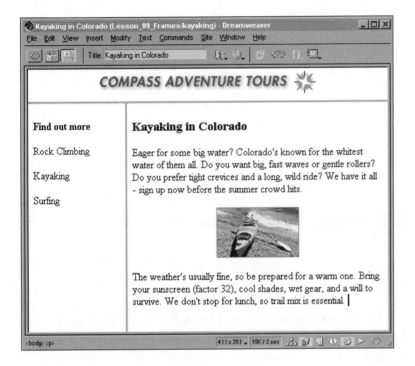

Leave these files open.

## CREATING OTHER CONTENT DOCUMENTS

You now need to create additional documents to open in the content frame.

**1) Choose File > New to create a new document. Save the file as surfing.htm in the Lesson_09_Frames folder and title it Surfing in California.**

The document title bar changes to reflect the new title and file name.

**2) In the surfing.htm document, type *Surfing in California* and press Enter (Windows) or Return (Macintosh). Format this text as a heading 3 and save the file.**

You will open this document in the content frame in the next exercise.

**3) Repeat steps 1 and 2 to create climbing.htm. Type *Rock Climbing in Wyoming* for both the title and heading, and then save the file.**

You can close both surfing.htm and climbing.htm. Leave the other files open to use in the next exercise.

## OPENING AN EXISTING PAGE IN A FRAME

You've already started several content pages, so you need to make sure they fit in the content frame. You can open those files directly in the frame to check or edit them.

**1) In the frameset.htm document window, click inside the content frame.**

This is where you want the surfing page to appear.

**2) Choose File > Open in Frame. Choose surfing.htm from the dialog box.**

The page is loaded into the content frame and is available for editing.

**3) Copy the text from Lesson_09_Frames/Text/calif_surf.txt and paste it below the heading.**

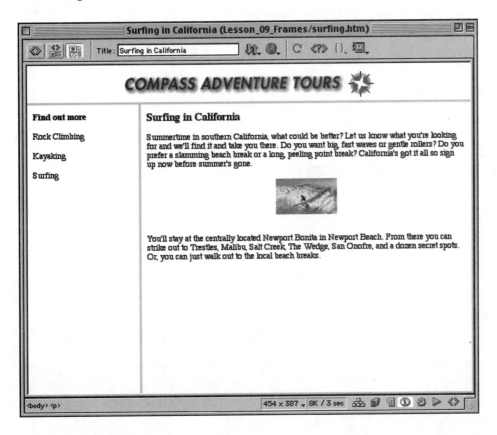

You are editing this document inside the frame as you would edit any standard HTML document.

**4) Use the Assets panel to place the surf image (from the Favorites Lesson 9 folder) between the two paragraphs and center the image. Save the file.**

**NOTE** *In the Assets panel, the image is called surf. You can drag the image from the list into the document window. You can also use the Insert Image icon on the objects panel to browse in the Lesson_09_Frames/Images folder for surf.jpg.*

Depending on the size of the text and of the window in which your frameset is displayed, the content on this page may require scrolling. With the frame properties set to auto scroll, the browser will use scroll bars only if they are needed.

**5) Open climbing.htm in the content frame. Copy the text from Lesson_09_Frames/ Text/wyo_climb.txt and paste it below the heading. Place the climber graphic between the paragraphs, and then save the file.**

You might have noticed the Save All Frames command in the File menu. Exercise caution when using this command. It saves all open pages contained in your frames and the frameset. Remember that the frameset is the file you use when linking. The number of frames and the files that initially appear within each frame are defined in the frameset. If you choose File > Save All Frames while you are editing other pages within the frames (by using File > Open in Frame), you will redefine the frameset.

## CHECKING FRAME CONTENT

As you create and edit pages within a frame, it's easy to accidentally place the wrong content in a frame. You can use the property inspector to ensure that the correct pages will be loaded into each of the frames for the initial view of your Web page.

**1) Select the logo frame by clicking the top frame in the Frames panel. In the Src text field, make sure logo.htm is selected. If it isn't, click the folder icon to find and select it.**

The property inspector shows frame properties for the logo frame.

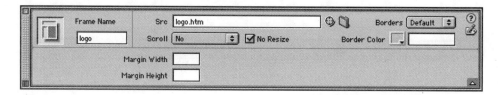

**2) Select the nav frame by clicking the bottom-left frame in the Frames panel. In the Src text field, make sure nav.htm is selected. If it isn't, click the folder icon to find and select it.**

The property inspector shows frame properties for the nav frame.

**3) Select the content frame by clicking the bottom-right frame in the Frames panel. In the Src text field, make sure climbing.htm is selected. If it isn't, click the folder icon to find and select it.**

The property inspector shows frame properties for the content frame.

## CONTROLLING FRAME CONTENT WITH LINKS

After you have created the content document pages, you need to link the navigation elements to the pages that should display in the content area of your Web page. To get the content to appear in its proper location, you need to target the link.

**1) In nav.htm, select the word "Kayaking." Create a link to kayaking.htm by typing kayaking.htm in the Link text field on the property inspector, or by clicking the folder icon next to the Link text field and browsing to find kayaking.htm in the Lesson_09_Frames folder.**

By default, links are targeted to the frame or window in which they are located. However, you want this link to open in the content frame, not the nav frame.

**2) In the property inspector, select content from the Target drop-down menu.**

This option forces the Kayaking document to be placed in the content frame (the bottom-right frame) when the Kayaking link is clicked in the browser. Whenever you create a new frame, the name of that frame is automatically added to the Target drop-down menu.

**NOTE** *If you are working on a document that will be loaded in a frame, and you are not working on it inside the frameset as you are in this exercise, you won't have the option in the Target menu to select the names of any frames. Dreamweaver only displays the names of frames that are available in the current document in the Target menu. In this case, you will need to type the exact name of the frame which you want to target into the Target text field.*

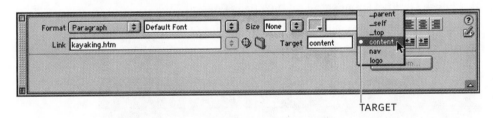

TARGET

There are other options available in the Target drop-down menu.

_blank loads the linked document in a new, unnamed browser window.

_parent loads the linked document in the parent frameset of the frame that contains the link. If the frame containing the link is not nested, the linked document loads into the full browser window.

_self loads the linked document in the same frame or window as the link. This target is implied, so you usually don't have to specify it.

_top loads the linked document in the full browser window, thereby removing all frames.

**3) Save the file and preview it in the browser.**

When you click the Kayaking link, the kayaking document displays on the right.

**4) Repeat steps 1 and 2, linking Surfing to surfing.htm and Rock Climbing to climbing.htm.**

Remember to select the target so that these pages will open in the content frame.

**5) Save your file and preview it in the browser.**

If your pages don't appear where you expect them, check to see that you have selected content from the Target drop-down menu in the property inspector for each link in the navigation.

## CREATING NOFRAMES CONTENT

In Dreamweaver, you can create content that will be ignored by frames-capable browsers and displayed in older and text-based browsers or in other browsers that do not support frames. The NoFrames content you create is placed in the frameset file. When a browser that doesn't support frames loads the frameset file, the browser displays only the NoFrames content.

**1) Select the frameset.**

This is the page the browser will load initially, so the NoFrames content will be specified here.

**2) Choose Modify > Frameset > Edit NoFrames Content.**

The document window changes to display the NoFrames page, and the words "NoFrames Content" appear at the top.

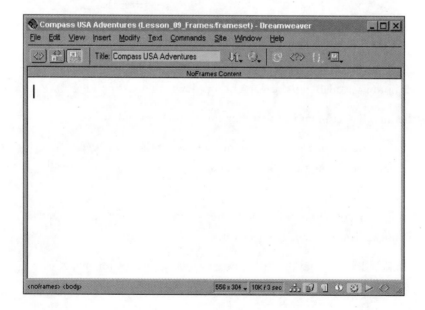

### 3) Create the NoFrames content in the document window.

Create alternative content of your choice in this document. This content can contain elements from a standard html page and will be enclosed between the `<noframes>` and `</noframes>` tags. Only browsers that do not support frames will see this content. The content should be relatively simple—browsers that do not support frames are likely to not support JavaScript, image maps, and other types of complex elements. Some Web sites use NoFrames content to provide simple alternative pages or to direct users to a text-based version of the Web site; other sites use NoFrames content to display a message to users that the site is only available to frames-capable browsers.

### 4) Choose Modify › Frameset › Edit NoFrames.

The document window changes to hide the NoFrames content and returns to the normal view of the frameset document.

**NOTE** *When you finish editing the NoFrames content, you might be inclined to close the window because you can't see the original document. If you do, you will close the frameset and all the frame pages. You will then have to open them up again if you wish to continue editing them.*

## WHAT YOU HAVE LEARNED

**In this lesson, you have:**

- Created a frameset to define the layout of frames within your document (pages 194–196)

- Saved a frameset and learned how to save other frames individually (pages 196–197)

- Resized frames by dragging borders in the document window and changing the dimensions in the property inspector (pages 198–200)

- Changed frameset and frame properties using the Frames panel and the property inspector (pages 201–202)

- Created documents within frames by inserting elements directly into the frames and by opening existing documents in the frames (pages 203–204)

- Targeted frame content into other frames to control where the pages appear (pages 205–210)

- Created NoFrames content for browsers that are unable to display frames (pages 210–211)

# creating layers

## LESSON 10

A layer is a rectangular container for HTML content that you can position at an exact location in the browser window. Layers can contain a wide variety of elements: text, images, tables, and even other layers. Anything you can place in an HTML document you can also place in a layer. Layers are especially useful for placing elements atop each other or making them overlap. Layers are only supported by 4.0 or later browsers. They can control layout and appearance when used in combination with CSS, and they provide interactivity when used in combination with behaviors and timelines.

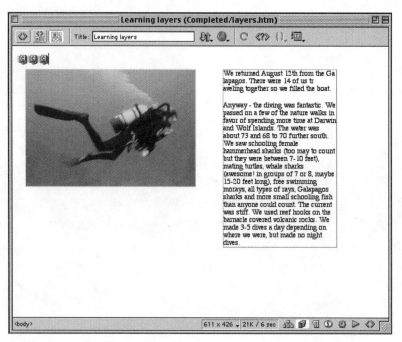

*In this project, you will work within pages like this one to create layers, place text and images in them, move them to exact locations, and change their properties.*

In this lesson, you will learn several ways to create layers in Dreamweaver. You will draw a layer on the page to the size you want and place a layer on the page using a predetermined width and height. You will learn to modify layer attributes including size, placement, and visibility. You will also convert your layers to tables in order to make it possible for users with older browsers to view your pages.

To see an example of the finished page, open layers.htm from the Lesson_10_Layers/ Completed folder.

## WHAT YOU WILL LEARN

**In this lesson, you will:**

- Create layers

- Name layers

- Modify layer sizes and locations

- Use layers to control content on your page

- Change the stacking order of layers

- Nest and unnest layers

- Change layer visibility

- Set rulers and grids

- Use a JavaScript fix for a Netscape bug

- Make pages designed with layers compatible with earlier browsers

## APPROXIMATE TIME

This lesson should take about one hour to complete.

## LESSON FILES

**Media File:**
*Lesson_10_Layers/Images/diver.jpg*

**Starting File:**
*Lesson_10_Layers/Text/dive.txt*

**Completed Project:**
*Lesson_10_Layers/Completed/layers.htm*

*Lesson_10_Layers/Completed/ layers_table.htm*

## CREATING LAYERS

There are several different ways to create layers. Which method you choose may depend on how you plan to use the layer and where you plan to place it.

**1) Create a new document. Save the file as layers.htm in the Lesson_10_Layers folder. Title the document Learning Layers.**

In this exercise, you will create several layers on this page and insert content into two of them.

**2) Click the standard view button in the View area of the Objects panel.**

DRAW LAYER

STANDARD VIEW

You must be in the standard view in order to create a layer.

**3) Click the draw layer button from the Common category of the Objects panel. Move the pointer into the document window (the pointer becomes a cross hair), and then click and drag to create a new layer on the right side of the page.**

The pointer changes to a cross hair (+) when you move the pointer into the document window. After you drag and release the pointer, the new layer displays as a rectangle with a tab at the top left. The tab is the layer selection handle.

LAYER MARKER

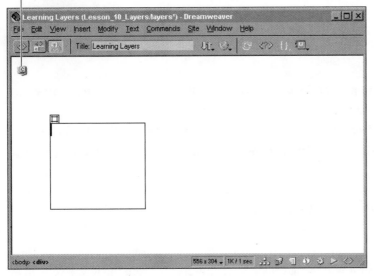

You should also see a yellow layer marker at the top of the document window. If the layer marker isn't visible, choose View > Visual Aids > Invisible Elements.

**NOTE** *You can use the layer marker for selecting the layer, but if your layer is positioned at the top left of the document window, the marker could get in the way and may appear to shift the position of the layer. This shift only happens in the document window. When the page is viewed in the browser, all elements will be in their correct positions. Turn the markers off by using View > Visual Aids > Invisible Elements. A check next to the command in the menu indicates the option is on.*

By default, the layer code is inserted at the top of the page, just after the <BODY> tag. There are four tags you can set for your layers using the Tag drop-down menu in the property inspector: <DIV>, <SPAN>, <LAYER>, and <ILAYER>. The <DIV> and <SPAN> tags are the most common and widely supported; they allow the largest possible audience to be able to view your layers. Dreamweaver uses the <DIV> tag by default to create layers that use absolute positioning to determine the placement of the layer in relation to the top and left sides of the browser window. <SPAN> uses relative positioning to determine the placement of the layer depending upon the position of other elements around it. The <LAYER> and <ILAYER> tags are only supported by certain versions of Netscape and are outside of the scope of this book.

**4) Place the insertion point in the layer. Open dive.txt from the Lesson_10_Layers/ Text folder, copy the first two paragraphs of text ("We returned..." through "...but made no night dives."), and paste it into the layers.htm document.**

215

The text will paste into the layer at the insertion point. The layer will expand if necessary to accomodate all the text. Layers expand to show you all of their content unless you change the overflow setting in the property inspector. You will change these settings in the Modifying Layers exercise.

**5) Place the insertion point in the document outside the layer and use the draw layer button on the Objects panel to draw a second layer on the page, to the left of the other layer. From the Lesson_10_Layers/Images folder or from the Image Favorites list in the Lesson 10 folder in the Assets panel, insert diver.jpg into the layer.**

**TIP** *To draw multiple layers continuously without clicking the draw layer button more than once, hold down Ctrl (Windows) or Command (Macintosh) as you draw the first layer. You can continue to draw new layers until you release the modifier key.*

If the insertion point is within a layer when you insert the layer, the new layer will be nested inside the other layer. Nested layers can cause problems in browsers, so it is best to avoid using them.

At this point, your document should look similar to the example shown here.

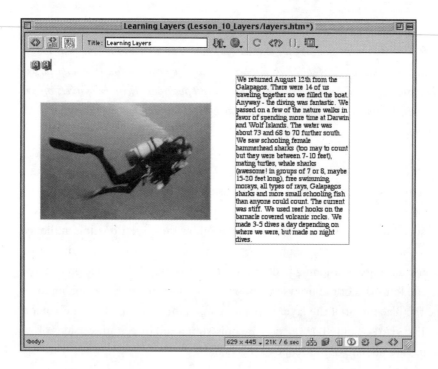

**NOTE** *Layers that are not selected and not activated will be displayed with a faint, thin gray line marking their borders. You can turn this on or off by choosing View > Visual Aids > Layer Borders. A check next to the command in the menu indicates the option is on.*

**6) Place the insertion point in the document outside the first and second layers and choose Insert › Layer.**

The layer appears in the top left corner of the document window with the default width and height specified by the layer preferences.

**NOTE** *Dreamweaver's default is 200 pixels for the width and 115 pixels for the height, but you can change this in the Layers category of the Preferences dialog box. To open the Preferences dialog box, choose Edit > Preferences and choose the Layers category.*

A layer marker appears at the pointer location to show where the layer code has been inserted.

**TIP** *You can also insert a layer by dragging the draw layer icon from the Objects panel into the document window. A layer with the default width and height will be created in the top-left corner of the document window.*

**7) Save the document.**

Leave this file open for the next exercise.

## NAMING LAYERS

Dreamweaver assigns generic names automatically in numeric order: Layer1, Layer2, and so on. These names are not very descriptive, especially when you create complex pages with multiple layers. It is best to get in the habit of giving your layers short, descriptive names.

**1) In the layers.htm document, choose Window › Layers.**

The Layers panel gives you a list of the layers on the page. You can use it to select a layer, name a layer, change the layer's visibility, change the stacking order, or select multiple layers on the page. When you create a layer, it is placed at the top of the list on the Layers panel, before other layers, if there are any. If the layer is hidden or placed off the page, the Layers panel is the easiest method of selecting the layer.

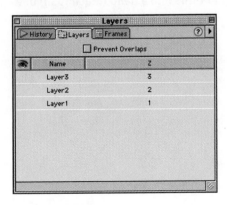

*If the insertion point is inside a layer, that layer's name will appear in bold on the Layers panel and the selection handle will appear in the document window to indicate that the layer is active but not selected.*

The layers you just created are named Layer1, Layer2, and Layer3.

**2) Double-click Layer1 in the Layers panel, type *textlayer* for the layer name, and press Enter (Windows) or Return (Macintosh). Double-click Layer2 in the panel, type *picturelayer*, and press Enter (Windows) or Return (Macintosh).**
Don't change the name for Layer3.

Do not use spaces or special characters (including the underscore character) for layer names. A layer name must be unique—don't assign the same name to more than one layer or to a layer and another element, such as a graphic. It is a good idea to use a consistent naming scheme for all layer names.

**NOTE** *You can also type the name in the Layer ID text field on the property inspector if the layer is selected.*

**3) Save the document.**
Leave this file open for the next exercise.

## MODIFYING LAYERS

After you create a layer, you might want to add a background to it, move it around, or resize it. One of the advantages of using layers is that you can place them in precise locations on the page. You can use the property inspector and type in numbers for placement, and you can align layers to other layers. You need to select a layer first before you can make any modifications to it. There are several methods for selecting a layer. Which method you use may depend on the complexity of your layout.

**1) In the layers.htm document window, position the pointer over the text layer's border and click the border line when the pointer turns into a hand (Macintosh) or a cross hair with arrows (Windows).**

**NOTE** *If no layers are active, Shift-clicking inside a layer will select it. Simply clicking inside a layer places the insertion point in the layer and activates it, but does not actually select the layer itself. Other ways to select a single layer are to click the yellow layer marker that represents the layer's location in the HTML code (invisible elements must be showing) or to click the name of the layer in the Layers panel.*

SELECTION HANDLE

SIZING HANDLES

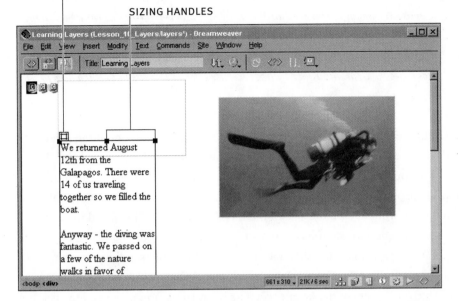

The layer becomes selected; square, black sizing handles appear around the layer. The name of the selected layer is highlighted in the Layers panel. The property inspector changes to indicate the properties of the selected layer. To see all properties, click the expander arrow in the lower-right corner of the property inspector.

**NOTE** *To delete a layer, select it in the document window and press Backspace (Windows) or Delete (Macintosh).*

**2) Resize the text layer by typing *182* for the width in the W text field of the property inspector and pressing Enter (Windows) or Return (Macintosh).**

In the property inspector, the W and H text fields display the specified width and height of the layer. Resizing a layer will change these values. The default unit of measurement is px (pixels).

**NOTE** *You can also specify the following units: pc (picas), pt (points), in (inches), mm (millimeters), cm (centimeters), or % (percentage of the parent's value). The abbreviations must follow the value without a space (for example, 3mm). Pixels or percentage are the recommended units.*

You can also resize the layer by dragging any of the sizing handles.

**TIP** *To resize the layer one pixel at a time using the keyboard, select the layer and press Ctrl+right-arrow (or down-arrow) key for Windows or Option+right-arrow (or down-arrow) key for Macintosh. To resize the layer by the current grid increment, press Shift+Ctrl+right-arrow key (or down-arrow) for Windows or Shift+Option+right-arrow (or down-arrow) key for Macintosh. See the Grid and Ruler Settings exercise later in this lesson to learn how to set the grid increment.*

By default, layers will expand to fit their content: When the content of the layer exceeds the specified size, the values for width and height will be overridden. The Overflow setting on the property inspector controls how layers behave when this occurs. There are four Overflow options: visible, hidden, scroll, and auto. Visible, the default option, will increase the size of the layer, expanding it down and to the right as much as is needed for all of its contents to be visible. Hidden maintains the size of the layer and clips any content that doesn't fit. Scroll will add scroll bars to the layer whether or not the contents exceed the layer's size. Auto will make scroll bars appear only when the contents of the layer exceed its boundaries. You may need to click the expander arrow on the property inspector to make these options visible. Overflow is not supported by all browsers, so use these options with caution.

**NOTE** *You can also set the clipping area to specify the part of the layer that is visible. The Clipping Area can be smaller, larger, or the same size as the layer. Use the property inspector to define the visible area by typing values in all four Clip text fields: L (left), T (top), R (right), and B (bottom). Any content outside of the clipping area will be hidden. This setting is available with all four Overflow options, but is not supported by all browsers.*

**3)** **With the text layer still selected, type *345* in the L text field and *37* in the T text field on the property inspector. Select the picture layer and type *22* in the L text field.**

**NOTE** *Be sure to use the L and T text fields on the top half of the property inspector. Do not use the Clip text fields for this step.*

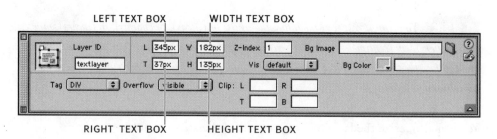

The L text field on the top half of the property inspector defines the space between the layer and the left side of the browser window. The T text field on the top half of the property inspector defines the space between the layer and the top side of the browser window.

**TIP** *You can also drag the selection handle or border of the selected layer to move it to a different location on the page. To move a layer from the keyboard one pixel at a time, select the layer and use the arrow keys. Hold the Shift key and press an arrow key to move the layer by the current grid increment.*

**4) Select Layer3 and drag the selection handle down on the page so the layer appears below the first two layers. Paste the remaining text from dive.txt into this layer.**

You can use any of these methods to move layers atop each other. If you overlap layers, you will need to adjust the order in which they are overlaid (their stacking order), as demonstrated in the next exercise.

**NOTE** *If <LAYER> or <ILAYER> (Netscape 4.x layers only) are selected in the Tag drop-down menu, the property inspector will display radio buttons for you to choose from Top, Left or PageX, PageY. These two options allow you to position a layer in relation to its parent. Top, Left places the layer in relation to the top left corner of its parent (the outer layer if it is a nested layer, or the document window if it is not nested). PageX, PageY places the layer in the absolute location relative to the top-left corner of the page, whether or not it is a nested layer.*

**5) Select the text layer. In the property inspector, click the Bg Color box and select the lightest gray, or type #CCCCCC into the text field beside the color box.**

The background of the layer changes to light gray.

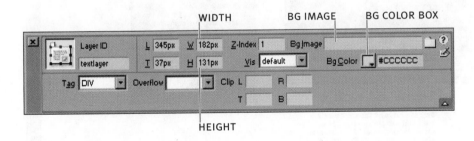

There are two options for the backgrounds of layers. When using either option, test your pages in all browsers since the results may not be what you expect, depending on the content of the layer.

Bg Image specifies a background image for the layer. Type the path for the image in the text field or click the folder icon to select a source image. The background of a layer might not display in all browsers.

Bg Color specifies a background color for the layer. Leave blank to specify transparency.

**NOTE** *If <LAYER> or <ILAYER> (Netscape 4.x layers only) are selected in the Tag drop-down menu, the property inspector will include the Src option. Src will display another HTML document within the layer. Type the path of the document or click the folder icon to browse to and select the document. Note that Dreamweaver does not display this property in the document window.*

**6) Select the picture layer first, and then select the text layer by holding down Shift and clicking inside or on the border of the layer, or hold down Shift and click the picturelayer name in the Layers panel.**

If the Layers panel is not visible, you can choose Window > Layers to display the Layers panel.

Since multiple layers are selected, the most recently selected layer appears with black handles—the other layer has outlined handles.

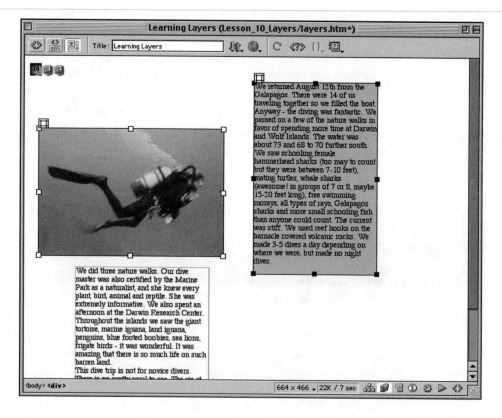

**NOTE** *To resize multiple layers at once, select two or more layers in the document and choose Modify > Align > Make Same Width or Make Same Height. The first selected layers change to the width or height of the last selected layer. You can also enter width and height values in the property inspector to apply the values to all selected layers.*

### 7) Choose Modify › Align and choose Top from the alignment options.

When you choose an alignment option, all the selected layers are aligned to the last layer selected. The alignment options in this menu also include Left, Right, and Bottom.

The tops of textlayer and picturelayer are now aligned to each other.

### 8) Save the document.

Leave this file open for the next exercise.

## CHANGING THE STACKING ORDER OF LAYERS

You can use either the property inspector or the Layers panel to change the stacking order of layers by adjusting the z-index of each layer. The **z-index** determines the order in which layers are drawn in a browser. A layer with a higher z-index number appears to be laid over the top of layers with lower z-index numbers. Values can be positive or negative. This is particularly useful when you have overlapping layers and you need to specify which layer(s) will be atop others. It is also possible for more than one layer to have the same z-index number, in which case the layer that appears in the code first will appear on top.

### 1) In the layers.htm document, select textlayer and change the z-index text field located on the property inspector to 3, or select picturelayer in the Layers panel and drag it downward in the list. Stop dragging and release the layer when a highlighted area appears between the layers.

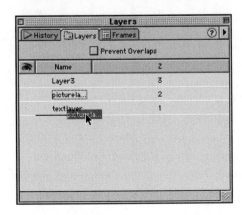

You can change the z-index for each layer separately by using the z-index text field on the property inspector. However, using the Layers panel to change the stacking order of layers is much easier than entering specific z-index values on the property inspector, because you don't have to keep track of the values or the order in which they appear in the code.

### 2) Save the document.

Leave this file open for the next exercise.

## NESTING AND UNNESTING LAYERS

There may be times when you accidentally nest a layer. This exercise demonstrates the process of nesting and unnesting layers. Nesting is a way to group layers together. A nested layer moves with its parent layer and inherits the parent's visibility. Although the concept of nested layers sounds like a good idea, especially when creating animations (covered in Lesson 14), it is not recommended because the results may be unreliable. Be cautious: Nested layers may not display correctly in all browsers. The more layers that you have nested, the longer it will take the browser to display them and the more likely they will be to display incorrectly. If you do choose to nest layers, test your pages with all browsers to be sure the result is what you expected.

**1)  In the layers.htm document, use the Layers panel to select textlayer and drag it over Layer3 while pressing the Ctrl key (Windows) or the Command Key (Macintosh). When the Layer3 name is highlighted, release the text layer.**

**TIP**  *Don't release when the area between the layers is highlighted—doing so changes the stacking order of the layers instead of nesting the layers.*

In the Layers panel, textlayer appears indented below its parent layer, Layer3. Next to Layer3 is a plus sign (Windows) or a blue triangle (Macintosh). You can click the plus sign or blue triangle to hide the list of nested layers. The position of textlayer in the document window may shift.

PARENT LAYER
NESTED LAYER

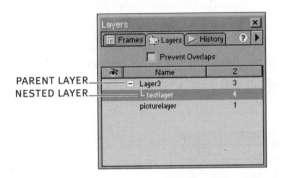

**NOTE**  *You can also create a layer within an existing layer by selecting Draw Layer on the Objects panel and drawing the layer within an existing layer. For this to work, Nest When Created Within A Layer must be selected in Preferences. To change the Preferences, choose Edit > Preferences and select the Layers category.*

**2)  On the Layers panel, select the nested textlayer layer and drag it above or below another layer so that the area between the layers is highlighted.**

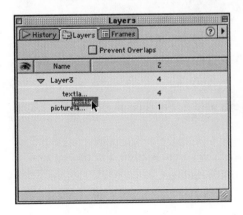

The nesting of a layer is removed, and the layer no longer appears indented in the Layers panel. If textlayer shifted position, it will now be moved back to its original location.

### 3) Save the document.

Leave this file open for the next exercise.

## CHANGING LAYER VISIBILITY

You can change layer visibility in order to show or hide a layer. This can be useful when using layers to add user interactivity. You may need to change the visibility of a layer if you are creating dynamic content that displays in response to user interaction. For example, you can use Timelines (covered in Lesson 14) to hide a layer until the user clicks a button or rolls over an image.

### 1) In the layers.htm document, click in the column to the left of the Layer3 name in the Layers panel to change the visibility of that layer. Click until you see a closed-eye icon.

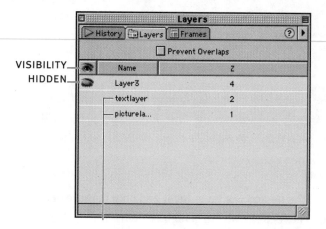

To change the visibility of all layers at once, click the eye icon at the top of the column. There are three visibility options on the Layers panel: inherit, visible, and hidden.

Inherit uses the visibility property of the layer's parent. For this option, there is no icon displayed in the visibility column.

Visible displays the layer contents, regardless of the parent's value. For this option, there is an open-eye icon displayed in the visibility column.

Hidden displays the layer content as transparent, regardless of the parent's value. If you set a layer to hidden, the layer markers and the Layers panel may be the only ways for you to select that layer. For this option, there is a closed-eye icon displayed in the visibility column. Even though you have set Layer3 to hidden, you will still see scroll bars, because hidden layers take up the same space as if they were visible.

On the property inspector, there is a fourth visibility option: Default does not specify a visibility property, but most browsers interpret this as inheriting the parent's value.

**NOTE** *Choose Edit > Preferences and select the Layers category to set the default visibility for new layers.*

## 2) Save the document.

Leave this file open for the next exercise.

## SETTING GRID AND RULER OPTIONS

When you work with layers, you might want to use grids and rulers as visual guides for placement of layers on your page.

## 1) In the layers.htm document, choose View > Grid > Show Grid.

The grids will display in the document window. A check next to the command indicates the option is on.

## 2) Choose View > Grid > Snap To Grid.

This option will turn snapping on or off. A check next to the command indicates the option is on. When this option is on, the layers will snap to the grid lines when you move them close.

## 3) Choose View > Grid > Edit Grid.

The Edit Grid dialog box appears. Use this dialog box to change grid settings. You can change the color, set the spacing value and units (pixels, inches, or centimeters), and switch the grid display to lines or dots. The grid can be useful when you need to align layers.

## 4) Choose View > Rulers > Show.

The rulers will display in the document window. A check next to the command indicates the option is on. The units for rulers can be set by choosing View > Rulers > Pixels, Inches, or Centimeters. A check next to a unit of measure indicates which one is set.

**5) Click in the square between the vertical and horizontal rulers. Drag the zero point downward and to the right, and then release.**

ZERO POINT

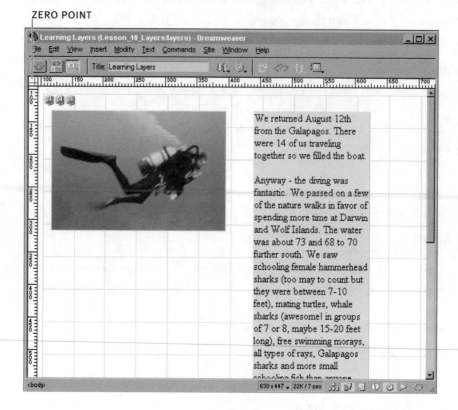

This enables you to set the zero point at the desired location. The **zero point** is where the horizontal and vertical rulers intersect. The default location for the zero point is the upper-left corner of the page, where the top and left sides of the page meet. When the zero point is moved to a point inside the document, you will see negative values appear upward and to the left of the zero point.

**NOTE** *Choose View > Rulers > Reset Origin to reset the zero point.*

**6) Save the document.**

Leave this file open for the next exercise.

## USING THE NETSCAPE RESIZE LAYER FIX

Netscape 4.x versions have a problem with layers when you resize the browser window: The layer changes its shape when the browser window is resized. This can cause problems with your page when the user resizes the browser window. You can fix the problem by inserting the Netscape Resize Fix JavaScript code in your document when you add layers. The code fixes the Netscape problem and will not affect Internet Explorer.

**1) In the layers.htm document, choose Commands › Add/Remove Netscape Resize Fix. If the option is to Add, click the Add button. If the option is to Remove, click the Cancel button.**

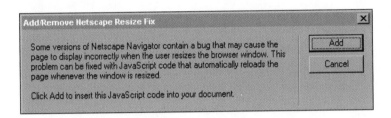

In the Add/Remove Netscape Resize Fix dialog box that opens, you can either add or remove the JavaScript code. The code will cause the page to reload if the user resizes the browser window. Dreamweaver may have added this code to your page automatically; if not, you can add it easily with this dialog box.

**2) Save the document.**

Leave this file open for the next exercise.

## CONVERTING LAYERS TO TABLES

Layers can be an easy way to design your page; however, because not all browsers support them, your audience may be limited. Earlier browsers display layer contents without any positioning and without any control as to the placement. If you decide to design your page using layers, you may want to convert the layers to a table to provide an alternate page for those viewers with browsers that do not support layers. After you have converted the layers to a table, you can switch to Layout view to complete any design changes. You can then use the Check Browser behavior to redirect users based on their browser version (as you did in Lesson 5).

The following exercise shows you how to convert layers, but the recommended method of creating tables is using Layout view to draw tables and table cells or Standard view to create tables (as you did in Lesson 4).

A few restrictions apply when you're converting layers to tables: You can't have nested layers, and the layers can't overlap. Dreamweaver displays an alert and will not create the table if these conditions exist. You also cannot convert a single layer—the entire page will be converted.

**NOTE** *Another way to convert your layers to pages that are compatible with older browsers is to choose File > Convert > 3.0 Browser Compatible. This method will open the converted file in a new window.*

**1) In the layers.htm document, choose File › Save As and type *layers_table.htm* in the Name text field. Save the file in the Lesson_10_Layers folder.**

The layers in this document will be converted and replaced with a single table.

**NOTE** *The conversion to a table will remove the layer names.*

**2) Click in the document window. On the Layers panel, select Prevent Overlaps.**

Overlapping layers cannot be converted to a table. If you select this option before you begin drawing layers, Dreamweaver will prevent them from overlapping. By using the Prevent Overlaps option, you can move layers as close as possible to other layers.

If you already have layers that overlap, checking the Prevent Overlaps checkbox will not move those layers. You will have to move them in order to stop them from overlapping.

### 3) Choose Modify > Convert > Layers to Table.

The Convert Layers to Table dialog box opens with several options.

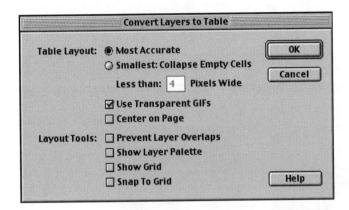

Most Accurate will create a table cell for every layer, plus any additional cells that are necessary, to preserve the space between layers.

Smallest: Collapse Empty Cells specifies that the layers' edges should be aligned if they are positioned within the specified number of pixels. If this option is selected, the resulting table may have fewer empty rows and columns.

Use Transparent GIFs will fill the last row of the table with transparent GIFs. This ensures that the table will display the same in all browsers. When this option is selected, you cannot edit the resulting table by dragging its columns. When this option is deselected, the resulting table will not contain transparent GIFs, and its appearance might vary slightly in different browsers.

Center on Page will center the resulting table on the page. If this option is deselected, the table is left-aligned.

Layout Tools will allow you to set any desired layout or grid options.

**4) Select the desired options and click OK. For this exercise, keep the default settings of Most Accurate and Use Transparent GIFs.**

Any hidden layers will be deleted. After you convert your layers to a table, use Layout View to make any necessary adjustments to the table.

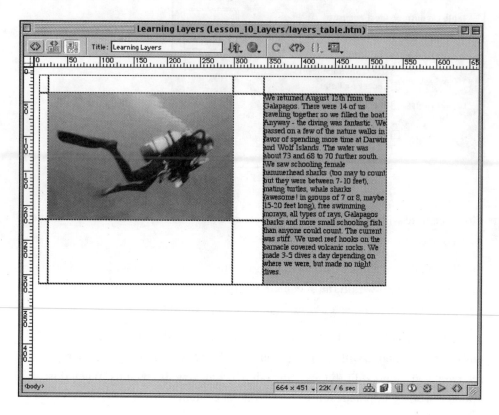

**NOTE** *You can also convert a table to layers by choosing Modify > Convert > Tables to Layers while in Standard View. The Convert Tables to Layers dialog box opens, and there you can select the desired options and then click OK. Empty cells in the table will be ignored and not converted to layers. Any content on the page outside the table will be converted to a layer.*

**5) Choose Commands › Add/Remove Netscape Resize Fix.**

When you convert layers to a table, you should use the Add/Remove Netscape Resize Fix option to remove the JavaScript code you added in the previous exercise, because it is no longer needed.

**6) Save the document.**

You can close this file.

## WHAT YOU HAVE LEARNED

**In this lesson, you have:**

- Created layers by drawing them in the document window and by inserting default, pre-sized layers (pages 214–217)

- Named layers to keep track of them in the Layers panel (pages 217–218)

- Selected single and multiple layers, modified their sizes and locations, and aligned them relative to each other (pages 218–223)

- Changed the stacking order of layers in order to specify the order in which they display from top to bottom (pages 223–224)

- Nested and unnested layers to understand how layers can work in groups or become nested accidentally (pages 224–226)

- Changed layer visibility to hide and show entire layers (pages 226–227)

- Set rulers and grids to help when moving layers on the page (pages 227–228)

- Inserted a JavaScript to remedy a Netscape bug that causes viewing problems with layers (page 229)

- Made pages designed with layers compatible with earlier browsers by converting the layers to a table (pages 229–232)

# using style sheets

Cascading style sheets (CSS) enable you to define how type is displayed on your Web pages. The term "cascading" refers to the ordered sequence of styles. A **style** is a group of formatting attributes, identified by a single name. Styles in HTML documents give you a great deal of control over text formatting. The advantage of using styles is that when you make a change to an attribute of the style, all of the text controlled by that style will be reformatted automatically. You can make adjustments on a wide variety of settings from standard HTML attributes such as font, size, color, and alignment to unique attributes such as the space between characters (tracking), the space between lines (leading), and additional size and font options.

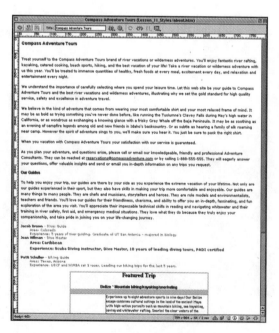

*In this project, you will use three types of styles—HTML tag styles, custom styles, and CSS selector styles—to apply a variety of format options to the text in this document.*

Using style sheets, you can, for example, create a paragraph with a half-inch margin, 20 points between the lines, and the text displayed in a 12-point blue Verdana font. This would not be possible without the use of CSS, which is mainly supported by 4.0 or later browsers. Most earlier browsers ignore CSS, although Internet Explorer 3.0 recognizes some style attributes.

You can use an **embedded style**—one that is stored inside the document—when you need to format a single page, or you can use an **external style sheet**—one that is stored outside of the document and linked to the current page—when you need to control several documents at once in order to keep the same style of text formatting on multiple pages. It is ideal to keep the treatment of text consistent throughout your site because drastic changes in appearance may give viewers the impression they have landed on another site.

To see an example of the finished page for this lesson, open about.htm from the Lesson_11_Styles/Completed folder.

## WHAT YOU WILL LEARN

**In this lesson, you will:**

- Create an external style sheet
- Add styles to an existing style sheet
- Edit a style
- Create a custom style
- Link to an external style sheet
- Create an embedded style
- Convert embedded styles to external styles
- Convert CSS to HTML

## APPROXIMATE TIME

This lesson should take about two hours to complete.

## LESSON FILES

**Starting Files**

*Lesson_11_Styles/about.htm*

*Lesson_11_Styles/biking.htm*

**Completed Project**

*Lesson_11_Styles/Completed/about.htm*

*Lesson_11_Styles/Completed/lessonstyle.css*

## CREATING EXTERNAL STYLE SHEETS

Style sheets can be stored externally and linked to one or more documents. When you create an external style sheet for a document, the style sheet is automatically linked to the document for which it was created. An external style sheet is a text file that only contains style specifications. One advantage of creating an external style sheet for a document is that you can link that style sheet to other documents in the site in order to ensure consistency from page to page. Another advantage of using an external style sheet is that you can easily edit your styles, because any modifications will be made automatically to all documents that link to that style sheet. Use an external style sheet to standardize the appearance of text on multiple pages and to make changes that will be applied to all linked documents.

In this exercise, you will create a new style in an external style sheet by redefining an HTML tag. By redefining the heading 3 (<h3>) HTML tag in this exercise, you are telling the browser that any text using the <h3> tag should be displayed with the formatting you specify. This is useful because it allows you to alter the basic heading 3 format so all text that uses the heading 3 format will be formatted with the style attributes you specified.

### 1)  Open the about.htm file from the Lesson_11_Styles folder.

This document contains paragraphs, headings, and a definition list.

### 2)  Place the insertion point within the Compass Adventure Tours heading.

Look at the tag selector at the bottom left of the document window. You'll see the HTML tag <h3> that has been applied to the heading. The redefinition of the <h3> tag will be the first style you create.

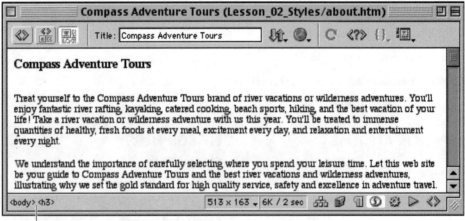

TAG SELECTOR

236

### 3) Choose Window > CSS Styles to open the CSS Styles panel.

The CSS Styles panel opens.

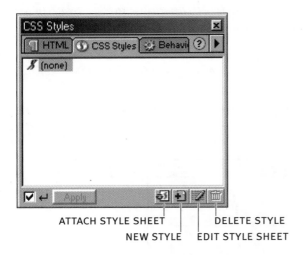

ATTACH STYLE SHEET          DELETE STYLE
              NEW STYLE    EDIT STYLE SHEET

**TIP.** *You can also open the CSS Styles panel by clicking the CSS Styles button located on the mini-launcher at the bottom right of the document window.*

### 4) Click the new style button at the bottom of the CSS Styles panel.

The New Style dialog box opens.

**TIP** *You can also open this dialog box by choosing Text > CSS Styles > New Style.*

### 5) In the Type area, select Redefine HTML tag.

You are going to redefine the <h3> tag. Since your insertion point was within the heading when you clicked the new style button, the <h3> tag is automatically selected and shown as h3 in the Tag text box. If h3 is not displayed, choose h3 from the drop-down menu.

**6) In the Define In area, select New Style Sheet from the drop-down menu and click OK.**
The Save Style Sheet File As dialog box opens.

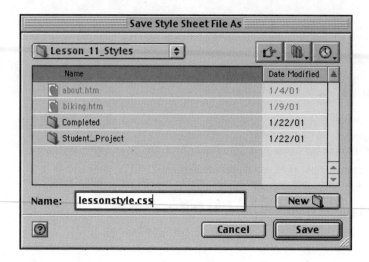

**7) Navigate to the Lesson_11_Styles folder. Type *lessonstyle.css* in the Name box and click Save.**

This creates the external style sheet file and opens the Style Definition dialog box for the selected <h3> tag. In the Style Definition dialog box, you define the way you want your heading 3 tags to appear. The options you want to select for the next step are located in the Type category. Make sure the Type category is selected in the category list on the left side of the dialog box.

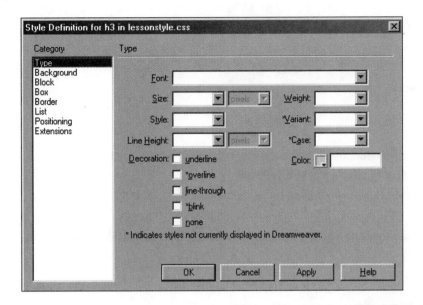

**8) For this exercise, select Arial, Helvetica, Sans-serif from the Font drop-down menu. Select 14 from the first Size drop-down menu and change the measurement to points in the second Size drop-down menu. Select a medium blue for the color by clicking the color box.**

When you click, color swatches appear and the pointer becomes an eyedropper that you can use to select a color.

**9) Click OK.**

The changes you have made are now reflected in the first heading on your page. Redefined HTML tag styles are not displayed in the CSS Styles panel.

**NOTE** *Dreamweaver has some style attributes it cannot render in the document window. These attributes appear with an asterisk (*) before the name in the Style Definition dialog box. Dreamweaver also has some attributes that are in the CSS specification but are not supported by all current browsers. Some of the options you see are not supported by any browser. Make sure you check your styles in both Netscape Navigator and Internet Explorer to see if the attribute you chose is supported.*

**10) Save this document.**

Leave this file open for the next exercise.

## ADDING A STYLE TO AN EXISTING EXTERNAL STYLE SHEET

When you create an external style sheet for a page, it is attached (linked) to that page. You can add new styles to make changes to not only this page but to all pages that use the style sheet.

In this exercise, you will add new styles to the style sheet.

**1) In the about.htm document, place the insertion point within the first paragraph below the heading Compass Adventure Tours.**

You will create a style for all paragraphs on the page.

**2) Click New Style on the CSS Styles panel and select Redefine HTML Tag from the Type area.**

The New Style dialog box opens.

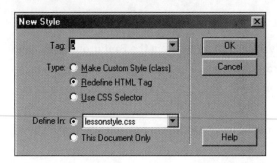

Since your insertion point was within the paragraph, the <p> tag is automatically selected and shown as p in the Tag text box. If p is not displayed, choose p from the drop-down menu. The <p> tag represents paragraph.

The tag selector at the bottom left of the document window will display the HTML tag <p>, indicating that the insertion point is within the paragraph.

**3) In the Define In area, choose lessonstyle.css from the drop-down menu and click OK.**

The Style Definition dialog box opens. By using the Style Definition dialog box, you are redefining the way text formatted with paragraph tags should appear.

**4) For this exercise, select Verdana, Arial, Helvetica, Sans-serif from the Font drop-down menu. Select 10 from the Size drop-down menu and change the measurement to points in the second Size drop-down menu. Type *16* in the Line Height text box and change the measurement to points. Choose a dark blue from the color box and click OK.**

Style Definition for p in lessonstyle.css

Category | Type

Type
Background
Block
Box
Border
List
Positioning
Extensions

Font: Verdana, Arial, Helvetica, sans-serif

Size: 10    points    Weight:

Style:    *Variant:

Line Height: 16    points    *Case:

Decoration: ☐ underline    Color: ■ #000066
☐ *overline
☐ line-through
☐ *blink
☐ none

* Indicates styles not currently displayed in Dreamweaver.

Help    Apply    Cancel    OK

Any text that is contained within paragraph tags in the document appears with the formatting you defined in the external style sheet. Any text that has a different format applied to it, such as the subheading "Our Guides," is not affected by the style sheet.

**TIP** *Click Apply to see your selections appear on the page while the dialog box is still open. If you want to make changes, you can do so before closing the dialog box. Click OK when you finish.*

### 5) Select the subheading "Our Guides" and repeat steps 2 through 5 to apply a style with format attributes of your choice for that heading.

This subheading is a heading 4. You can see the tag displayed <h4> in the tag selector at the bottom left of the document window, and you can also see heading 4 displayed in the Format drop-down menu on the property inspector. You should choose a font, size, and color from the Style Definition dialog box. Most of the text on the page now has been formatted with styles. The next section of text is a definition list and still needs formatting.

### 6) Place the insertion point in the first line of the definition list "Jacob Brown – River Guide." In the tag selector, click <dl>.

This selects the definition list tag that controls the HTML formatting of the text. By selecting the <dl> tag, you will apply the formatting to both the definition term <dt> and the definition data <dd> at the same time. You also avoid a browser difference between Netscape 4.0 (and later) and Internet Explorer 4.0 (and later). Netscape 4.0 (and later) does not display style formatting if you create separate styles for the <dt> and the <dd> tags. Formatting the <dl> tag works in both browsers.

**7) Use steps 2 through 6, as you did for the other tags on this page, to apply a style for the <d1> tag with format attributes of your choice.**

At this point, your document should look similiar to the example shown here, although you may have chosen different formatting attributes for some of the styles.

**8) Save this document.**

Leave this file open for the next exercise.

## EDITING AN EXISTING STYLE

You may need to modify the styles that are in an existing style sheet. Editing an external style sheet will affect all documents that are linked to it. This is useful because the appearance of text can be changed in several pages or an entire site by editing only the external style sheet.

In this exercise, you will edit a style in the external style sheet that you created in the first exercise.

### 1) In the about.htm document, click Edit Style Sheet icon at the bottom of the CSS Styles panel.

If the CSS Styles panel is not visible, choose Window > CSS Styles.

The Edit Style Sheet dialog box opens.

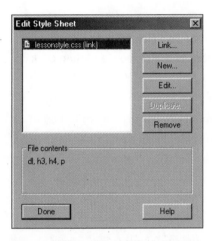

**NOTE** *The styles contained in the style sheet you select will be displayed in the File contents area of the Edit Style Sheet dialog box.*

### 2) Select the external style sheet lessonstyle.css (link) from the list and click Edit.

The lessonstyle.css dialog box appears with a list of all the styles contained in this external style sheet. In this case, all the styles are redefined HTML tags.

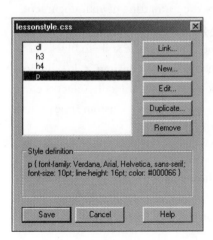

**3)  Select p from the list to edit the paragraph tag and click Edit.**

**NOTE** *When you select the p style from the list, the attributes of that style are displayed in the Style Definition area of the lessonstyle.css dialog box.*

The Style Definition dialog box opens. This is the same as the Style Definition box you used in the previous exercise to choose formatting attributes.

**4)  In the Style Definition dialog box, change the size from 10 points to 11 points by typing *11* in the Size text box. Change Line Height to 18. Click OK in the Style Definition dialog box, click Save in the lessonstyle.css dialog box, and then click Done in the Edit Style Sheet dialog box.**

Your changes are applied to the document. The font size in now slightly larger, and the space between each line of text is greater. This style sheet is not yet linked to from any other documents; if other documents were linked to this style sheet, any text in those documents using the <p> tag would be formatted according to the modifications you just made.

**TIP** *You can use the Reference panel to learn more about the CSS elements. Open the Reference panel by choosing Window > Reference. In the Book drop-down menu, choose O'Reilly CSS Reference. Use the Style drop-down menu to choose CSS terms and read their descriptions. All references to CSS styles are placed between the* <HEAD> *and* </HEAD> *tags of the document.*

**5)  Save this document.**

Leave this file open for the next exercise.

## CREATING CUSTOM STYLES

Custom styles give you more specific control over the formatting of your document. You apply custom styles the same way you apply styles in a word processor: by selecting the text and then applying the style. You can apply the style to blocks of text or to individual words within the text. When you create a custom style, you do not have to preselect text as you did in the previous exercise. You only select the text in order to apply the style to it, after the style has been created. Custom styles can be created in either external or internal style sheets.

In this exercise, you are going to make a custom style in the external style sheet that will apply a bold style to any text to which you choose to apply it.

**1)  In the about.htm document, click New Style on the CSS Styles panel.**

The New Style dialog box opens.

**2) Select Make Custom Style from the Type area.**

The text box that displayed tags in the previous exercises now becomes a Name text box for creating a custom style. Dreamweaver assigns generic names automatically in a numeric order: .unnamed1, .unnamed2, etc. These names are not very descriptive, and they can be especially unhelpful when you create multiple custom styles. It is best to get in the habit of giving your styles short, descriptive names.

**3) Type *boldit* in the Name text box for the name of your custom style.**

A period before the name is required; Dreamweaver automatically adds it for you. If you delete the period, Dreamweaver will automatically include it at the beginning of the name, even if it isn't shown.

**4) The Define In area should still show lessonstyle.css. If not, choose lessonstyle.css from the drop-down menu. Click OK.**

The Style Definition dialog box opens.

### 5) Change Weight to bold and pick a dark red color from the Color drop-down menu. Then click OK.

You'll see the custom style you just created displayed on the CSS Styles panel. Only custom styles are displayed in this panel because they are the only styles for which you can select text in the document window and apply a style as if you were using a word processor. HTML tag styles and CSS selector styles are applied automatically when they are defined or changed in the style sheet.

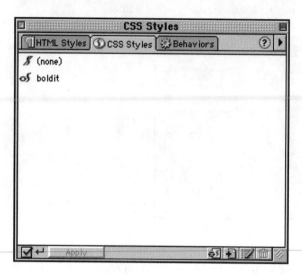

In the next steps, you'll apply the boldit custom style you just created to the guide names in the definition list.

### 6) Select Jacob Brown's name and click the boldit custom style on the CSS panel.

The selected text changes to reflect the boldit style. There are now two styles affecting this text: the first style applied which redefines the <dl> (definition list) tag, and the custom style—the second style applied—which specifies bold and color formatting. When you apply more than one style to the same text, those styles might conflict and produce unexpected results. Browsers apply style attributes according to the order in which styles are applied and the following rules:

CSS is applied in an ordered sequence. When two or more styles are applied to the same text, the browser will display the attributes of each style in combination with each other.

If there is more than one style applied to the same text with conflicting attributes, the browser uses the specifications from the innermost style (the style closest to the text itself). The most recent styles are nested inside earlier styles. Since the last formatting attributes you apply are physically the closest tags to the text, they take precedence over earlier styles and control the final look of the text. The order of styles is as follows:

1. External styles (this is the style that is farthest away from the text)

2. Embedded styles (sometimes known as internal styles)

3. Custom styles applied to text on the page

4. Local formatting, such as bold or italics, applied to text on the page from the property inspector (this is the style that is closest to the text)

If you have an external style sheet containing redefined HTML tags linked to your document, those styles are applied across your document. Suppose, for example, the external style sheet has definitions for heading 3 and heading 4, and that you've also created an embedded style within your document that redefines the heading 3 tag. The embedded style takes precedence if the attributes conflict with those in the external style.

Text formatting applied manually to ranges of text can also take precedence over styles. Suppose, in the example just presented, that you've used the property inspector to apply a different color on one of the heading 3 lines. That is local formatting, and it overrides other styles if they specify color as well. However, the attributes from custom styles overrule attributes from HTML tag styles. To make sure that your styles control the formatting for a paragraph, you may need to remove all other formatting settings if they conflict.

### 7) Repeat step 6 for the remaining guide names in the list.

The custom style changed only the color and weight of the text. The text inherits additional font formatting from the style you defined previously for the paragraph.

**NOTE** *After you apply a custom style, you might want to remove the style. If you apply the custom style to the entire paragraph, make sure the insertion point is in the paragraph, and then click None on the CSS Styles panel. The style and its formatting are removed. If you're removing the custom style that has only been applied to selected text within a paragraph, make sure the insertion point is within a word that uses the custom style, and then click None on the CSS Styles panel.*

### 8) Save this document.

Leave this file open for the next exercise.

## CREATING CSS SELECTOR STYLES FOR LINKS

You can use styles to change the appearance of links on your page. CSS Selector styles can be used for controlling the dynamic link tag (<a>) with specific attributes for the different states that can be applied to it. The different states of the <a> tag are activated when a user performs an action such as clicking the link. In the CSS Selector drop-down menu in the New Style dialog box, Dreamweaver provides four standard states for the <a> tag that make it easy to change the formatting of links on your pages. This type of CSS selector is known as a **pseudo-class**.

In this exercise, you will create a CSS selector style in the external style sheet in order to change the look of a link on the page.

**1)  In the about.htm document, click New Style on the CSS Styles panel.**
The New Style dialog box opens.

**2)  In the New Style dialog box, select Use CSS Selector from the Type area, choose lessonstyle.css from the drop-down menu in the Define In area, and choose a:link from the Selector drop-down menu.**

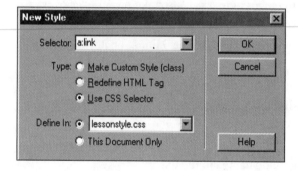

The four states applicable to links appear in the Selector drop-down menu. They change based on user activity. The choices in the drop-down menu are a:active, a:hover, a:link, and a:visited.

The Active selector controls the link when the link is selected or as it is clicked by the user; the default color is red. It is displayed in the Selector menu as a:active.

The Link selector controls the normal state of a link; the default color is blue. It is displayed in the Selector menu as a:link.

The Visited selector controls the link after it has been clicked by the user; the default color is purple. It is displayed in the Selector menu as a:visited.

The Hover selector controls the link when the user moves the pointer over the link; the default color is red. It is displayed in the Selector menu as a:hover. Currently, only Internet Explorer 4.0 and later support the Hover option.

**3) Click OK in the New Style dialog box. In the Style Definition dialog box that appears, change the font and size to values of your choice. Use the color box to change the color to a dark green and click OK.**

You are using a color other than the default so you can see your style changes.

You will not see the changes that you make to links within Dreamweaver. You need to preview the page in your browser to see those formatting changes.

**4) View your page in the browser to see the change in the formatting of the e-mail link (reservations@compassadventure.com) on the page.**

The e-mail link is displayed with the formatting attributes that you chose in the Style Definition dialog box. If there were any other links on this page, or in documents that linked to the same external style sheet, they too would display these formatting attributes.

CSS selector styles are not displayed in the CSS Styles panel.

**NOTE** *Using CSS selector styles, it is possible to remove the default underline that appears on all links, but this practice is not recommended. When creating Web sites, you need to consider user expectations. Users have become accustomed to underlined links. If you remove the underlines, your users might overlook the links and miss the information. Conversely, if you underline other words in your text, users might try to click them, expecting links. If it is necessary, you can remove the underline in your Style Definition for the link you just created in this exercise by following these steps: In the lessonstyle.css dialog box that you used in this exercise select a:link and click Edit. In the Style Definition dialog box that opens, select None in the Decoration area to remove the underline from the link.*

**5) Save this document.**

Leave this file open for the next exercise.

## CREATING CSS SELECTOR STYLES FOR TAG COMBINATIONS

CSS selector styles also enable you to format combinations of tags—tags that appear within other tags. In this lesson, for example, you want to give text paragraphs within a table a different format than the other paragraphs on the page. Since you already created a style for the <p> tag, the paragraphs within the table currently reflect that formatting. Place the cursor in a paragraph within the table, and you will see by looking at the HTML code that there are <td> tags for the table cell and <p> tags for the paragraphs within the cell. The tag selector at the bottom left of the document window shows the hierarchy of the code: <body><table><tr><td><p>—body, table, table row, table cell, and paragraph, respectively.

In this exercise, you will create a style that changes only the formatting of the paragraphs within the table cells so they look different from the rest of the paragraphs on the page.

**1) In the about.htm document, click New Style on the CSS Styles panel.**
The New Style dialog box opens.

**2) Select Use CSS Selector in the Type area and type *td p* in the Selector text box.**

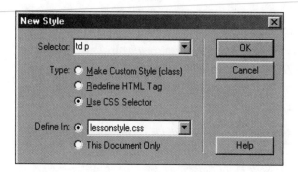

The td p you typed in the Selector text box represents the table cell and the paragraph tags inside it. Wherever this specific combination of tags appears in the document, the formatting you are going to choose in the following steps will be applied. By using td p, you are specifying that only paragraphs located within table cells will be affected.

**3) Select lessonstyle.css in the Define In area and click OK.**
The Style Definition dialog box opens.

**4) Set the font to Geneva, Arial, Helvetica, san-serif. Select 10 points for the size and 14 points for the line height. From the color box, select a dark green color and click OK.**

Your changes are reflected in the text that is located in the table.

**5) Save your changes and close the file.**

Because CSS selector styles allow you to format tags that appear after another tag, the changes you made for the paragraph in the table do not affect the other paragraphs on the page. The text in the table uses a <p> tag, which appears after the <td> tag in the HTML code, so the td p CSS selector style is applied to that text. The paragraphs outside the table, however, do not have a <td> tag that appears before the <p> tag, so that text remains unaffected by the selector style.

## LINKING TO AN EXISTING EXTERNAL STYLE SHEET

You now have an external style sheet with several Style Definitions. Because it is external, you can link to this file from other documents. The Style Definitions, except for custom styles, will be applied automatically to all documents that are linked to this style sheet. You will need to manually apply any custom styles to paragraphs or selected text.

**1) Open the biking.htm file from the Lesson_11_Styles folder.**

In the following steps, you will link this document to the external style sheet you've been working with so the text formatting will be consistent between both pages.

**2) Click the attach style sheet button at the bottom of the CSS Styles panel.**

ATTACH STYLE SHEET

The Select Style Sheet File dialog box opens.

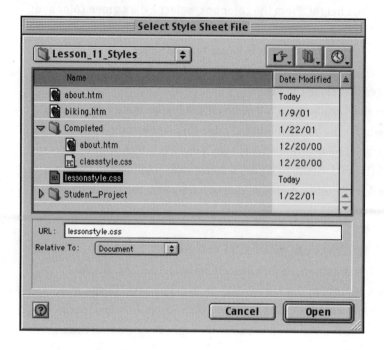

**3) Locate the lessonstyle.css file you created at the beginning of this lesson in the Lesson_11_Styles folder and click Select (Windows) or Open (Macintosh).**

The external style sheet has now been linked to this document. Any tags in the current document are changed to the styles in the external style sheet.

Notice that not all the text in biking.htm has changed from its default formatting. The document had some HTML tags that were not included in your style sheet. In the following steps, you will edit the external style sheet to add the HTML tags that appear in this new page.

**4) Click Edit Style Sheet at the bottom of the CSS Styles panel. Add styles with format attributes of your choice for the heading "Mountain Biking Adventures" and the bullet lists that appear on the Mountain Biking Adventures page.**

Use the steps you learned in the Adding a Style to an Existing Style Sheet exercise earlier in this lesson to complete this step. The text on the page changes as you specify styles for the heading and bullet list.

**5) Use the steps you learned in the Creating Custom Styles exercise earlier in this lesson to apply the boldit custom style to the definition terms, starting with "Horsethief Bench."**

Save this file and leave it open for the next exercise.

## CREATING EMBEDDED STYLES

Embedded styles are used only in the current document. If you want to create Style Definitions for only one page in your site, you should create an embedded style. If you want your site to have a consistent look, you should use an external style sheet and link that style sheet to each document.

In this exercise, you will add an embedded style that will be available only for the current document.

**1) In the biking.htm document, click New Style on the CSS Styles panel.**

The New Style dialog box opens.

**2) Select This Document Only in the Define In area and change the Type to Make Custom Style (class).**

"This Document Only" specifies that you are adding a new embedded style.

**3) Type *highlight* in the Name text box and click OK.**

The Style Definition dialog box opens.

**4)  In the Style Definition dialog box, click Background in the Category list on the left.**

The Style Definition dialog box changes to display background options.

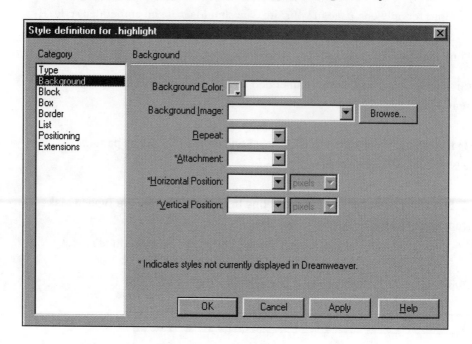

**5)  Change the color in the Background Color field to pale yellow (#FFFFCC) or pale blue (#CCFFFF) and click OK.**

**NOTE**  *There are a total of eight categories available for Style Definition. You've used two: Type—basic text format options such as font, size, and style; and Background—options for background appearance such as color and image. The other six categories are: Block, which provides additional text spacing and positioning options; Box, which provides additional options to control placement; Border, which provides options to control borders; List, which provides options to control the formatting of ordered and unordered lists; Positioning, which provides options for CSS layers; and Extensions, which provides additional options that are not widely supported.*

The highlight custom style you just created appears in the CSS Styles panel. There are now two custom styles: boldit and highlight. Notice the icon to the left of each name. The custom style in the external style sheet (boldit) has a small link image on the icon to represent the link to the external style sheet.

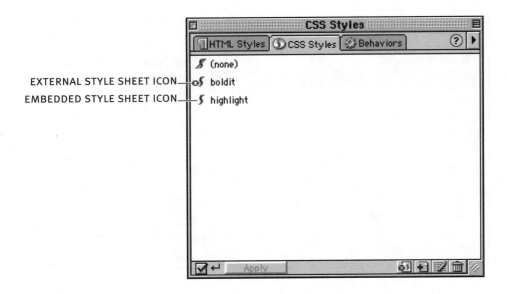

EXTERNAL STYLE SHEET ICON

EMBEDDED STYLE SHEET ICON

**6) Select Compass Adventure Travel on the first line below the Mountain Biking Adventures heading at the top of the page and click highlight on the CSS Styles panel to apply the style.**

The text appears to be highlighted with the pale color.

**7) Save your file, and then open the about.htm file.**

Look in the CSS Styles panel. You will not see the highlight custom style you just created because it is an embedded style and appears only in the document where it was created.

**NOTE** *To remove embedded or external styles, click the Edit Style Sheet icon on the CSS Styles panel to open the Edit Style Sheet dialog box. Select the style you want to remove and click Remove. If the style is an embedded style, it is deleted from the document. If you remove an external style sheet, the link to the style is removed from the document. The actual external style sheet file is not deleted from your site.*

## CONVERTING EMBEDDED STYLES TO EXTERNAL STYLES

If you have a document with all embedded styles and you decide you want to use those styles in other pages, you can easily export those styles to an external style sheet.

**1) In the biking.htm document, choose File > Export > Export CSS Styles.**

The Export Styles as CSS File dialog box opens.

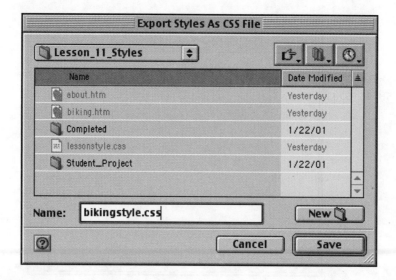

### 2) Name your style sheet bikingstyle.css and click Save.

An external style is created from the internal styles in the current document.

**NOTE** *If you want to use this external style sheet in your current document, first remove all internal styles, and then click the Attach Style Sheet button at the bottom of the CSS Styles panel to link to the external file you just created.*

## CONVERTING CSS TO HTML

CSS is a great way to control the text throughout your Web site, but not all browsers are capable of CSS. Earlier browsers will ignore CSS formatting. If you decide to use CSS, you may want to convert your page to 3.0 browser-compatible files in order to display the page with formatting as close to the CSS styles as possible. You can then use the Check Browser behavior to redirect users based on their browser version (as you did in Lesson 5). This exercise shows you how to convert from CSS to HTML tags.

### 1) In the about.htm document, choose File > Convert > 3.0 Browser Compatible.

The Convert to 3.0 Browser Compatible dialog box opens.

### 2) Select CSS Styles to HTML Markup and click OK.

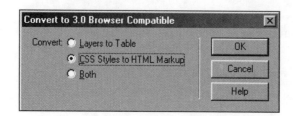

The converted file is opened in a new, untitled document and your original file remains unaltered. The styles that were applied in the about.htm document are reproduced as closely as possible using standard HTML tags. However, it is not possible to convert some types of CSS formatting to HTML tags. For example, line height—also known as leading—has no equivalent in HTML. There is no way to adjust the spacing between lines of text with the standard HTML formatting attributes. Any attributes that cannot be converted will be discarded.

**NOTE**  *After the file is converted and placed into a new document, any changes made to the original won't be reflected in the converted document. Changes made by editing the CSS styles will not appear in converted 3.0 browser-compatible documents. You will have to reconvert the original document to match the edits as closely as possible.*

### 3) Save the document.
You can close this file.

## WHAT YOU HAVE LEARNED

**In this lesson, you have:**

- Created an external style sheet specifying text formatting that can be used to maintain consistency in the look of text throughout a Web site (pages 235–239)

- Added multiple styles to an existing style sheet by redefining HTML tags (pages 240–242)

- Edited a style in the external style sheet to affect all documents linked to it (pages 242–244)

- Created a custom style that can be applied to different kinds of text formats (pages 244–251)

- Linked to an external style sheet from another document to use the same text formatting (pages 251–255)

- Created an embedded style to use the same text formatting quickly and easily (pages 253–255)

- Converted embedded styles to external styles so they can be used by other documents (pages 255–256)

- Converted CSS to HTML to make the pages compatible with 3.0 browsers (pages 256–257)

# using find and replace

The Find and Replace feature in Dreamweaver provides you with a powerful searching tool. You can search the current document, a specified folder, or the entire site. The extensive options enable you to search for text, HTML tags, or even HTML tags with certain attributes. After you've found what you are looking for, you can modify or replace it. The Find and Replace feature can save a lot of time when you need to make massive changes to a document or an entire site.

In this lesson, you will use Find and Replace to make a wide variety of changes to several documents. You will use Find and Replace to apply CSS styles and attach

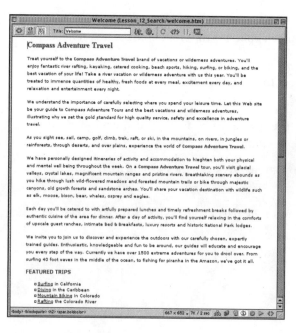

*In this project, you will use Find and Replace to change a company name in this document and remove the color from that name. You will also adjust the formatting attributes of text in this document by using Find and Replace to automate the process of linking to an external style sheet and applying a custom style to text.*

external style sheets to a number of documents all at once. You'll find and replace text, change text formatting, learn to save your searches to use at a later time, find dates, and replace names.

To see an example of the finished page for this lesson, open welcome.htm from the Lesson_12_Search/Completed folder.

## WHAT YOU WILL LEARN

**In this lesson, you will:**

- Find and replace text
- Find text within HTML tags
- Use Find and Replace to apply a custom style
- Use Find and Replace to attach external style sheets
- Save and reuse your search settings
- Search for patterns in text
- Find variations of a name

## APPROXIMATE TIME

This lesson should take about one hour to complete.

## LESSON FILES

**Starting Files**

*Lesson_12_Search/welcome.htm*

*Lesson_12_Search/pattern_search.htm*

*Lesson_12_Search/Files_to_Style/…
   (all files)*

**Completed Project**

*Lesson_12_Search/Completed/welcome.htm*

259

## SEARCHING YOUR DOCUMENT

In this exercise, you will perform a simple search in order to find and replace a company name in the text of a document.

### 1) Open the welcome.htm file from the Lesson_12_Search folder.

This file gives the company name as Compass Adventure Tours. The name needs to be changed to Compass Adventure Travel.

### 2) Choose Edit › Find and Replace.

The Find and Replace dialog box opens.

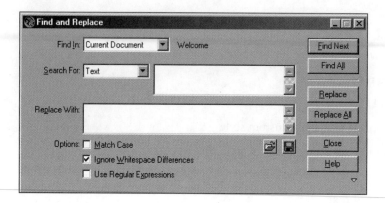

### 3) In the Find In drop-down menu, choose Current Document. In the Search For drop-down menu, choose Text. In the Search For text box, type *Compass Adventure Tours*. In the Replace With text box, type *Compass Adventure Travel*. Check the Match Case box and uncheck the other two boxes.

> **TIP** *Selecting a portion of text before opening the Find and Replace dialog box will automatically cause the selected text to appear in the Search For text box.*

Find in Current Document will search the entire document. This can only be used from a single document while it is open. The Find In drop-down menu also has additional options.

Entire Local Site will search the whole current site.

Selected Files in Site will search files you specify and should be used while viewing the site window so you can select the files.

Folder will allow you to browse in order to select a folder and search all the contents of that folder.

**NOTE** *Dreamweaver remembers the settings from your most recent search. If you close and reopen the dialog box, the text and options you set the last time the dialog box was open will still be there.*

There are three other options at the bottom of the Find and Replace dialog box.

Match Case limits the search to the exact case of the words. Because you checked Match Case, the search will look for a phrase with the exact capital and lower-case letters of the phrase you entered.

Ignore Whitespace Differences ignores all spaces. If this is checked and you are searching for two words, Dreamweaver will also find all instances where those two words have additional spaces between them.

Use Regular Expressions provides patterns to describe character combinations in the text. Use this option to select sentences that begin with "The" or attribute values that contain a number.

### 4) Click Find Next.

The first occurrence of the phrase after the insertion point is highlighted.

### 5) Click Replace.

The phrase is changed to "Compass Adventure Travel," and the next occurrence of the phrase is highlighted.

### 6) Click Replace All.

The remaining names are all changed and a message box appears, reporting the number of items found and replaced in your document. A list of all the changed text appears at the bottom of the Find and Replace dialog box. You can double-click any of the items in the list; the replaced text highlights in the document window to let you know the location of the changes made.

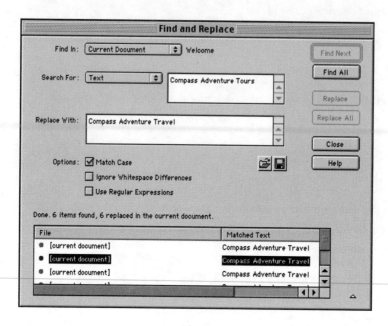

**NOTE** *When replacing text in your document, always click Replace first and check the new text to make sure you typed the correct information in the Replace field. After you verify the search criteria, then use Replace All.*

### 7) Click OK to close the message box and click Close to close the Find and Replace dialog box. Save this document.

Leave this file open for the next exercise.

## REMOVING AN HTML TAG

In this same file, the text "Compass Adventure Travel" is a purple color that has been applied using local formatting. Local formatting is applied using the property inspector to define the text attributes as opposed to using CSS. In this exercise, you will use Find and Replace to remove the HTML font tag that applies the color.

In a later exercise, you will use Find and Replace to apply a custom CSS style to the text, but first you need to remove the local formatting. Remember that in CSS styles, local formatting overrides any internal or external styles, so you will want to remove the local formatting.

**1) In the welcome.htm document, select the first occurrence of the name "Compass Adventure Travel" in the text. Don't select the heading—select the text in the first paragraph.**

The text you have selected is purple.

**2) Choose View > Code and Design, or click Show Code and Design Views on the toolbar to view the HTML for the text.**

**NOTE** *Selected text in the document is also selected in the Code window. This makes it easier to spot the text and its HTML.*

The HTML tag that controls the color of the text is the <font> tag that appears before the selected text. This is the tag you will remove from this document.

**3) To make sure the first Find selects the first tag, click anywhere before the opening <font> tag in the Code View.**

If your insertion point is inside of or after the opening font tag (<font>) that defines the color, Dreamweaver will bypass that tag. You need to place the insertion point before the font tag in the HTML code in order to include the first instance of the purple text in your search.

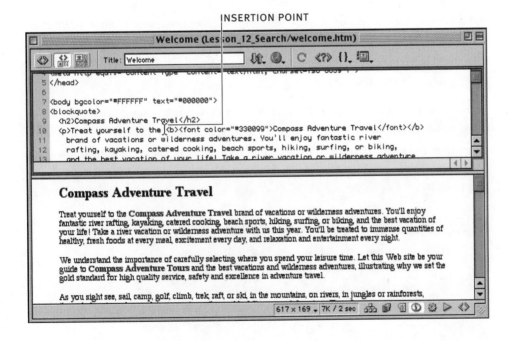

INSERTION POINT

**4) Choose Edit > Find and Replace to open the Find and Replace dialog box. Change the Search For drop-down menu to Specific Tag.**

**NOTE** *You can also use the shortcuts Ctrl+F (Windows) or Command+F (Macintosh) to open the Find and Replace dialog box.*

Choosing Specific Tag allows you to search Dreamweaver for a certain tag. The dialog box will change to reflect this search method. A set of options to choose from will be displayed in order to narrow the search and look for tags with specific attributes.

**5) Select font from the list of HTML tags in the drop-down menu to the right of Specific Tag. Select With Attribute in the drop-down menu directly below the Search For field and select color from the drop-down menu to the right of it. From the drop-down menu to the right of color, select = and, in the next drop-down menu to the right, select [any value]. In the Action drop-down menu, select Strip Tag. Deselect the check boxes for Match Case and Use Regular Expressions.**

**TIP** *You could also type* font *in the Search For field, instead of using the drop-down menu.*

Below the Search For field, there is a set of four drop-down menus and two text boxes for modifying the tag. Use these menus and text boxes to limit your searches and find unique occurrences of a tag. The additional options here include a number of qualifiers for an attribute; the ability to choose a specific attribute that can be used with the selected tag; less than (<), greater than (>), and not equal to (!=); and a place to set a value for the desired tag.

In this exercise, you have chosen to look for font tags. Since you want to remove only the tags that have color applied, you are looking specifically for the <font> tag with the attribute of color. If you don't want to limit the search, click the minus (–) sign to remove the tag modifier option. If you want to add additional modifiers, click the plus (+) sign.

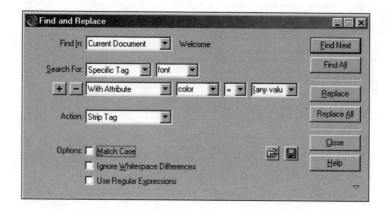

**6) Click Find Next to select the first occurrence, and then click Replace. Verify that the** <font> **tag was removed and click Replace All.**

The purple color attribute is discarded from any text with that color throughout the entire document.

**7) Click OK to exit the message box that reports the number of items replaced, and then click the Close box to exit the Find and Replace dialog box.**

The Compass Adventure Travel text still contains the bold (<b>) tag which also needs to be discarded.

**8) Choose Edit › Find and Replace to open the Find and Replace dialog box and make sure the Search For drop-down menu is set to Specific Tag. From the tag drop-down menu, select b (the bold tag) or type *b* into the text box.**

Dreamweaver will search for all bold tags in the welcome.htm file.

**9) Click the minus (–) sign to remove the tag modifier option and uncheck all three additional options below the Action drop-down menu.**

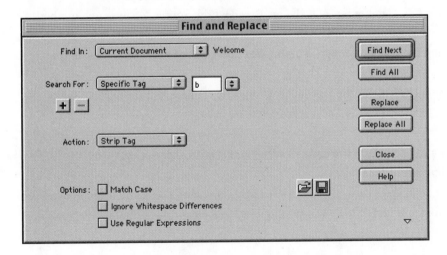

Since you are looking for a simple tag with no attributes, no modifiers are needed.

**10) Click Find Next to select the first occurrence, and then click Replace. Verify that the bold tag (<b>) was removed, and then click Replace All. Save the document.**

All bold tags within the document are removed. Leave this file open for the next exercise.

## USING FIND AND REPLACE TO APPLY A CUSTOM STYLE

Now that you have removed the local color and bold formatting from the text, you can apply a custom CSS style to it. In this lesson, you will use Find and Replace to locate the text in the HTML source window and apply the HTML tags for the custom style. You can do this even if you are not familiar with HTML.

**1) In the welcome.htm document, link to the external style sheet search_style.css, located in the Files_to_Style folder, by clicking the Attach Style Sheet button on the CSS Styles panel.**

If the CSS Styles panel is not visible, choose Window > CSS Styles.

This style sheet has three custom styles already created. You need to attach a style sheet first before you can apply any of the custom styles.

**2) Select the first occurrence of the phrase "Compass Adventure Travel" in the body text. Click the boldcolor custom style from the CSS Styles panel to apply it to the selected text.**

The text changes to reflect the bold and red attributes that are defined by the custom style.

**3) Choose Edit > Find and Replace, change the Search For drop-down menu to Source Code, and type *Compass Adventure Travel* in the text box.**

The dialog box that appears will change to reflect the Source Code search method.

**4) Leaving the Find and Replace dialog box open, click Show Code View on the toolbar.**

Look at the HTML for the custom style you just applied. You should see: <span class="boldcolor">Compass Adventure Travel</span>.

**5) Copy all the HTML in the code view beginning with** <span class="boldcolor"> **and ending with** </span>.

You must be in code view to copy the HTML along with the text; otherwise, you get just the text and no HTML. You should now have <span class="boldcolor">Compass Adventure Travel</span> selected.

**TIP** *You could choose Edit >Copy HTML to copy the HTML as well as the text without being in code view.*

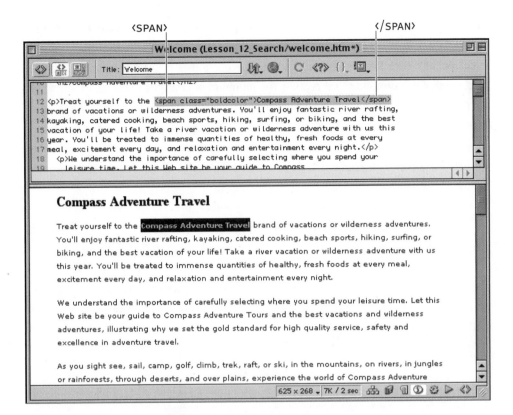

**6) Return to the Find and Replace dialog box. Paste into the Replace With text box the HTML code you copied in step 5. Uncheck the three additional options.**

Dreamweaver will replace all occurrences in the text with this code.

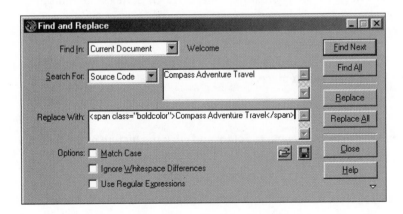

**7) Click Find Next to select the next occurrence of the words "Compass Adventure Travel." Click Replace to change the text and add the HTML. Verify that the change is correct and click Replace All to change all occurrences in your document. Click OK to close the message box that reports the numbers of changes made.**

All Compass Adventure Travel text is now formatted with the boldcolor CSS style. Using Find and Replace to apply styles in this way can save you a lot of time.

**8) Close the Find and Replace dialog box, and then click Show Design View to return to the design window. Save this document.**

Look back to the first occurrence of "Compass Adventure Travel" where you manually applied the custom style. You should see that now you have two <span> tags applied to this text because Find and Replace added the extra tag. Although the phrase appears to display properly in Dreamweaver, you need to remove the extra tag. Choose Commands > Cleanup HTML. Make sure Redundant Nested Tags is selected in the Cleanup HTML dialog box and click OK. Dreamweaver removes the extra <span> tag.

You can close this file.

## USING FIND AND REPLACE TO ADD EXTERNAL STYLE SHEETS

In Lesson 11, you created an external style sheet and attached that style sheet to another document. The steps to add a style sheet to a document are not difficult, but they could be time-consuming for multiple pages or an entire site. By using Find and Replace, you can accomplish that task in a matter of minutes.

In this exercise, you will attach an external style sheet, search_style.css, to multiple pages. For this exercise, you do not need to open a document.

**1) Open the Site Window by choosing Site > Open Site and selecting the name of your site. Choose Edit > Find and Replace.**

The Find and Replace dialog box opens.

**2) Change the Find In drop-down menu to Folder and click the picture of the folder.**

The Choose Search Folder dialog box opens.

**3) Locate the Files_to_Style folder in the Lesson_12_Search folder. In Windows, open the Files_to_Style folder and click Select. In Macintosh, select the Files_to_Style folder (but do not open it) and click Choose.**

There are four HTML documents in the Files_to_Style folder that need to have the external style sheet attached.

**4) Change Search For to Source Code. In the Search For text box, type `</head>`. In the Replace With text box, type the following code:** *<link rel="stylesheet" href="search_style.css"></head>*.

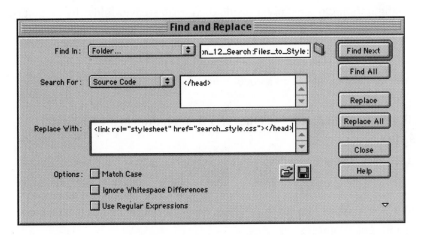

When you use the Attach Style Sheet icon, Dreamweaver adds the <link> tag within the <head> tag. You are using Find and Replace to search for the end head (</head>) tag and then add the <link> tag before it by replacing it with the <link> tag followed by a </head> tag.

**NOTE** *To get a new line when you are within the Replace With text box, press Shift+Enter (Windows) or Shift+Return (Macintosh). Using the Enter or Return key alone activates the Find Next button in the dialog box.*

**5) Click Find Next.**

The first document in the folder in which Dreamweaver finds the </head> tag opens. Dreamweaver will select the </head> tag.

**6) Click Replace All to add the style sheet link to each document in the folder. Click OK to close the message box that reports the numbers of changes made, and close the Find and Replace dialog box. Save this document.**

The style sheet is attached to all four documents.

**NOTE** *Replace All opens and changes all documents within the Files_to_Style folder. To be safe, you should always check your search criteria before replacing all pages in your site.*

## SAVING AND REUSING YOUR SEARCH CRITERIA

You might want to save your search criteria for other documents in your site, especially with complex search criteria. Saved search criteria, known as queries, are saved in the Configuration/Queries folder inside the Dreamweaver folder by default. They can, however, be saved in different places.

In this exercise, you'll save your search query in the Lesson_12_Search folder. For this exercise, you do not need to open a document.

**1)  Choose Edit › Find and Replace. Click the Save Query button in the Find and Replace dialog box.**

The Find and Replace dialog box will have the same settings that were used in the last exercise.

The Save Query button looks like a floppy-disk icon. This option makes it possible for you to save and reuse complex searches.

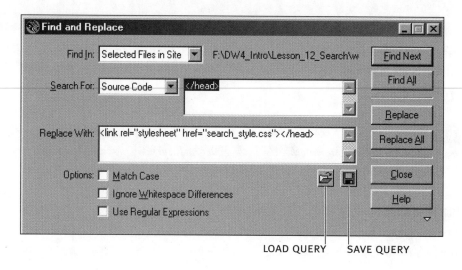

LOAD QUERY    SAVE QUERY

**2)  In the Save Query (Windows) or Save query to file (Macintosh) dialog box, locate and open the Lesson_12_Search folder. Then type *styles* in the File Name text box and click Save.**

The file is saved in the Queries folder inside the Configuration folder. The Configuration folder is located in the Dreamweaver program folder.

**3)  Click the Load Query button in the Find and Replace dialog box.**

The Load Query button looks like an open-folder icon.

**4) In the Load Query (Windows) or Load query from file (Macintosh) dialog box, locate and choose the highlight_query.dwr query in the Files_to_Style folder.**

This query will look for "Compass Adventure Tours" and add the highlight custom style from the external style sheet you just added to the files in the folder.

**5) Change the Find In drop-down menu to Selected Files in Site. Leaving the Find and Replace dialog box open, use your Site window to select kayaking.htm and biking.htm in the Files_to_Style folder.**

**NOTE** *You can Ctrl-click (Windows) or Command-click (Macintosh) each file name to select noncontiguous files in the Site window.*

Dreamweaver will use the search criteria you loaded from the saved query on both documents.

**6) Click Replace All to make the changes in the selected files. Click OK to close the message box that reports the numbers of changes made and close the Find and Replace dialog box.**

Both kayaking.htm and biking.htm are updated to include the highlight custom style.

## SEARCHING AND REPLACING WITH REGULAR EXPRESSIONS

Regular expressions are control characters that describe character combinations or patterns in text. For example, if you want to find all occurrences of years from 1900–1999, the pattern is "19" followed by any combination of two numbers from 0–9. You can use a number of special characters to define the search pattern. For example, the backslash (\), dollar sign ($), and question mark (?) are special characters. It is important to know these characters; if you are looking for a special character in your text, you need to precede that character with a backslash to indicate it is part of the character search and not used as a special character.

The Appendixes at the back of this book contain tables with all the special characters, regular expressions, and their meanings.

In this exercise, you will use patterned searches in a document.

**1) Open the pattern_search.htm file in the Lesson_12_Search folder and choose Edit > Find and Replace.**

**TIP** *You can also use Ctrl+F (Windows) or Command+F (Macintosh) to open the Find and Replace dialog box.*

The Find and Replace dialog box opens.

**2) Change Find In to Current Document. Change the Search For drop-down menu to Text. Select the Use Regular Expressions option.**

Notice that Ignore Whitespace Differences is disabled when you select Use Regular Expressions.

**NOTE** *The Ignore Whitespace Differences option, when selected, treats all whitespace as a single space for the purposes of matching. For example, with this option selected, "this text" would match "this  text" but not "thistext." This option is not available when the Use Regular Expressions option is selected; you must explicitly write your regular expression to ignore whitespace. Note that p and br tags do not count as whitespace.*

**3) In the Search For text box, type *19\d\d*.**

The first search will look for all years from 1900–1999. The search_pattern.htm file contains a list of years including years not between 1900 and 1999. You want to skip the other years such as 1875.

To search for any number between 0–9, you use \d (known as a wildcard) as the search pattern. Because you want to limit the search to only the 1900 years, precede the pattern character with the explicit text.

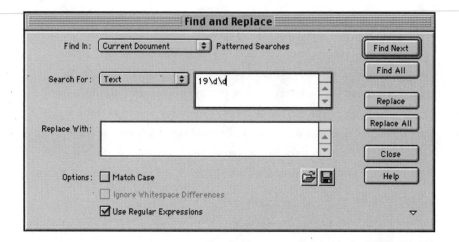

**TIP** *To distinguish decimal numbers from years—19.45 for example—when searching in the document, include a period in your search. A period is also a special character, so you need to precede it with a backslash in your search.*

**4) Click Find Next.**

Dreamweaver will select the first year (1945) in the document window.

### 5) Continue to click Find Next several times to see what gets selected.

The years 1875 and 2010 are not selected because they don't match the exact pattern.

### 6) In the Find and Replace dialog box, change Search For to Source Code.

The search now takes place in the code inspector.

In the Replace With text box, you will add the bold tags (<b> and </b>) around the text in the search. However, if you were to type <b>19\d\d<\b>, the text in the document window would be changed to 19\d\d. It would literally change the numbers in the year to \d. Instead, you need to isolate the search as a pattern by surrounding the pattern in parentheses.

### 7) In the Search For text box, insert a left parenthesis before the text and a right parenthesis after the text, like this: (19\d\d).

The parentheses create the first pattern.

### 8) In the Replace With text box, type *<b>$1</b>*.

To reference the pattern you created in the previous step, you use $1 in the Replace With text box. This adds the bold tags around the results of the first pattern search. If you were to create several patterns, the next pattern would be referenced in this text box with $2, and so on, in a sequential manner.

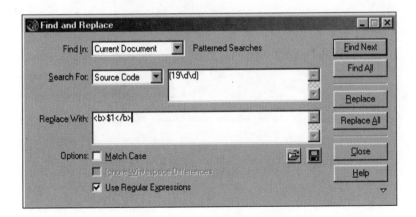

### 9) Click Find Next, and then click Replace.

The bold tags are placed around the year in the Code inspector. Click in the Document window to see the results.

### 10) Click Replace All to find and replace all occurrences in the document. Save the document.

Leave this file and the Find and Replace dialog box open for the next exercise.

**273**

## FINDING VARIATIONS IN A NAME

You can also look for variations in a name. For example, the company CEO is Richard Melton, but his name is misspelled throughout the site as Rick, Rich, Ricky, and so on. You want to make his name consistent and change it to Richard E. Melton.

**1) In the pattern_search.htm document, change Search For to Text in the Find and Replace dialog box. Type *R\w\* Melton* in the Search For text box.**

The \w searches for any alphanumeric character after the R, and the asterisk means you want to find any number of alphanumeric characters. Adding the last name Melton limits the search even further. If you leave off the last name, the search will also find "R2D2" in the document.

**2) In the Options, select Match Case and Use Regular Expressions.**

This limits the search to finding only words that begin with an uppercase R.

**3) In the Replace With text box, type *Richard E. Melton*. Click Find Next to find the first occurrence, and then click Replace to change it.**

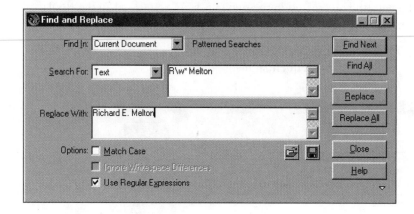

The first version of the name is found in this document and replaced with Richard E. Melton.

**4) Click Replace All to find and replace the remaining names. Save the document.**

You can close this document.

## WHAT YOU HAVE LEARNED

**In this lesson, you have:**

- Found and replaced text using detailed options to quickly modify a document (pages 260–262)

- Found text within HTML tags and learned how to change it using Find and Replace (pages 262–265)

- Used Find and Replace to quickly apply a custom style to a document (pages 266–268)

- Used Find and Replace to attach external style sheets to multiple pages within a site (pages 268–269)

- Saved your search settings for later use and loaded saved queries (pages 270–271)

- Searched for patterns in text to find specific text like dates and names (pages 271–273)

- Found multiple variations of a name and replaced them with one version (page 274)

# creating forms

## LESSON 13

Forms are a way to gather information from people who visit your Web site. Forms allow you to ask visitors for specific information or give them an opportunity to send feedback, questions, or requests to you. Common uses of forms include polls, e-commerce, feedback, and registration. A form contains fields in which users enter information. These fields can be text fields, radio buttons, checkboxes, menus, or lists.

Form data is usually sent to a database on a server or to an e-mail address. Data sent by a form is a continuous string of text from the information typed by the user. The data is usually processed by a CGI (Common Gateway Interface) script. CGI is a

*In this project, you will build a form with various text fields, checkboxes, radio buttons, submit and reset buttons, and a menu.*

standard protocol that acts as the communication link between the data from the form and the server. Dreamweaver does not create or edit CGI scripts. You will need to talk to your Web administrator to get information about what CGI scripts your server uses.

To see an example of the finished page for this lesson, open myform.htm from the Lesson13/Completed folder.

## WHAT YOU WILL LEARN

**In this lesson, you will:**

- Create a form on a Web page
- Add single-line text fields
- Add a multi-line text field
- Add checkboxes
- Add radio buttons
- Add list/menu items
- Add buttons
- Validate a form
- Create a jump menu
- Test a form

## APPROXIMATE TIME

This lesson should take about one hour to complete.

## LESSON FILES

**Media File**

*Lesson_13_Forms/Images/Banner.gif*

**Starting Files**

*Lesson_13_Forms/myform.htm*

*Lesson_13_Forms/about.htm*

*Lesson_13_Forms/gear.htm*

*Lesson_13_Forms/logs.htm*

**Completed Project**

*Lesson_13_Forms/Completed/myform.htm*

## BUILDING YOUR FORM

Before adding individual fields, you must place a form on the page. The form will contain fields into which users enter information, and it will specify what should be done with the data. In this exercise, you will create the form area.

**1) Open the myform.htm document from the Lesson_13_Forms folder. Position the insertion point below the text "Enter our drawing for a free adventure trip" and choose Insert > Form.**

**TIP** *You can also insert a form by clicking the Insert Form button from the Forms category in the Objects panel. Select the Forms category by clicking the down-arrow at the top of the panel and choose Forms from the list.*

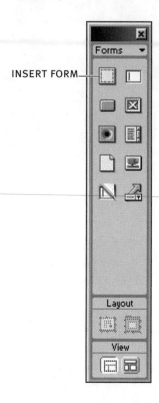

INSERT FORM

Red dotted lines visually define the form area in the document window; that area is located between the <form> and </form> tags in the code. These red lines are invisible elements that are only visible in Dreamweaver; when you view the page within a browser, there will be nothing to mark the form area. These red lines are not draggable. The size of the form area depends on what you place inside the form, and it will expand as much as necessary to accomodate the contents.

278

## 2) Select the form by clicking the red dotted line.

The property inspector changes to display form properties. There are several options on the property inspector.

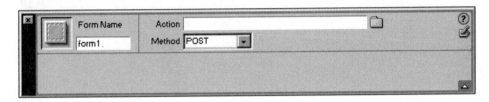

Form Name lets you give the form a name if you want to control it with a scripting application such as JavaScript. Dreamweaver assigns generic names automatically in a numeric order: form1, form2, etc.

*Action tells the browser what to do with the form data. It specifies the path or URL to the location and name of an application (usually a CGI script) that will process the information when the user clicks the Submit button. CGI scripts are located on the Web server that processes the data sent by a form.*

*Method defines how the form data is handled: GET, POST, or Default. Data sent by a form is a continuous string of text from the information typed by the user. GET appends form contents to the URL specified in the Action text box. GET is not a secure method of transferring data, so it should not be used for sensitive information such as credit card or social security numbers. Usually you'll use the POST option. POST sends the form value in the body of a message. Default uses the browser's default method, which is usually GET.*

Talk to your ISP (Internet Service Provider) or Web administrator to get the information you need to set the Action and Method options. You won't need this information in order to complete this lesson.

**3) Place the insertion point in the area between the red dotted lines. Click the Insert Table icon from the Common category of the Objects panel. In the Insert Table dialog box, make the table 8 rows, 2 columns, and 600 pixels wide. Set the border to 0, the cell padding to 5, and the cell spacing to 0. Click OK.**

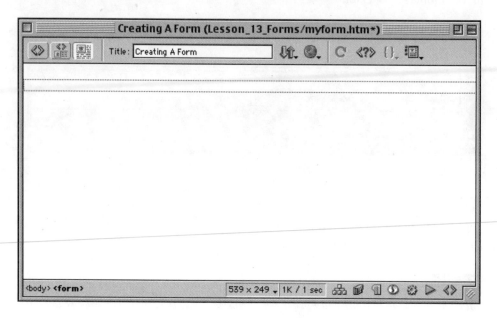

The table will improve the layout of the form and make it easy to align text or images with the form fields to label them. You can place a table inside a form or you can place a form in a table, but the table must completely contain or be contained by the form.

**4) Select the top four cells in the left column. From the Horz pop-up menu of the property inspector, choose Right to right-justify all four cells.**
These four cells will contain the text that label the form fields. You will add the labels to the table as you add the form fields, beginning with the first cell in the next exercise.

**5) Merge both cells in row 5. Repeat this step for rows 6, 7, and 8.**
The first four rows each have two cells. The last four rows now have a single cell each. Your document should now look like the example that follows.

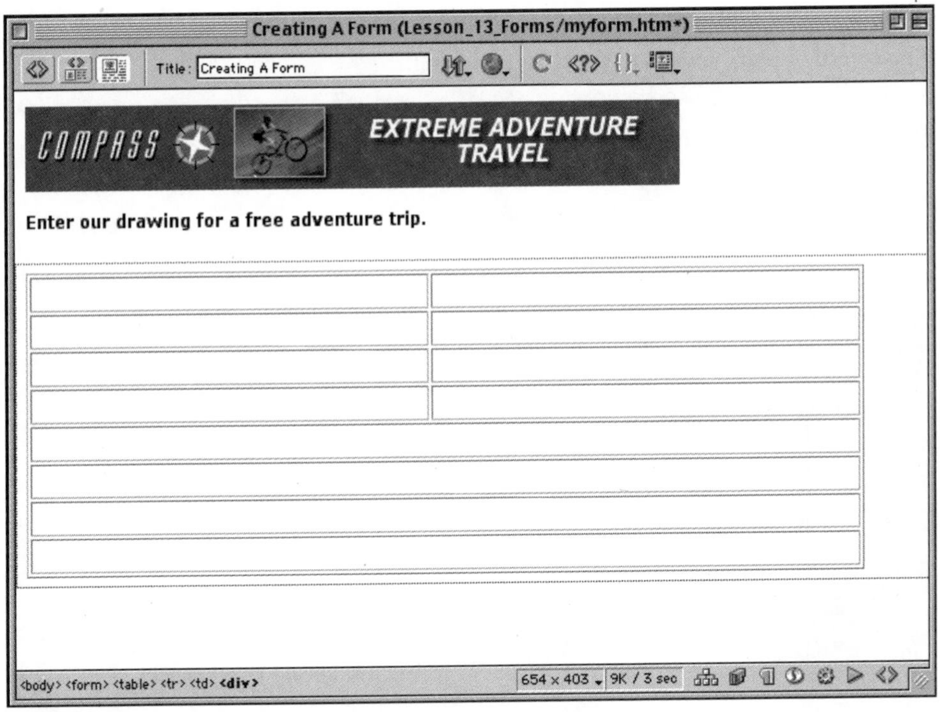

The screenshot shows a Dreamweaver document window titled "Creating A Form (Lesson_13_Forms/myform.htm*)". The Title field reads "Creating A Form". A banner displays "COMPASS" with a compass star, a cyclist icon, and "EXTREME ADVENTURE TRAVEL". Below the banner: "Enter our drawing for a free adventure trip." followed by a table layout. The status bar shows tags: `<body> <form> <table> <tr> <td> <div>` and "654 × 403", "9K / 3 sec".

## 6) Save the document.

Leave this file open for the next exercise.

**NOTE** *You can have multiple forms on one page. However, it is not possible to nest a form inside of another form in HTML. Because of this restriction, Dreamweaver prevents forms from becoming accidentally nested by disabling the insertion of a form into another form. The option to insert a form will not be grayed-out, but no form will be inserted if you attempt to place one form inside of another. If form tags have been inserted manually within a form, Dreamweaver will highlight the tags that are incorrect to bring the error to your attention.*

## ADDING SINGLE-LINE TEXT FIELDS

Text fields are for gathering information the user types at a keyboard. Typical single-line text fields collect name, address, and e-mail information from users.

You must place all form fields and buttons within the red dotted lines; otherwise, they will not be a part of the form. If you try to insert form fields outside of the red lines, Dreamweaver will display an alert box with Yes or No options asking if you want to add a form tag. If you choose No, the field or buttons will not function as a part of any form.

In this exercise, you will place two single-line text fields in the table inside the form.

**1) In the myform.htm document, type *Name:* in the left cell of row 1 and press Tab.**

The insertion point moves to the next table cell.

**2) Choose Insert > Form Objects > Text Field.**

> **TIP** *To place a single-line text field in the form, you can also click the Insert Text Field button from the Forms category in the Objects panel.*

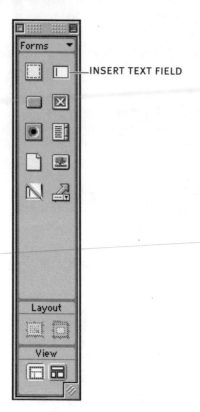

INSERT TEXT FIELD

A single-line text field is placed in the form. The property inspector displays Text Field properties whenever a text field is inserted or when you click on a text field in the document window. The default Type option is Single line.

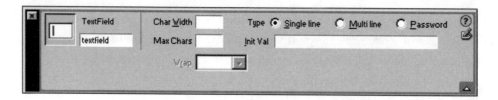

Leave the Init Val text box blank for this exercise. This option enables you to set text that will appear in the text field when the page loads. Although the user will be able to change this text, use this option with caution. Users who want to get through the form quickly may accidentally skip a field that already has text in it, perhaps thinking they have already filled it out. Init Val can, however, help to give the user an example of the kind of information that is being requested of them.

### 3) In the Name text box on the property inspector, replace textfield with *name*.

When the form is submitted, the name of the text field identifies the information that was entered into the field. In this case, "name" signifies that the information entered into this field is the visitor's name. Names are required for all fields. Do not use any spaces or special characters in the name, and remember that names are case-sensitive. Dreamweaver assigns generic names automatically in a numeric order: textfield, textfield2, etc.

It is important to remember to name all of your fields with short descriptive names. Suppose you have two text fields on a page with labels next to them prompting the user to enter a home phone number into one field and a work phone number into the other. If those fields are named textfield and textfield2, their names will not give you any indication as to which number is the home number and which is the work number. On the other hand, by giving the fields more descriptive names, such as worknumber and homenumber, you can avoid confusion over the identity of the information.

### 4) In the Char Width text box on the property inspector, type *40*.

The width of the text box increases to show approximately 40 characters. The initial width of the text field is approximately 24, even though the text box is blank. The actual size of the text field in the browser will vary because it is dependent upon the size to which the user has set their browser's default text. The height of the text box is also determined by the browser's default text size.

### 5) In the Max Chars text box on the property inspector, type *50*.

Max Chars limits the total number of characters a user can enter. Initially this text box is blank, and the number of characters a user can enter is unlimited. You may need to limit the number of characters if you are sending information to a database in which the number of characters for a field is limited in the database definition.

**NOTE** *If the Max Chars value is larger than Char Width, users can continue to type and the text will scroll within the area. The scrollable area ends at the Max Char value.*

**6) Type *E-mail* in the left cell of row 2 and press Tab. Add a single-line text field in the right cell and name the field *email*. Set the Char Width to 40 and the Max Char to 70.**

This field will accept the user's e-mail address.

**TIP** *Use care when setting the Max Char for fields that accept information such as e-mail addresses and URLs. Users won't be able to enter a complete URL, or any other information, if it is longer than the Max Char value because they won't be able to type past the limit you set.*

**7) Save the file and preview it in the browser.**

Leave this file open for the next exercise.

## ADDING MULTIPLE-LINE TEXT FIELDS

Multiple-line text fields are used to collect larger amounts of information from a user. Typical multiple-line text fields collect comments and feedback from users. In this exercise, you will place a multi-line text field in the table inside the form.

**1) In the myform.htm document, type *Address* in the left cell of row 3 and press Tab.**

The multiple-line text field will be inserted in same column as the single-line text boxes from the previous exercise.

**2) Choose Insert > Form Objects > Text Field.**

A single-line text field is placed in the form and the property inspector shows Text Field properties.

**3) On the property inspector, select Multi line for the Type option.**

In Dreamweaver, text fields are inserted as single-line fields by default; in order create multi-line fields, you must select Multi line from the property inspector.

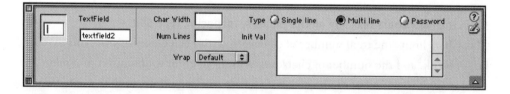

**4) In the Name text box on the property inspector, replace textfield with *address*. In the Char Width text box, type *40*.**

When you use multiple-line text fields you will see an additional option on the property inspector. The Wrap drop-down menu is only available for multiple-line text fields. It is grayed-out for both single-line and password text fields. Wrap specifies how text that is typed into a multiple-line field is displayed if there is more text than will fit in the visible area. The options are Default, Off, Virtual, and Physical.

Default will use the browser default. This option is selected automatically when you select Multi line for the Type option.

Off will stop text from wrapping to the next line. Text will continue on one line until the Return key is pressed. (Off is typically the default setting.)

Virtual will wrap text to the next line, but wrap will not be applied to the data when it is submitted.

Physical will wrap text to the next line, and wrap will be applied to the data when it is submitted.

### 5) In the Num Lines text box on the property inspector, type 4.

This option dictates how many lines will appear in the scrollable area. It does not limit the number of lines users can enter.

Your document should now look similar to the example shown here.

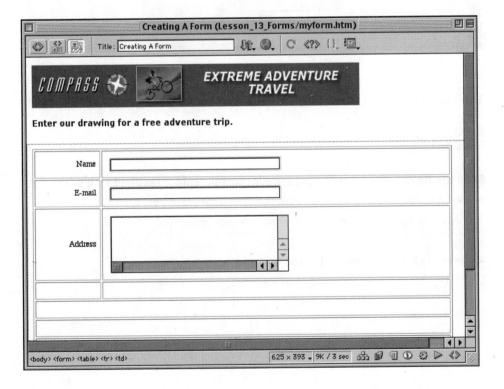

### 6) Save the file and preview it in the browser.

Leave this file open for the next exercise.

## ADDING A PASSWORD TEXT FIELD

A regular text field displays the information in the browser as you type it in. A password text field looks the same as any other text field, but the text displayed on the screen is hidden by bullets or asterisks as you type.

The password option only hides the text in the field from someone looking over your shoulder as you type—it does not encrypt or secure your data. To encrypt data, you must have secure server software running on the Web server. You should talk to your Web administrator for detailed information on securing data.

**1)  In the myform.htm document, type _Enter your password_ in the left cell of row 4, press Tab, and choose Insert > Form Objects > Text Field.**
A single-line text field appears in the cell.

**2)  On the property inspector, select Password for the Type option.**

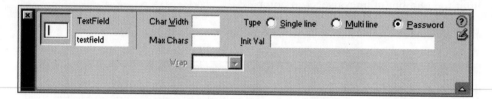

This option causes asterisks or bullets to appear when a user enters data in this field.

**NOTE**  _Password text fields can only be single-line text fields._

**3)  In the Name text box on the property inspector, replace textfield with _password_. In the Char Width text box, type _10_; in the Max Chars text box, type _10_.**
The Max Chars value for passwords should be set at the limit.

**4)  Save the file and preview it in the browser.**
Leave this file open for the next exercise.

## ADDING CHECKBOXES

Checkboxes allow users to choose one or more options in a group of related items. Checkboxes are typically used when you want the user to choose as many of the listed options as desired. If you want your user to choose only one selection, then you should use a radio button as demonstrated in the exercise that follows this one. In this exercise, you will insert a group of checkboxes.

**1) In the myform.htm document, type *Which adventure trips would you be interested in?* in row 5 of the table. Add a line break after the text by pressing Shift+Return.**

Recall from Lesson 1 that a line break will move the insertion point to the next line without inserting a blank line, as a regular paragraph return would do. The checkboxes will be place on this blank line in the following steps.

**2) Choose Insert > Form Objects > Check Box.**

A checkbox is inserted into the form, and the property inspector displays checkbox properties.

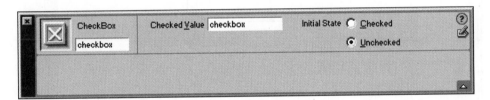

**3) In the document window, position the insertion point to the right of the checkbox and type *Mountain Biking*. Select the checkbox again by clicking it.**

The property inspector displays the checkbox properties again.

**4) In the Name text box on the property inspector, replace checkbox with *biking*. In the Checked Value text box, type *yes*.**

When the visitor to the page checks the biking checkbox, the name and value will be passed to the CGI to indicate that the checkbox has been selected.

**5) Position the insertion point on a line below Mountain Biking using a line break. Repeat steps 2 through 5, adding checkboxes for White Water Rafting, Sea Kayaking, and Rock Climbing, each on a separate line. In the Name text box on the property inspector, replace checkbox each time with *rafting*, *kayaking*, and *climbing*, respectively. Type *yes* in each Checked Value text box.**

Your document should now look similar to the example shown here.

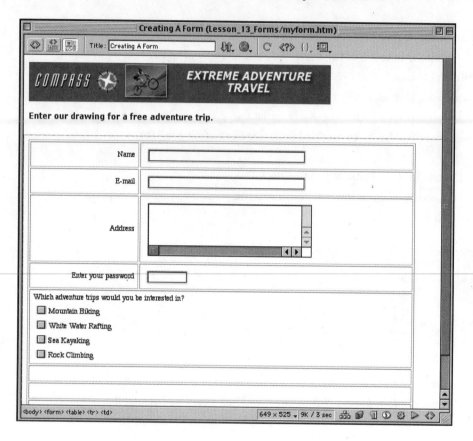

**6) Save the file and preview it in the browser.**

Leave this file open for the next exercise.

## ADDING RADIO BUTTONS

Radio buttons are a group of options in which selecting one option automatically deselects all other options. Typical uses for radio buttons are credit card selections and yes/no answers. In this exercise, you will insert a group of radio buttons in the table.

**1) In the myform.htm document, type *Have you ever taken an adventure trip before?* in row 6 of the table.**

In the next step, you will place the radio buttons on the same line as this text.

### 2) Choose Insert > Form Objects > Radio Button.

A radio button is inserted into the form. The property inspector displays radio button properties.

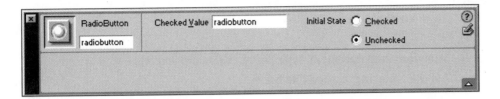

### 3) In the document window, type *Yes* to the right of the radio button you just inserted.

When inserting text labels in the document for radio buttons or checkboxes, make sure the text is close enough to the corresponding button or box and not too close to another. This will help to avoid confusing your Web site visitors.

### 4) Select the radio button. In the Name text box of the property inspector, replace radiobutton with *trip*.

When using radio buttons, you must use the same name for each group of items. Radio buttons are meant to allow only one selection. Using the same name for several radio buttons indicates that those buttons are part of the same group. If the names are not the same, the radio buttons will be treated as different groups and negate the purpose of using radio buttons. Keep in mind that names are case-sensitive, so "Trip" is not the same as "trip."

### 5) In the Checked Value text box, type *yes*.

When the form is submitted, this value will be sent to the script that processes the form on the server.

### 6) Repeat steps 2 through 5 for the "No" answer to the right of "Yes." Type *no* in the Checked Value text box.

Make sure you use the same name (trip) in the Name text box for both radio buttons. It is also important to be sure you give each radio button a different Checked Value so that you know which option the user chose.

### 7) Save the file and preview it in the browser.

To test the radio buttons, click each one in the browser. When you click one to select it, the other one should deselect. If not, that means you gave the radio buttons different names. The names need to be typed exactly the same for them to function correctly.

Leave this file open for the next exercise.

## ADDING LIST/MENU ITEMS

A list/menu enables users to pick options from a scrolling list or menu. A scrolling list gives you the option to allow users to make multiple contiguous or noncontiguous selections. A drop-down menu restricts users to one selection. In both types, items chosen by the user will be highlighted.

### 1) In the myform.htm document, type *Which region are you interested in exploring?* in row 7 of the table and insert a line break.

In the following steps, you will place a scrolling list with six menu options on the same line as this text.

### 2) Choose Insert > Form Objects > List/Menu. On the property inspector, select List for the Type option and change the Height to 4.

A small menu is inserted into the form, and the property inspector displays Menu properties. Dreamweaver inserts a drop-down menu by default. You've changed the format to a scrolling list. Check the Allow Multiple checkbox for the Selections option.

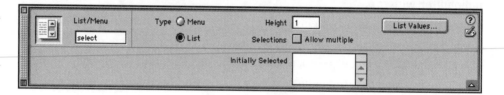

List has two additional options. You can choose to allow or not allow multiple selections by checking or unchecking the selections checkbox. This option is unchecked by default. If you check the selections box, users can make multiple noncontiguous selections by using Command-click on the Macintosh and Ctrl-click on Windows. Users may make contiguous selections by using Shift-click on both Macintosh and Windows.

You can also set a height for the scrolling list by typing in the Height text box the number of lines that you want to be visible. If you leave the selections checkbox unchecked, be sure to enter a line height value of more than one. Otherwise the scrolling list will display as a menu. You should always define the height for a scrolling list; if you don't, the number of lines displayed will be the browser default, which varies.

**3) In the Name text box, replace select with *region* and click List Values.**

The List Values dialog box opens. This dialog box is the same for both List and Menu.

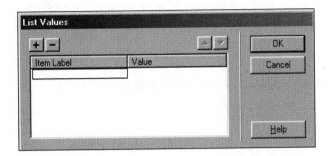

**4) In the Item Label field, type *Africa* and then press Tab.**

The longest item in the list values box determines the width of the list/menu.

**5) In the Value field, again type *Africa*.**

This text is sent to the CGI or server to indicate that the option has been selected.

**6) Press Tab or click the plus (+) sign in the dialog box to add another option to the menu.**

Use the minus (–) sign to delete items from the list values box.

**7) Repeat steps 4 through 6, adding Australia, North America, South America, Caribbean, and Europe to the list. Change the Value field to match the name of each region.**

Use the arrows above the Value field if you want to reorder the list.

**8) Click OK to close the dialog box.**

The list shows the regions you just added.

An additional option on the property inspector for list/menu items is the Initially Selected box. You can choose to have any one of the items in the list be selected when the page loads. This might not be desirable for scrolling lists, but for menu items it is helpful for the drop-down menu to have a sample choice or instruction appear on the first line.

**9) Save the file and preview it in the browser.**

Leave this file open for the next exercise.

## ADDING BUTTONS

Forms usually have two buttons, one to send the form data (Submit) and one to clear the form (Reset). The Submit button tells the browser to send the data according to the Action and Method specified. The Reset button clears all the information from the fields on the page.

**1)  In the myform.htm document, position the insertion point in the last row of the table and choose Insert > Form Objects > Button.**

**TIP**   *You can also click Insert Button from the Forms category in the Objects panel.*

INSERT BUTTON

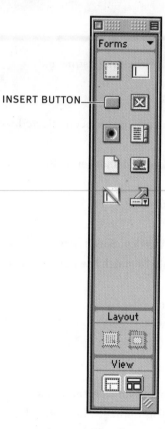

A Submit button is placed in the form, and the property inspector displays Button properties. Since a submit button is the default, you do not need to change any of the options for this button.

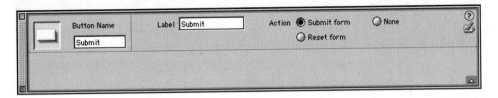

### 2) Position the insertion point on the same line just after the submit button and add another button to the page.

A second submit button is placed in the form. The only difference is the name—this button is called submit2 because no two buttons can have the same name. The only form objects that can have the same name are radio buttons, which can be grouped with other radio buttons. The button you are working with in this exercise is different in that it cannot be grouped with other buttons. It will have its own action assigned to it in the next step.

### 3) Choose Reset form as the Action on the property inspector.

The text in the Label text box will automatically change to Reset. The Button Name however, stays the same.

This action will cause all text fields, checkboxes, and radio buttons to clear and revert to their original state when the page was first loaded in the browser.

The third Action option is None. Unlike Submit and Reset, the None button option has no action attached to it. It can be used in conjunction with a script in order to perform another task. A JavaScript, for example, can be used to perform calculations such as totals or interest and return the end value to the user.

### 4) In the Label text box, type *Clear Form*; in the Button Name text box, type *Reset*.

It is a good idea to name your buttons clearly, with consideration for your user's expectations. Submit and Reset are standard form button labels that people understand because of their widespread use.

## 5) Save the file and preview it in the browser.

Your document should now look similar to the example shown here.

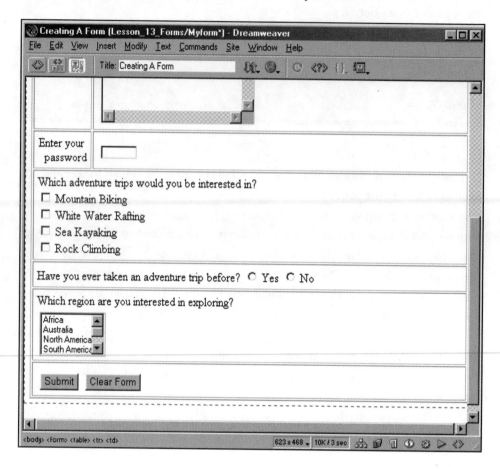

Leave this file open for the next exercise.

## VALIDATING FORMS

The Validate Form behavior checks the contents of text fields in a form to ensure the user has entered the proper information. Whether accidentally or intentionally, users sometimes enter the wrong information or skip a field entirely. Instead of waiting until the form has been sent, you can check data as the user enters it or just before the form has been sent to the server.

In this exercise, you will add a behavior that will check the information typed into a form to be sure all required text fields have been filled out and that the information is the right type of data.

**1) In the myform.htm document, click the e-mail field that you placed in the second row of the table to select it. Choose Window > Behaviors.**

The Behaviors panel opens.

**2) Choose Validate Form from the Actions drop-down menu on the Behaviors panel.**

The Validate Form dialog box opens with the first item selected by default.

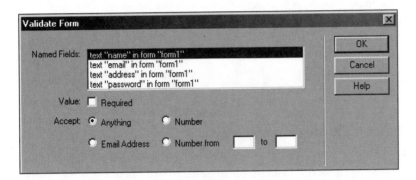

**3) Select the email text field from the Named Fields list on the dialog box. Check the Required box for the Value option.**

This specifies that it is necessary for the e-mail field to contain data. The Validate Form action is added to the Behaviors panel with the onBlur event. Now an error message will be displayed if the user tabs to the next field without filling in this one. The onBlur event is activated when the user leaves the text field. In this example, if the user tabs to the next field in the form, leaving the e-mail text field blank, an error message will be displayed. If the user clicks into specific fields (not tabbing through the form), this initial validation check is ignored.

**NOTE** *While it may seem like a good idea to validate each field as the user moves along through the form, use care as it may annoy your visitors. Many people skip questions and come back to them later, after filling out the rest of the form.*

**4) Choose Email Address from the Accept options and click OK.**

This option will check whether or not the text field contains an @ symbol. This only checks whether @ was included—it can't check that an e-mail address actually exists.

**5) Select the Submit button in the document window. Click the plus (+) button on the Behaviors panel to add an action and choose Validate Form from the drop-down menu.**

The Validate Form action is added to the Behaviors panel with the onSubmit event. Now when the user clicks the Submit button, the checks will be made.

**6) Select the Name text field from the Named Fields list and select Required from the Value option. Select Anything from the Accept option.**

Anything specifies that the field is required, but that it does not need to have a certain type of data.

**7) Select Password from the Named Fields list. Select Number from the Accept option.**

The Number option requires users to enter a number as the password. Number specifies that the field should only contain numbers.

There is a second Accept option regarding numbers. Number from specifies that the field should contain a number that is within the given range of numbers. This is particularly useful for years.

**8) Click OK. Save the file and test it in your browser.**

Click in the e-mail field and then press Tab without entering any data. You will see an error message generated by the Validate Form behavior. You may not want to rely on the individual field check to validate a form, because if you click to place the insertion point in another field, you will not see an error message.

**NOTE** *To add the e-mail field to the checks that occur when the Submit button is clicked, open the Validate Form dialog box again by double-clicking the Validate Form action in the Behaviors panel. Select the e-mail field and the desired option. Click OK when you are done.*

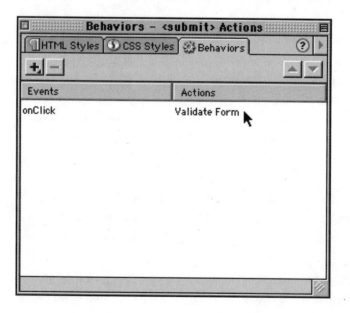

Leave this file open for the next exercise.

## CREATING JUMP MENUS

A **jump menu** is a drop-down menu that contains links to other pages in your site or to other Web sites. Like regular links, the jump menu can link to any type of file, including graphics or PDF files. The jump menu provides an easy-to-use interface for linking to pages in your site, if you don't make the list too long. A jump menu is embedded in a form and looks like a menu list in the browser.

**1) In the myform.htm document, place the insertion point at the top of the page, on a blank line between the banner and the text "Enter our drawing for a free adventure trip." Choose Insert > Form Object > Jump Menu.**

**TIP** *You can also click the Insert Jump Menu icon from the Forms category in the Objects panel.*

The Jump Menu dialog box opens. By default, there is one item listed in the menu, unnamed1. Dreamweaver assigns generic names automatically in a numeric order: unnamed1, unnamed2, etc.

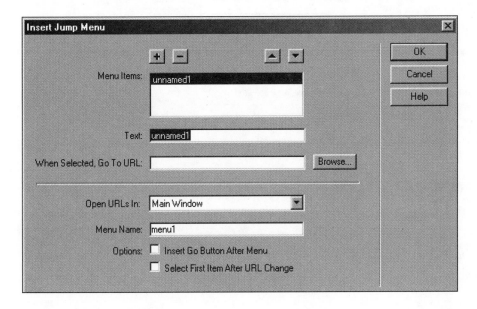

**2) In the Text text box of the Jump Menu dialog box, type *Pick One*. Leave the When Selected, Go To URL text box blank.**

The first item in the menu list will appear in the first line of the menu. Since the user will see this initially in the menu list, the first line should be a short description of the list or a short instruction to let the user know that this is a jump menu.

### 3) In the Options area, choose Select First Item After URL Change.

This forces the menu list to display the first menu item in the list when the user returns to this page; otherwise, the list displays the most recent option chosen.

### 4) Click the plus (+) button to add a new menu item. Type *About* in the Text field, press Tab, and type *about.htm* in the When Selected, Go To URL text box. Repeat this step, entering *Gear*, *gear.htm* and *Logs*, *logs.htm*. Click OK when you are done.

When these items are selected in the browser window, they will link to their appropriate pages. A link will be activated when the user selects the corresponding item.

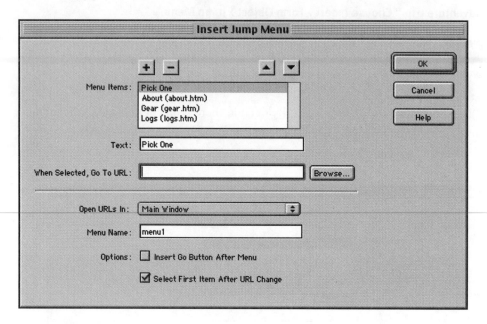

**NOTE** *If you want to add a Go button to your list, select the Insert Go Button After Menu checkbox. In most cases, you won't need a Go button, because choosing an item from the jump menu normally takes you to the appropriate URL. If you are using the jump menu within frames and jumping to a page that contains links, you will want to add a Go button. If the user wants to return to the first page by using the jump menu, the jump won't occur without the Go button.*

### 5) Save the file and preview it in the browser.

After you create the jump menu, you can make changes by using the property inspector or the Behaviors panel. The property inspector gives you limited editing capability; you can change the text the user sees and change the order in which the text appears in the list. For complete editing control, double-click the Jump Menu action on the Behaviors panel.

Leave this file open for the next exercise.

## TESTING YOUR FORMS

You can send a form to an e-mail address even if you don't have a CGI script running on your server. This should only be used to test your forms.

**1) In the myform.htm document, select the form below the text "Enter our drawing for a free adventure trip" by clicking on the red lines. In the Action field of the form on the property inspector, type *mailto:* followed by your e-mail address.**

You should remember to include the colon and no spaces. It should appear as mailto:info@mysite.com with your e-mail address replacing info@mysite.com. This is the same way you inserted manual e-mail links in Lesson 3.

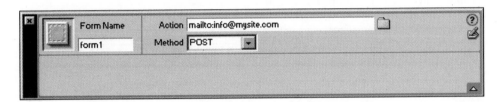

**2) Choose POST from the Method drop-down menu.**

You should then also set the encode type to plain text; otherwise, the text sent will be encoded into an almost unreadable form.

**3) Switch to split Code and Design view by choosing View > Code and Design or clicking the Show Code View icon on the document window tool bar.**

Look for the form tag. You can find it easily, because all the form code from the <form> to </form> tags in the code is highlighted because you selected the form. Scroll to the top of the highlighted area and deselect the code by placing the insertion point inside the <form> tag.

**4)  Type** *enctype="text/plain"* **within the** <form> **tag.**

The code should look like this:

```
<form method="post" action="mailto:info@mysite.com" enctype="text/plain">
```

The enctype defines how the data in the form is encoded. The text/plain value formats the information with each form element on a separate line. Using this value will make it easier to read the results in an e-mail. If you don't define an enctype value, browsers will use a default value that formats the data. Because the default is the one that should be used in most circumstances, you will usually not need to specify an enctype. This example is an exception, because you are sending the data in an e-mail to test the form.

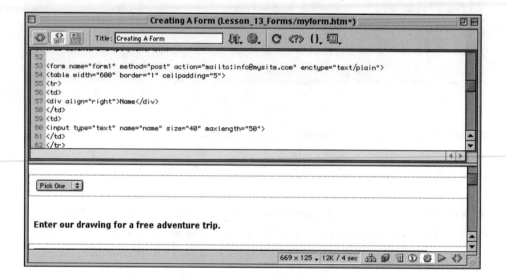

To add a subject line, change the action like this:

```
action="mailto:info@mysite.com?Subject=Title for Subject goes here"
enctype="text/plain">
```

You can uses spaces in the subject, but do not use any other special characters such as quote marks, apostrophes, periods, or slashes because they will interfere with the HTML code.

This form action might not work in all browsers. Use it only for testing. You should always use a CGI script to send your forms. If your computer is not configured to send e-mail, you will not be able to test this form in this manner.

**5)  Save the file and test it in the browser.**

You can close this file.

## WHAT YOU HAVE LEARNED

**In this lesson, you have:**

- Created a form on a Web page to place form fields within, enabling visitors to send information to you (pages 278–281)

- Added single-line text fields using options including width and maximum number of characters (pages 281–284)

- Added a multi-line text field and set options for the number of lines, maximum characters, and wrap method (pages 284–286)

- Added checkboxes to allow users to select multiple choices (pages 287–288)

- Added radio buttons to limit users to a single choice (pages 288–289)

- Added scrolling lists and drop-down menus with multiple items and specified an item to be selected initially (pages 290–291)

- Added buttons for Submit and Reset in order for users to send or clear the form (pages 292–294)

- Used a behavior to validate individual fields and multiple fields to make sure that all required fields are filled out with the correct kind of data (pages 294–296)

- Created a jump menu that allows users to navigate through the site (pages 297–298)

- Tested a form with a mailto action to be sure it is functioning correctly (pages 299–300)

# animating with timelines

HTML pages are generally motionless unless you add an animated GIF or a Macromedia Flash movie. You can roll over a button that might appear to move slightly as it swaps out with another image, but it remains static on the page. With Dynamic HTML (DHTML), you can add simple animations to your Web page. You can have an object come in from the left of the browser and disappear off the right of the browser. The animation is controlled completely with JavaScript within the HTML page, without the need of a plug-in. The limitation on DHTML animations is that users must use a 4.0 or later browser to view your pages.

All objects that you want to include in an animation must be contained in layers. The layers are placed in a timeline that allows you to control the timing and movement of

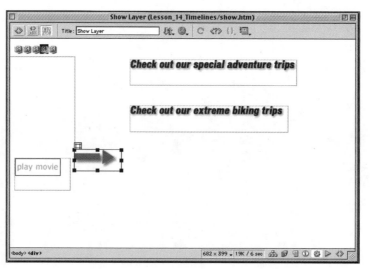

*In this project, you will create an animation by placing multiple layers in a timeline, and you will use keyframes to control visibility and create movement.*

the layer. The timeline consists of a series of frames, much like frames in a movie. Each frame displays on the Web page at a point in time depending on how many frames per second you specify and how long the animation is. You can control the placement and properties of each layer in a frame. A frame can also trigger a behavior during the animation.

To see an example of the finished pages for this lesson, open moveit.htm and show.htm from the Lesson_14_Timelines/Completed folder.

## WHAT YOU WILL LEARN

**In this lesson, you will:**

- Add layers to the timeline
- Make layers move around the page
- Alter the timeline with keyframes
- Change the speed and duration of the animation
- Record the path of a layer as you move it
- Control when the animation starts
- Change the visibility of layers during the animation
- Add behaviors to the timeline
- Make it possible for the viewer to start the animation

## APPROXIMATE TIME

This lesson should take about two hours to complete.

## LESSON FILES

**Media File**
*Lesson_14_Timelines/Images/…(all files)*
**Completed Project**
*Lesson_14_Timelines/moveit.htm*
*Lesson_14_Timelines/show.htm*

## ANIMATING OBJECTS

To create animations on your Web pages, you need to use layers and the Timelines inspector. This exercise demonstrates how to add objects in layers to a timeline and how to work with those elements once they are a part of the timeline.

**1) Create a new page and save it as moveit.htm in the Lesson_14_Timelines folder. Title the document Move It.**

In the following steps, you will animate an image on this page.

**2) Click the Draw Layer button on the objects panel and draw a layer on the bottom-left side of the page. Use the Layers panel to name the layer *carL*.**

DRAW LAYER

Layers must be used to create an animation using timelines. Keep in mind that using layers will limit your audience to those using 4.0 or later browsers.

**3) Insert the coupe.gif image from the Lesson_14_Timelines/Images folder or from the Assets panel Favorites Lesson 14 folder.**

To animate an object (text or graphic), the object must be contained in a layer.

**4) Choose Window > Timelines to open the Timelines panel.**

304

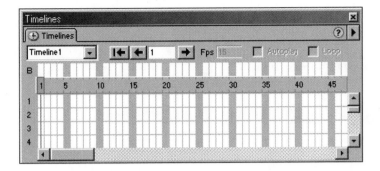

The Timelines panel represents the properties of layers and images over time.

Each row on the Timelines panel is called an **Animation channel** and represents elements on the page. Because you can only animate layers, each row on the timeline can only contain layers. You can use the Timelines panel to control a layer's position, dimension, visibility, or stacking order.

Each column on the Timelines panel is called a **frame** and represents a unit of time. Frame numbers indicate the number of frames each animation occupies.

**5) Select the carL layer. Choose Modify > Timeline > Add Object To Timeline to put the layer on the timeline.**

**TIP** *You can also use the layer selection handle to grab the layer and drag it from the document window into the Timelines panel.*

When you use Modify > Timeline > Add Object To Timeline, the layer is added to the Timelines panel in the first Animation channel (the first row). When you drag a layer into the Timelines panel, the layer will appear in whichever animation channel (row) that you drop it into.

A message box appears to tell you what layer attributes the Timelines panel can animate.

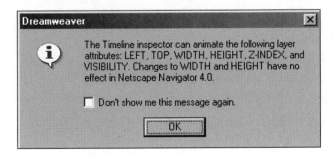

A horizontal, blue animation bar appears in the new channel on the timeline and displays the name of the layer in the bar. You should see "carL" displayed in the bar.

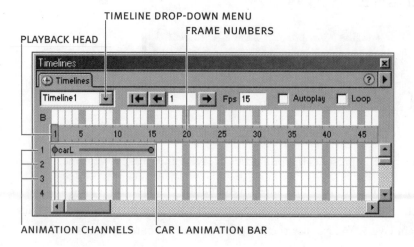

If you were to continue to add layers to the timeline using the Modify menu, the next layer would be placed in the next Animation channel, in the row below the preceding bar.

**NOTE** *You can also add more timelines to a page by choosing Modify > Timeline > Add Timeline. The timeline drop-down menu allows you to select a timeline if you have created more than one.*

**6) You can move the animation bar on the timeline by dragging the solid area of the bar. For this exercise, make sure the animation bar is positioned in the first row, starting in frame 1 with the playback head in the first frame.**

Since you used the modify menu to add the layer to the timeline, the animation bar will be in the first row and begin at frame 1. If you drag a layer into the Timelines panel, you can drop it anywhere; you may need to adjust the placement of the animation bar.

Animation bars show the duration of each object. A single row can include multiple bars, representing different objects. Different bars cannot control the same object in the same frame. The animation bar can be relocated to any frame and any channel. The initial placement of the animation bar in the channel is based on the position of the playback head. The playback head shows which frame of the timeline is currently displayed on the page. If the playback head is in frame 1, the animation bar begins in frame 1; if the playback head is in frame 8, the animation bar begins in frame 8. As you move the animation bar, the playback head will also move.

**7) Save the file.**

Leave this file open for the next exercise.

## USING KEYFRAMES

All animations are controlled by keyframes. **Keyframes** are the pivotal instances that define what happens in the animation. After you place a layer on the timeline, you use keyframes to control the movement of that layer on the page. A keyframe marks a point in the animation when a change is made to specified properties (such as position or size) for the layer. Dreamweaver interpolates values for all frames between keyframes.

By default, there will always be a beginning keyframe and an ending keyframe, which are indicated by open circles at the beginning and end of the animation bar. An animation with only these two keyframes will move in a straight line. To create an animation that doesn't move in a straight line, you need to add keyframes at other frames in the timeline.

In this exercise, you will select the last keyframe and move the layer on the page to the ending position of the animation. That movement will control the animation of the layer from the first keyframe to the last keyframe.

**1) In the moveit.htm document, click the keyframe marker at the end of the bar to select the last keyframe.**

The playback head jumps to that frame. The keyframe turns dark to indicate it is selected; the rest of the animation bar remains lighter.

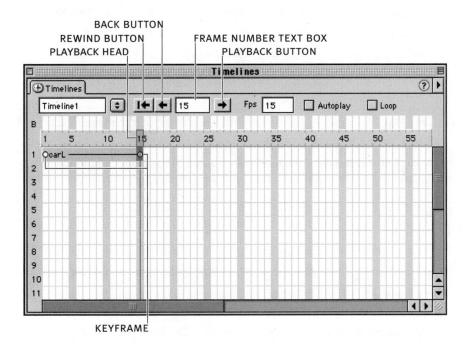

**2) In the document window, use the layer selection handle to drag the carL layer to the right side of the page.**

When you release the mouse button, you should see an animation line extending from the first location to the last. If you don't see the animation line, you didn't select the last keyframe before moving the layer. Since you are only using two keyframes in this exercise, the animation will move in a straight line.

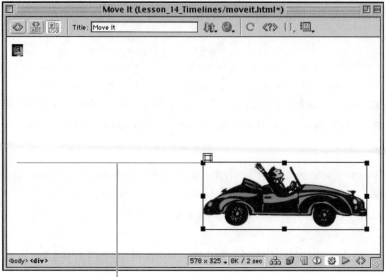

ANIMATION LINE

### 3) Click Rewind on the Timelines panel, and then hold down Play to preview the animation on the page.

When you click the Rewind button, the carL layer will jump back to its original position in the document window, and the playback head will move to the first frame in the Timelines panel.

If you click the Play button once, you will see the layer move one frame per click, and the playback head will advance one frame to the right. When you click and hold the play button, you will see the animation play continuously. The animation will repeat for as long as you continue to hold down the Play button.

As the animation plays, the playback head shows which frame of the timeline is currently displayed on the page.

**TIP** *You can also use the Back button to move one frame to the left or back. Hold down the back button to play the timeline backward.*

### 4) To make the animation play when the page loads in the browser, click Autoplay.

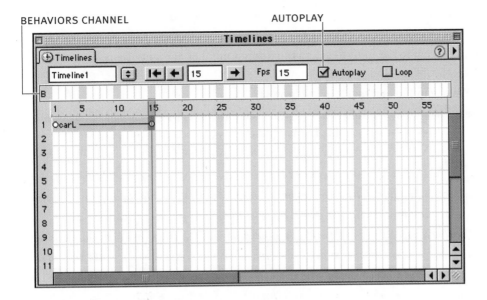

Autoplay uses JavaScript to make a timeline play when the page loads. A behavior is attached to the page's <body> tag; the behavior automatically executes the Play Timeline action when the page loads in a browser. A message box appears when you click Autoplay, alerting you that the Play Timeline action is being inserted in the <body> tag of your document using an onLoad event. The onLoad event will cause the animation to begin once the document has finished loading in the browser. Click OK to close the message box. You might not see the message box if the option to not display the message box again was selected previously.

**NOTE**   *If you select Loop on the Timelines panel, a behavior is added in the last frame that returns the playback head to frame 1 and plays the timeline again. The behavior is added to the Behaviors channel and appears as a dash above the last frame. You can edit the parameters for this behavior to define the number of loops by selecting the dash in the Behaviors channel and double-clicking the corresponding action in the Behaviors panel. A dialog box will allow you to set how many times the animation will loop and what frame it will begin from for the loops.*

Events don't have to start at the beginning of the timeline. You can use the timeline to delay action on the page until a certain time after the page loads by moving the animation bar to the right to create the desired number of empty frames.

**5) Save your file and test it in the browser.**
The car should move from the beginning point to the ending point and then stop. You can click Refresh or Reload in the browser to see the animation again.

**NOTE** *Users with a Macintosh and Internet Explorer 5.0 might notice a trail as the car moves across the screen. Internet Explorer 5.0 on a Macintosh is unable to calculate the layer dimensions as it moves across the page if the layer is the same size as the image. To fix this, you will need to change the size of the carL layer (or the layer you are animating) to make it larger than the image. When the layer is on the timeline, you have to change the size of the layer at each keyframe. Use the property inspector to exactly match the sizes of the layer at each keyframe. If you have a timeline with more than two keyframes, it might be easier to remove the layer from the timeline and start again.*

Leave this file open for the next exercise.

## POSITIONING AN OBJECT

In this exercise, you will change the car animation so it comes into the browser window from the left and moves out of the browser window to the right.

**1) In the moveit.htm document, select the first keyframe on the timeline for the carL layer. Click the title bar of the document window to make it active, and use the arrow keys or type a negative number in the L (Left) text box at the top of the property inspector to move the layer to the left, off the screen.**

**TIP** *The arrow keys will move the layer one pixel at a time. Holding down the Shift key and pressing an arrow key will move the layer by the current grid increment.*

L TEXT BOX

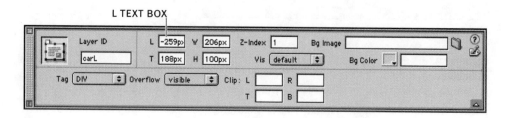

You have selected the first keyframe and moved the carL layer to the left where it is not visible. This will cause the animation to come into the browser window from the left. The top-left corner of the browser is the zero point (covered in Lesson 10), where Dreamweaver's horizontal and vertical rulers intersect when they are visible. Anything to the right of or below that point is a positive value; anything to the left of or above that point is a negative value. In order to make the carL layer begin outside the visible window of the browser, you have set the starting point of the layer to a negative horizontal value. You've placed this value in the L text box because the horizontal location of layers on a Web page is defined by their distance from the left side of the browser window.

**NOTE** *You can select any frame or keyframe by clicking it in the animation bar, or by typing the desired frame number into the frame number text box. The frame text box is a good indication of the exact frame that is selected.*

**2) Select the last keyframe on the timeline for the carL layer. Use the arrow keys or type a larger number in the L text box of the property inspector to move the layer to the right, off the screen.**

Selecting the last keyframe and moving the carL layer to the right where it is not visible will cause the animation to move out of the browser window to the right. Selecting a keyframe in the Timelines panel will automatically select the corresponding layer in the document window. Keep in mind that whether the carL layer moves out of the browser window or simply stops on the far right side of the page will depend on how large the browser window is when it is open. When it is important for an animation to completely leave the right side of the screen, make sure that the value is large enough to make this happen for those with large monitors.

**3) Save your file and test it in the browser.**

The car should come in from the left and move off the screen to the right.

**4)  Drag the last keyframe on the timeline to the right to make the carL animation bar longer. Hold down the Play button to preview the animation.**

The car animation now lasts longer and has slowed down. By default, when you add a layer to the Timelines panel, the animation bar is 15 frames long. The frame numbers show the duration of the animation. You can control the speed and length of the animation by setting the total number of frames and the number of frames per second (fps). Set the total number of frames by dragging the last keyframe to the right as you did in this exercise. Set the number of frames per second in the Fps text box. The default setting of 15 frames per second is a good average rate to use—faster rates might not improve performance. Browsers always play every frame of the animation, even if they cannot attain the specified frame rate on the user's system.

FPS TEXT BOX

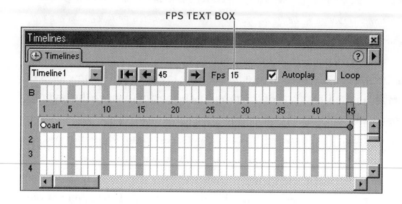

**TIP**  *If you want to shorten and speed up the animation, drag the last keyframe to the left to shorten the animation bar.*

**5)  Save the file.**

Leave this file open for the next exercise.

## CHANGING AN ANIMATION WITH KEYFRAMES

Animating a timeline can do more than just move an object from point A to point B. The important thing to remember is that all movement is controlled by keyframes. For the car animation, you set the position of the layer for the first and last keyframes, and Dreamweaver calculated the placement for all the frames in between. To make the movement more fluid and follow a more complex path, you need to add more keyframes.

In this exercise, you will add another layer to your file and animate that layer on a curved path. You will add a layer containing an image of a wasp and make it appear to chase the car across the page.

**1)  In the moveit.htm document, draw a layer and place it at the top left of the page. Name the layer waspL. Insert the wally_wasp.gif image from the Lesson_14_Timelines/Images folder or from the Assets panel Favorites Lesson 14 folder.**

Make the layer slightly larger than the image to ensure the animation will play correctly for viewers with a Macintosh and Internet Explorer 5.0.

**2)  Select the first frame in the Timelines panel by clicking the 1 in the row of frame numbers. Use the Layers panel to change the stacking order of the layers so the waspL layer is underneath the carL layer.**

The playback head moves to frame 1 when you select the first frame.

The carL layer should have a higher z-index number in order to be above the waspL layer. The z-index (covered in Lesson 10) determines the order in which layers will overlap each other, designating their level not horizontally or vertically, but in the third dimension. To change it, you can either change the z-index numbers themselves on either the layers panel or the property inspector, or you can drag the waspL layer below the carL layer on the Layers panel.

The waspL layer was created after the carL layer, so it was originally on top of the carL layer. You changed the stacking order because the wasp should be behind the car in this animation. If you wait until you place the wasp layer in the timeline, you have to select each keyframe in the timeline and then move the layer in the Layers panel. It is easier to move layers before you place them in the timeline.

**3)  Select the waspL layer in the document window by clicking the borders of the layer. Choose Modify > Timeline > Add Object To Timeline to add it to the timeline.**

The waspL layer now appears in the second animation channel on the Timelines panel. It is 15 frames long.

**4)  In the Timelines panel, select the last keyframe in the Wasp layer and drag it until the waspL animation bar is the same length as the carL animation bar. In the document window, move the waspL layer underneath the car.**

**TIP** *You can also choose Modify > Timeline > Add Frame or Remove Frame to add or remove frames on the timeline and make the animation longer or shorter.*

313

The waspL layer is selected and appears to be in front of the carL layer. It only appears in front because the layer is selected—when you preview the document in the browser, you will see the waspL layer is actually behind the carL layer.

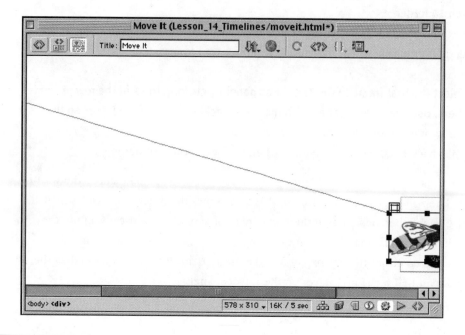

**NOTE** *You may need to deselect Prevent Overlaps in the Layers panel to correctly position the waspL layer.*

**5) Click Rewind, and click and hold on Play in the Timelines panel to see the animation.**

The wasp should move from left to right, following the car in a straight, diagonal line. To make the layer move in a curve, you will add more keyframes and move the layer at each new keyframe in the following steps.

**6) While in the Timelines panel, hold down Ctrl (Windows) or Command (Macintosh) until the pointer changes to a circle. Then click in the waspL animation bar.**

314

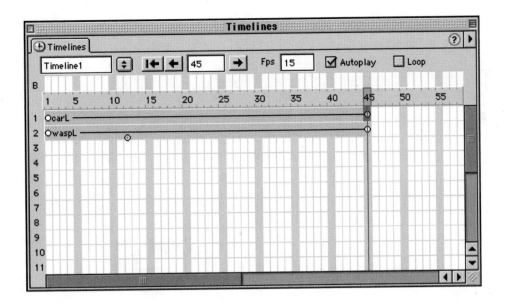

A new keyframe is added at the frame you clicked. If you want to move the new keyframe on the timeline, drag it left or right to a new frame. The frame text box will tell you which frame number the keyframe is on.

**TIP** *You can also add a new keyframe by clicking a frame on the animation bar or typing the number of the frame into the frame text box to select it and choosing Modify > Timeline > Add Keyframe. To remove a keyframe, select the keyframe and choose Modify > Timeline > Remove Keyframe.*

### 7) With the new keyframe selected, move the waspL layer on the page.

The animation line starts to change shape.

### 8) Add more keyframes, moving the waspL layer at each new keyframe.

**TIP** *Right-click (Windows) or Control-click (Macintosh) on the Timelines panel (or use the Timeline drop-down menu) to open a shortcut menu that includes all the relevant commands.*

Your document window will now have a more freeform animation line, similiar to the example shown here.

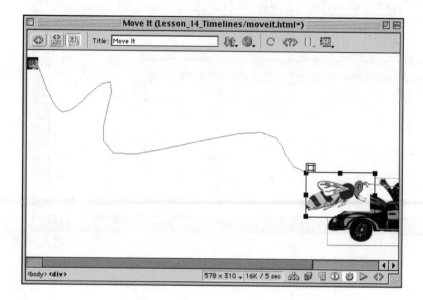

If you were to extend or shorten the animation bar to change the duration of the waspL animation, all the keyframes you added would automatically move in order to stay in the same position relative to the other keyframes.

Your Timelines panel will now have more keyframes on the waspL animation bar, similiar to the example shown here.

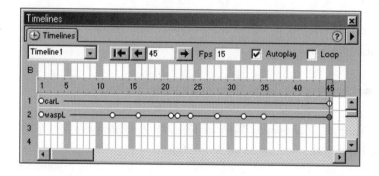

### 9) Save your file and preview it in the browser.
Leave this file open for the next exercise.

**NOTE**  *To change the start time of an animation, select the animation bar (click in the middle of the bar and not on a keyframe) and drag left or right. Press Shift to select more than one bar at a time.*

## RECORDING THE PATH OF A LAYER

The method you just used in the last exercise for animating a layer works great when you want to control the movement of the layer in a few frames. You can also use another method that follows your pointer as you drag the layer on the page. Dreamweaver tracks your movement and creates the keyframes on the timeline for you. Dreamweaver also matches the time you take when dragging the layer. The more slowly you drag, the more keyframes are added and the longer the animation bar becomes. You can then alter the time or the keyframes on the timeline.

In this exercise, you will add a second wasp to the animation and drag the layer to create the path.

**1)  In the moveit.htm document, draw another layer on the page and name it wasp2L. Insert the same wally_wasp.gif image into the wasp2L layer. Select the first frame in the Timelines panel by clicking the 1 in the row of frame numbers. Select the wasp2L layer in the layers panel and move it beneath the carL layer.**

The playback head moves to frame 1 when you select the first frame.

Use the selection handle on the wasp2L layer to select the layer. You should see the selection handle as well as the black square sizing handles that indicate the layer is selected. If you don't see the black square sizing handles, then the layer is only active, not selected.

The position of the wasp2L layer will be the starting point of the animation. If you want the animation to begin in a different place you should move the layer.

**2)  Select the wasp2L layer in the document window and choose Modify > Timeline > Record Path Of Layer.**

This option will allow you to create an animation by dragging a layer. Recording the path of a layer will automatically add that layer to the timeline.

**3)  Click the selection handle and drag the wasp2 layer on the page to form the path of the animation.**

As you drag the layer, a gray dotted line will show the resulting path. You can drag the layer in any direction, cross back over the path you are creating, and vary the speed with which you drag the layer to affect the way the path is recorded.

When you stop dragging and release, the dotted line is converted to the animation line. Dreamweaver adds the layer to the timeline with the necessary keyframes to control the layer's movement.

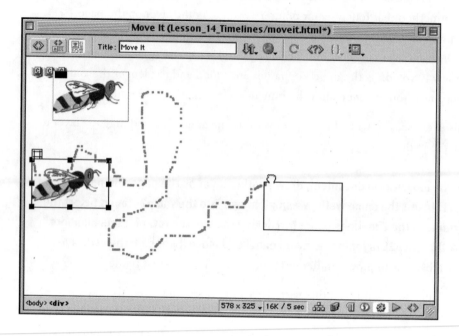

### 4) Drag the last keyframe to the left to shorten the time for the animation.

The animation bar for this new animation may be very long. The longer the path you create, the longer the animation will be. Keep in mind that long, complicated animations and pages with many different animation channels will take much longer to load and increase the possibility of crashing the visitor's browser.

As you shorten the animation bar, all the keyframes in the animation shift, so their relative positions remain constant. The keyframes will stay in the same positions relative to other keyframes, and the beginning and end of the animation bar.

**TIP** *To prevent the other keyframes from moving, press Ctrl (Windows) or Command (Macintosh) while dragging the keyframe at the end of the animation bar, also known as the* **end marker**. *If you drag the keyframe without the modifier keys, all the other keyframes in the animation move proportionally. The modifier keys restrain the movement to only the last keyframe. This is useful if you have a short animation bar and need to extend it without the keyframes moving to other frames.*

### 5) Save your file and test it in the browser.

You can also preview the path of the layer in Dreamweaver by clicking and holding down the Play button.

**NOTE** *To shift the location of an entire animation path, select the animation bar on the timeline and then drag the layer on the page. Dreamweaver adjusts the position of all keyframes. Making any change when an entire bar is selected changes all the keyframes.*

You can close this file.

## CHANGING THE VISIBILITY OF A LAYER

Timelines allow you to do more than simply moving layers. You can also use timelines to change the visibility of a layer. For example, you might want a layer to be displayed only after another layer animates across the screen. The initial state of the second layer would be hidden and would then become visible at a certain frame.

In this exercise, you will create four layers with graphics in each. Three of the layers will be hidden until the fourth layer, an arrow, animates and points to the others. The arrow layer will move to reveal each layer one by one. The show.htm file in the Lesson_14_Timelines/Completed folder demonstrates the effect.

**1) Create a new page and save it as show.htm in the Lesson_14_Timelines folder. Title the page Show Layer. In the top center of the document, draw three layers on the page. Place the layers vertically, one below another, and align their left edges.**
The layers should be left justified so that the left edge of each layer aligns with the left edges of the others. Your document should now look like the example shown here.

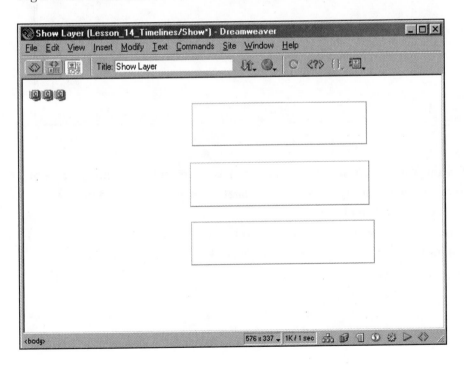

**2)  Name the top layer specialL, the middle layer bikingL, and the bottom layer raftingL. From the Lesson_14_Timelines/Images folder or from the Assets panel Favorites Lesson 14 folder. Insert the specials.gif, ext_biking.gif, and ww_rafting.gif images into their corresponding named layers.**

These layers now contain the graphics that will appear as the layers become visible in the browser during the animation.

**3)  Draw another layer and name it arrowL. Insert the arrow.gif image from the Lesson 14 Favorites Assets panel. Place this layer to the left of the top layer in the vertical list.**

In the finished animation, the arrow layer will move to reveal one by one the other layers.

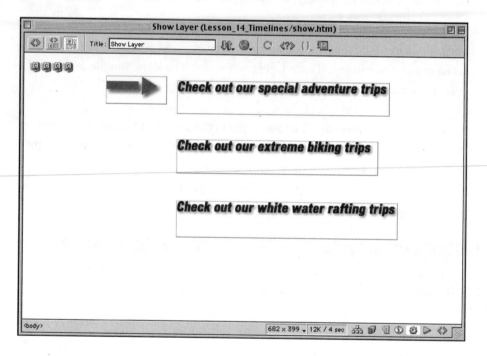

**4)  Starting with the arrowL layer, add all the layers except for the raftingL layer to the timeline. Place each layer in its own animation channel, starting each one in frame 1. Check the Autoplay box.**

The timeline now contains three animation channels: arrowL, specialL, and bikingL. The animation is set to begin when the page loads.

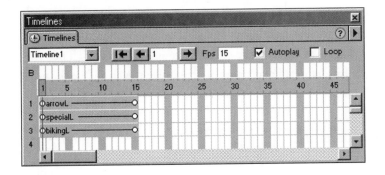

**5) Drag the last keyframe of the arrowL animation bar to frame 35. Hold down Ctrl (Windows) or Command (Macintosh) until the pointer changes to a circle and click the arrowL animation bar to add new keyframes at frames 15, 20, 25, and 30.**

These keyframes indicate a change in the movement of the arrowL layer.

**6) Select the last keyframe in the arrowL animation bar at frame 35. Drag the layer in the document window straight down to the left of the raftingL layer.**

This is the ending position of the arrowL layer.

**7) Select the keyframe at frame 30 and drag it straight down to the left of the bikingL layer. Look at the property inspector and make a note of the resulting value in the T text box. Select the keyframe at frame 25 and change the value in the T text box to match the value you made a note of.**

**TIP** *Turning the grid on by choosing View > Grid > Show Grid may help you to move the arrowL layer in a straight line.*

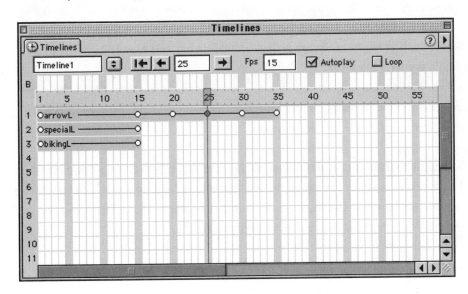

**ANIMATING WITH TIMELINES**

This is the third position of the arrowL layer. The keyframe at frame 25 will move the arrow layer to the left of the bikingL layer. The keyframe at frame 30 will be the point at which the layer begins to move to the ending position at frame 35. The block of five frames between frame 25 and frame 30 will cause the arrowL layer to pause in the third position.

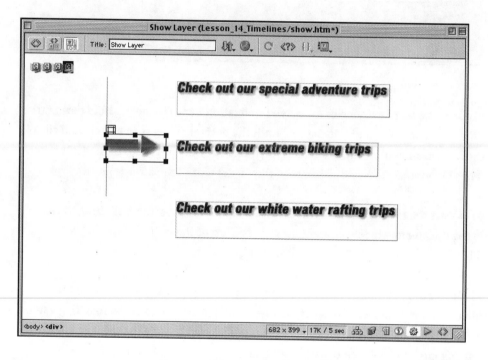

The second position is already set at frames 15 and 20, because you created the arrowL layer there. The arrowL layer will move until it is in the second position at frame 15 and pause until frame 20; at that point, it will begin to move to the third position.

**8) Select the first keyframe in the arrowL animation bar and type _–125_ in the L text box of the property inspector.**

This is the first position of the arrowL layer; the arrow is off the left side of the page. When the document is viewed in the browser, this will cause the arrow to appear to come in from the left side of the window.

**9) Select the first keyframe of the specialL layer and use the Vis drop-down menu on the property inspector to change the visibility of the layer to hidden. Select the last keyframe of the specialL layer; make sure it is on frame 15, and then use the same drop-down menu to change the visibility to visible.**

The default length of an animation bar is 15 frames, so the specialL layer should already be 15 frames long.

In this step, you have changed the visibility of the specialL layer so it will be hidden when the page loads initially. This layer will appear when the arrow moves to its second position in frame 15.

**10) Select the first keyframe of the bikingL layer and change the visibility of the layer to hidden. Select the last keyframe of the bikingL layer, drag it to frame 25, and change the visibility of the layer to visible.**

The visibility of the bikingL layer is changed to visible when the last keyframe is selected, because the layer should only appear at that point.

Your Timelines panel should now look like the example shown here.

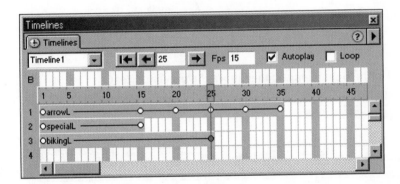

**11) Save your file and test it in the browser.**

The arrow moves into the browser window from the left and stops at the second position. Then the specialL layer appears. As the arrow moves down and stops at the third position the hidden bikingL layer becomes visible. The arrow continues down, reaching the last layer, raftingL, which has been visible during the entire animation.

**NOTE** *If the animation doesn't play, make sure Autoplay is selected in the Timelines inspector.*

Leave this file open for the next exercise.

## ADDING BEHAVIORS TO THE TIMELINE

Adding a behavior to the timeline is similar to adding a behavior to any other object, except that you attach the behavior to a single frame in the timeline and not to the entire animation bar. The behavior is added to the Behaviors channel and appears as a dash.

In the previous exercise, the two layers that appeared when the arrowL layer moved near them were added to the timeline. In this exercise, you will make the raftingL layer stay hidden and appear when the arrowL layer moves near it without adding the raftingL layer to timeline. You will use a behavior to display the layer.

**1) Select the raftingL layer and use the property inspector to change the visibility to hidden.**

The raftingL layer disappears.

**2) Select the end keyframe of the arrowL animation bar on the Timelines Panel.**

The arrowL layer is in the third position, to the left of the hidden raftingL layer.

**3) Click frame 35 in the Behaviors channel above the playback head.**

The frame in the Behaviors channel above the playback head turns black to indicate that it is selected.

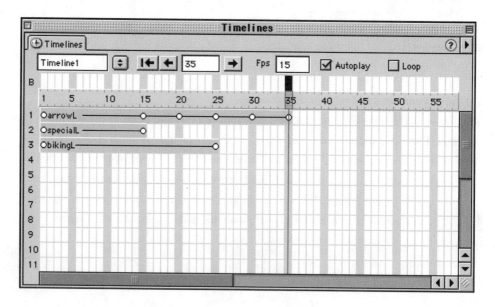

**4) Choose Window > Behaviors to open the Behaviors panel. Click the plus (+) sign to add a behavior and choose Show-Hide Layers from the pop-up menu.**

The Show-Hide Layers dialog box appears with a list of the layers on the page.

**5) Select the raftingL layer from the Named Layers list and click the Show button. Then click OK.**

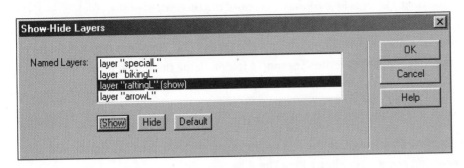

When you click the Show button, "(show)" displays next to the layer raftingL. This behavior will be triggered when the arrowL layer reaches frame 35 and cause the raftingL layer to become visible.

**NOTE** *You can make multiple layers appear and disappear all at once by selecting other layers in the Named Layers list and clicking the Show or Hide buttons. Default will restore the layer's default visibility. Layers do not have to be in the Timelines panel in order to show or hide them with this behavior.*

**6) Save your file and test it in the browser.**

Leave this file open for the next exercise.

## MAKING THE TIMELINE PLAY

In the previous exercises, the timeline automatically played in the browser because you selected the Autoplay option. At times you might want the user to control the playback of the timeline. You can add a Start Timeline button to play the animation when the user rolls over a button or clicks an image.

**1) In the show.htm document, deselect Autoplay on the Timelines panel. Select the first frame in the Timelines panel by clicking the 1 in the row of frame numbers.**

The playback head moves to frame 1 when you select the first frame. When you deselect Autoplay, the JavaScript Play Timeline action, which used an onLoad event to start the animation once the page loaded, is removed from the <body> tag.

**2) Draw a layer on the page where it won't overlap any of the objects as they animate on the page. Name the layer startL.**

The object to which you attach the Play Timeline behavior does not have to be contained in a layer. It can be any text, graphic, or object on the page. In this exercise, using a layer is an easy way to control the placement of the graphic.

### 3) Insert the play_movie.gif image from the Lesson_14_Timelines/Images folder or from the Assets panel Favorites Lesson 14 folder. Name the image play.

This is the graphic that you will attach the Play Timeline behavior to in the next step.

### 4) Select the play image. In the Behaviors panel, click the plus (+) sign to add a behavior and choose Timeline > Play Timeline behavior.

The Play Timeline dialog box appears.

### 5) Click OK. Save your file and test it in the browser.

When you click Play, the animation should begin. If the animation does not begin, go back to the document and make sure that the play movie graphic does not overlap any of the objects as they animate on the page.

**NOTE** *You can make the pointer change to a pointing hand when you move it over the button in the browser by selecting the graphic and typing a number (#) sign in the Link field of the property inspector. Keep in mind that this may cause the behavior not to work in Netscape. Test your pages to be sure everything works as you expect.*

You can close this file.

## WHAT YOU HAVE LEARNED

**In this lesson, you have:**

- Added layers to the Timelines panel to create animations that would add more dynamic action to your pages (pages 304–306)

- Made layers move around the page in straight lines and in freeform curves (pages 307–316)

- Altered the timeline with keyframes to create points in the animation when a layer's properties, such as direction and visibility, changed (pages 307–310)

- Changed the speed and duration of the animation by shortening or extending the animation bar on the Timelines panel (pages 310–312)

- Recorded the path of a layer as you moved it around the page so keyframes would automatically be created (pages 317–319)

- Used keyframes on the Timelines panel to control when layers were visible and when they were hidden (pages 319–323)

- Added behaviors to the timeline to control when layers were visible or hidden (pages 324–325)

- Made it possible for the viewer to start the animation by attaching a behavior to a graphic that would play the timeline when it was clicked (pages 325–326)

# extending dreamweaver

Throughout this book, you have tested your Web pages by previewing them in the browser as you have completed each exercise. As you've built individual pages or sections, you've had a chance to see how those pages looked and you've been able to make modifications as needed. Before making a site available to the public or to your intended audience, however, you should go further and test your entire site. Take the extra time to be sure you've worked out all the potential problems. If you have access to a testing server, it is a good idea to load the site onto that server and access the pages from all computer types and from as many versions of browsers as you can find. Test the pages under real user conditions. If you think a majority of your users will use

*In this project, you will use two Dreamweaver extensions that you will install during this lesson to quickly generate a calendar like this for your page and to automatically change the colors of all rows in the table.*

a modem, make sure you use a modem to test the speed at which the pages load. If you are the primary Web developer, have others test your pages. Watch how other people try to navigate your site. Make sure to test every link and fix any broken ones. Try to break your forms by entering bad data. Remember that users don't think like you do—try to prepare for the unexpected as you check the entire site.

On any site, large or small, the task of thorough testing can be daunting. You've worked hard on the content and the design, but if users get frustrated because of broken links, pages that don't work in their browsers or pages that are large and very slow to load, you've lost them. In this lesson, you will learn how to use Dreamweaver in your testing process by running reports on your site in order to find out if the pages are compatible with certain browsers. You'll also learn how to check links throughout the site and expand Dreamweaver's capabilities with the use of extensions.

To see examples of the finished pages for this lesson, open calendar.htm and catcopy.htm from the Lesson_15_Custom/Completed folder.

## WHAT YOU WILL LEARN

**In this lesson, you will:**

- Test your site for browser compatibility
- Test the links in your site
- Create site reports
- Use the Reference panel
- Add extensions using the Extension Manager
- Use new extensions
- Create your own objects

## APPROXIMATE TIME

This lesson should take about one hour to complete.

## LESSON FILES

### Media File

*Lesson_15_Custom/Images/...(all files)*

### Starting Files

*Lesson_15_Custom/bgtest.htm*

*Lesson_15_Custom/welcome.htm*

*Lesson_15_Custom/Check_browser/...*
  *(all files)*

*Lesson_15_Custom/Reports/...(all files)*

*Lesson_15_Custom/Objects/...(all files)*

### Extensions

*Lesson_15_Custom/MacExtensions/...*
  *(all files)*

*Lesson_15_Custom/WinExtensions/...*
  *(all files)*

### Completed Project

*Lesson_15_Custom/Completed/calendar.htm*

*Lesson_15_Custom/Completed/catcopy.htm*

## CHECKING BROWSER COMPATIBILITY

Many elements you can add to your Web pages will only work in the later versions of browsers. CSS and layers, for example, are only supported in 4.0 or later browsers. Before making a site available to the public, you should test your pages so you have a chance to fix errors and be sure that your audience will be able to view the pages as they are intended to be seen. To develop an accessible site, you can identify target browsers and design your pages with those browsers in mind. Current browsers support tables and frames, but earlier versions of browsers do not. If you know or suspect that a significant number of your users are still using Netscape Navigator 2.0, for example, you would want to check your pages in that browser. If your pages are geared toward people who may be using hand-held devices, readers, or ways other than standard browsers to access your pages, you should test your site with those devices and software applications.

In this exercise, you will use the Target Browser feature in Dreamweaver to test the HTML in your pages against a browser profile and determine whether or not that browser supports the code in your page. You can run a browser check on a saved file, a folder, or the entire site. Dreamweaver only reports the errors—it does not make any changes to your files.

### 1) Open the check_browser.htm file from the Lesson_15_Custom/Check_browser folder.

In the following steps, you will run a target browser check on this file.

### 2) Choose File > Check Target Browsers.

The Check Target Browsers dialog box opens.

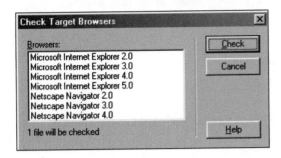

### 3) Choose Netscape Navigator 3.0 from the list to check against your page and click Check.

**TIP** *You can choose more than one browser in this dialog box. Make multiple, noncontiguous selections by using Command-click on the Macintosh or Ctrl-click in Windows. Make contiguous selections by using Shift-click on both Macintosh and Windows.*

The test runs, and a report page displays in your primary browser.

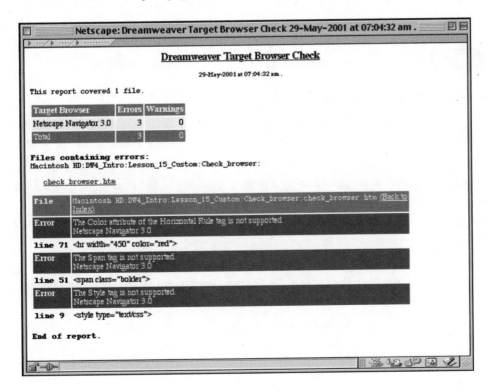

Close the check_browser.htm file.

### 4) Select the Lesson_15_Custom/Check_browser folder in the Site window.

In the following steps, you will run a target browser check on this folder.

### 5) Choose File > Check Target Browsers.

The Check Target Browsers dialog box opens.

### 6) Choose the browser from the list to check against the pages in the selected folder. Then click Check.

The test runs and a report page displays in your primary browser.

There will be differences in the way your site displays in every browser version. You may have to make trade-offs on how the pages appear. Certain JavaScripts, for example, will produce error messages in browsers that do not support them. Other JavaScripts will simply not work, and the visitor may never know it. To reach the widest audience possible, you will want to create a Web site that is error-free for older browsers. It is far better for visitors to miss certain features than to have error messages appear. If you have an audience using a wide variety of browsers, you may want to make sure the navigation of your pages does not rely on features that may not be supported in older browsers. You may also want to provide alternative pages for those who are not using the latest versions.

**NOTE** *If you want to save this report, you need to save it from the browser.*

## CHECKING LINKS IN YOUR SITE

It is not uncommon for a Web designer to add, delete, or change the filenames of pages in the site during the development process. Overlooking a page that links to a deleted or renamed file is very easy. Your users will get very frustrated if they get the "404: File Not Found" error message indicating a page is missing when they click on a link. In this exercise, you will use the Check Link feature to find those missing links. Dreamweaver can only verify links to files within the site. External links are listed, but it is up to you to test those links and make sure the external link is a valid URL.

### 1) Open links.htm from the Lesson_15_Custom/Reports folder. Choose File > Check Links.

The Link Checker report window opens.

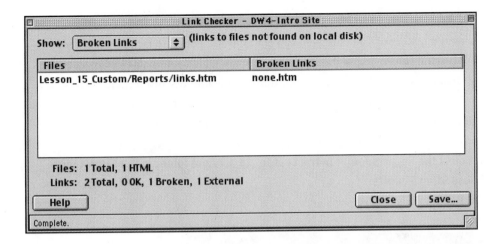

**2) Choose Broken Links from the Show drop-down menu.**

In this exercise, only one broken link is displayed in the Broken Links column.

**3) Select the broken link (none.htm).**

The filename highlights, and a folder icon appears next to the broken link.

**4) Change none.htm to ad_page.htm. Then press Enter (Windows) or Return (Macintosh).**

**TIP** *You can also click the folder icon and browse to the correct file to link to.*

If there are other broken references to this file, a dialog box opens asking if you want to fix the other references as well. Click Yes to have Dreamweaver fix all the references to this file. Click No to have Dreamweaver fix only the current reference.

**NOTE** *You can also check files or folders by selecting them in the Site Window and choosing File > Check Links. If you want to view the document or fix the links by using the property inspector, double-click the filename in the Link Checker window to open the file.*

You can close this file.

## GENERATING REPORTS FOR A SITE

During the testing of your site, you can compile and generate reports on several HTML attributes by using the Reports command. This command lets you check several options, including to search for untitled documents and redundant nested tags. You can run reports on a single document, a folder, or the entire site to help you troubleshoot and find potential problems before publishing your site.

**1) Select the Reports folder in the Lesson_15_Custom folder in the Site window. Choose Site > Reports.**

The Reports dialog box opens.

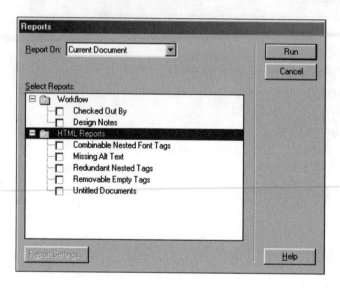

**2) Choose Selected Files In Site from the Report On drop-down menu. Leave all the options in the Workflow area unchecked. Check all the options in the HTML Reports area.**

You can choose to run reports on the Current Document, Entire Local Site, Selected Files In Site, and Folder.

**3) Click Run to create the report.**

A list of results displays in the Results window.

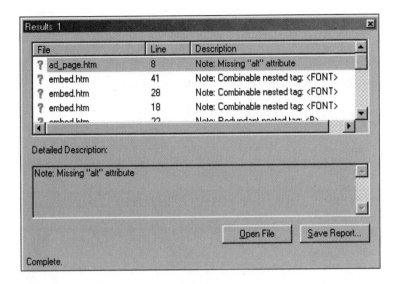

**4) Click Save Report to save the report.**

All reports are saved as XML files with the .xml file extension.

The Reports command lists problems in your pages but does not fix them.

**TIP** *After running the reports, you can use Clean Up HTML by opening an individual page and choosing Commands > Clean Up HTML. This command fixes many but not all of the problems found in the site report. A dialog box will appear with a number of items you can chose to have Dreamweaver remove: Empty Tags, Redundant Nested Tags, Non-Dreamweaver HTML Comments, Dreamweaver HTML Comments, and Specific Tag(s). You can also choose to combine nested <font> tags when possible and to show the log on completion. The log will give you a detailed list of what changes were made to the document.*

You can close this file.

## USING THE O'REILLY REFERENCE PANEL

Dreamweaver provides most of the common HTML tags you will use when you design your pages. Occasionally you might want to add additional HTML or JavaScript to your pages. If you are familiar with HTML or JavaScript, that task is easy; you simply switch to code view or the code inspector and add the additional code. If you need some help in determining the correct code, you can use the built-in O'Reilly Reference panel. In the next exercise, you will add some code to the <body> tag to change the way a background image scrolls on the page. This change works only in Internet Explorer and does not affect the page if viewed in Netscape Navigator.

**335**

**1) Open the bgtest.htm file in the Lesson_15_Custom folder. Preview this file in Internet Explorer.**

This file contains a background image and some text in a table. As you scroll down the page in the browser, notice how the background image scrolls along with the text.

**2) Switch to code view and select the <body> tag. Click the Reference button on the toolbar.**

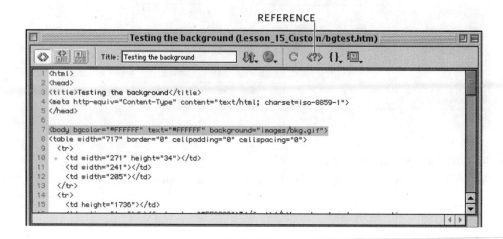

The Reference panel opens, displaying information about the <body> tag you selected.

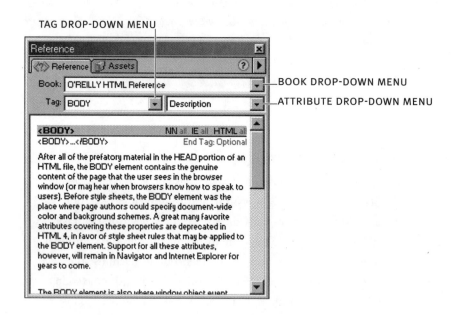

The Book drop-down menu displays the name of the book the reference material comes from: O'Reilly CSS Reference, O'Reilly HTML Reference, or O'Reilly JavaScript Reference. The Tag drop-down menu displays the tag you selected in the code view (or code inspector). To the right of the Tag drop-down menu is a menu that contains the list of attributes for the tag you choose. The default selection is Description, which displays a description of the chosen tag.

### 3) Choose bgproperties from the Attribute drop-down menu.

The description of bgproperties appears in the window, along with the browser support for this option.

### 4) Use the information from the Reference panel to change the <body> tag by adding the bgproperties attribute to change the background image to a fixed position.

Your code should look like this:

```
<body bgcolor="#FFFFFF" text="#FFFFFF" background="images/bkg.gif"
bgproperties="fixed">
```

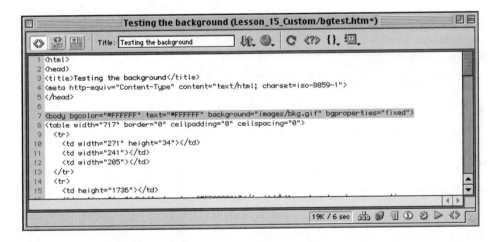

### 5) Save the file and preview it in Internet Explorer.

Scroll down the page to see the result. You can close this file.

## EXTENDING DREAMWEAVER

Dreamweaver was designed to be extensible, allowing users of the program to expand functionality by adding extensions. An **extension** is a piece of software you can add to Dreamweaver to enhance Dreamweaver's capabilities. There are several different kinds of extensions, from simple HTML you can add to the Objects panel and the Insert menu, to JavaScript commands you can add to the Command menu or Behaviors panel.

Advanced users who are proficient in JavaScript can create new behaviors and insert them into Dreamweaver. Even with only a basic understanding of HTML, you can create simple objects or commands for use within Dreamweaver. You can also use extensions created by others by using the Dreamweaver Extension Manager to download and install extensions from the Dreamweaver Exchange Web site. In this exercise, you will install several extensions that have been provided for you on the CD that accompanies this book.

**1) Choose Commands > Manage Extensions to launch the Extension Manager.**

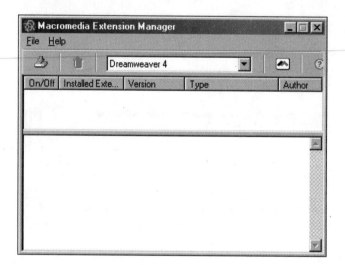

The Extension Manager enables you to install extensions, remove extensions, find out more information about an installed extension, and write a review of an installed extension. It also provides a convenient way to bring up the Dreamweaver Exchange Web site, which will help you find more extensions.

**338**

**2) Choose File > Install Extension in the Extension Manager, or click Install New Extension (Windows only).**

The Select Extension to Install (Windows) or Install Extension (Macintosh) dialog box opens.

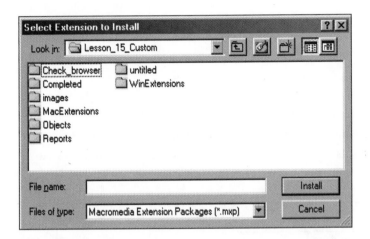

**TIP** *Double-click or open the package file from Windows Explorer (Windows) or the Finder (Macintosh) to launch the Extension Manager automatically.*

**3) Locate and open the Extensions folder in the Lesson_15_Custom folder.**

The extensions are grouped in the WinExtensions folder and the MacExtensions folder.

**4) Choose ChangeCase.mxp from the list, and then click Install (Windows) or Open (Macintosh).**

**NOTE** *The actual extension name will begin with MX, followed by a number and then the extension name.*

Dreamweaver will begin to install the extension.

**5) Read any legal information the extension author has provided.**

To continue with the installation, click Accept.

If you click Decline, the extension will not be installed.

*If you already have another version of the extension installed—or another extension with the same name—the Installer asks whether to remove the one already installed. If you click Yes, the previously installed extension is removed and the new extension is installed. If you click No, the installation is canceled, leaving the existing extension in place.*

If the installer doesn't encounter any problems, it displays a message to inform you that the extension has been successfully installed.

### 6) Click OK.

The Macromedia Extension Manager displays the extension name, version number, type, and author. The Type column tells where the extension is installed: commands indicates the extension was installed in the Command menu, objects indicates the extension was installed in the Objects panel, and so on.

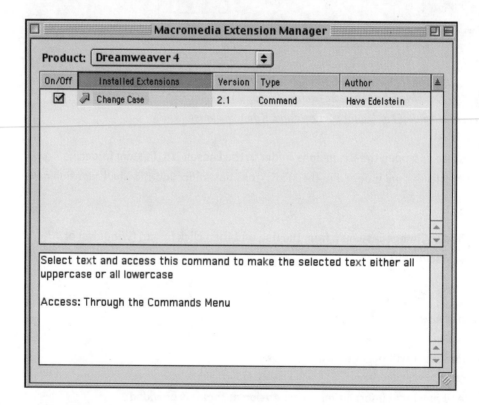

### 7) Repeat steps 2 through 6 to install Calendar.mpx, Scrubber.mpx, and AlternateTableRows2.mpx.

The Macromedia Extension Manager will now display a list of the four extensions you have installed.

**NOTE** *To find more extensions, open the Macromedia Extension Manager. Choose File > Go to Macromedia Exchange to open the Macromedia Exchange for Dreamweaver Web page in your browser. You must be a member of macromedia.com to download, submit, or review extensions. This is a free membership. You can sign up and log in at the Dreamweaver Exchange home page. Macromedia provides the Dreamweaver Exchange Web site as a repository for all kinds of extensions. When you find an extension you're interested in on that site, you can download it via your Web browser and then install it in Dreamweaver by using the Extension Manager as you have done in this exercise. Macromedia creates some extensions, while others are created by third parties. Those extensions that are created or authorized by Macromedia are marked on the Dreamweaver Exchange Web site with a small Macromedia icon in the Approval column.*

*If you find an extension you want, the file you download is an extension package file, and its name ends with .mxp. When you click an extension's name to download it, some Web browsers provide the option of opening the package file directly from its location on the Web instead of simply downloading the file. If you download the package file and save it on your disk, you'll have it handy in case you need to reinstall it later, but you'll have to open it explicitly (by double-clicking the file's icon on your desktop, for example) to install it. If you choose to open the package file from its current location, the Macromedia Extension Manager automatically launches to enable you to install the extension, but you won't retain a copy of the package file for later use. It's up to you which approach you prefer.*

**8) Click Close or choose File > Exit (Windows) or File > Quit (Macintosh) to exit the Extension Manager. Restart Dreamweaver.**

When you restart Dreamweaver, you will be able to use the new extensions.

**NOTE** *To remove an extension, choose File > Remove Extension while the Extension Manager is active. Select an extension from the list of installed extensions and confirm that you want to remove the extension by clicking Yes in the confirmation dialog box. Only extensions that appear in the list can be removed with the Extension Manager. If you manually installed an extension, you will need to manually remove it. Restart Dreamweaver for the changes to take effect.*

## USING EXTENSIONS

After you restart Dreamweaver, all four extensions you installed are ready to use. The extensions will appear in the Commands menu, the Insert menu, the Objects panel, or the Behaviors panel, depending on the extension type. Some extensions may appear in more than one place. The next several exercises take you through using the extensions you just installed.

**1) Open the welcome.htm file from the Lesson_15_Custom folder.**

The heading is lowercase. You'll change it to uppercase using the Change Case extension in the following steps.

**2) Select the title "compass adventure tours" and choose Commands > Change Case.**

The Change Case dialog box opens.

**3) Select UPPERCASE and click OK.**

The text is converted to all uppercase.

**4) Create a new document and save it as calendar.htm in the Lesson_15_Custom folder. Title the page Calendar of Events.**

In the following steps, you will use the calendar extension to automatically build a calendar. The extension builds a table with the dates of the month you choose already inserted in the table cells.

**5) Choose Insert > Calendar.**

The Insert Calendar dialog box opens.

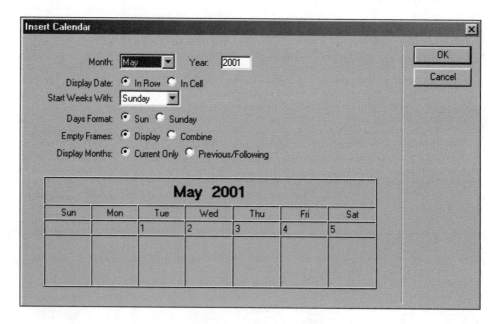

**6) Choose the month and the year you want for your calendar. For this exercise use the default options (Display Date: In Row; Start Weeks With: Sunday; Days Format: Sun; Empty Frames: Display; Display Months: Current Only). Click OK.**

A calendar is built using tables. The calendar appears in your document.

**7) Select the table and choose Commands > Alternate Table Rows. Type *tan* for the first color and *#FFFFCD* for the second color. Don't select the Include First Row option. Then click OK.**

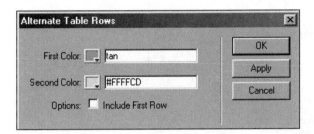

In the dialog box that opens, you can enter alternating colors you want for the table rows. Note that you can enter either a color name (such as white, yellow, tan, or blue) or the hexadecimal value for the color.

**8) Save the document.**

You can close both the welcome.htm and calendar.htm files.

## USING THE LINK SCRUBBER EXTENSION

The Link Scrubber extension removes the outlines on links that appear in Internet Explorer when you click a text link, a graphic link, or an image map. First, you need to understand the purpose of the outlines so you can determine whether you want to remove the outlines or leave them as designed. The outlines are added as part of Microsoft's efforts to aid user accessibility. In Internet Explorer, if you press Tab or Shift+Tab on a page with links, you jump to the next (or previous) link (text or graphic). The link is then outlined to indicate that it has been selected. To go to the linked page, you then press Enter. This enables users to access Web pages by using only the keyboard.

**1) Open the disjointed.htm file you created in Lesson 5.**

If you don't have this file, you can use the file in the Lesson_05_Behaviors/Completed folder.

Preview the file in Internet Explorer and click one of the rollover buttons in the browser window with the white arrows (either biking, kayaking, or surfing). You should see an outline around the image after you click it.

### 2) Press Tab to jump to the next link.

The next link will highlight with an outline around the image.

### 3) Return to Dreamweaver and choose Commands > StudioVII > IE Link Scrubber. Click the Scrub Em! button to add the code to your page.

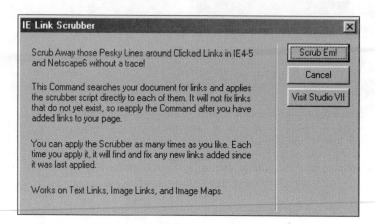

A custom script is added to the Behaviors panel for all three images with links.

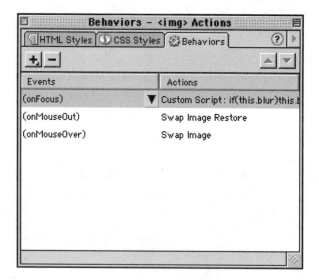

**4) Preview the page in Internet Explorer and test the results.**

The outlines should be removed.

**NOTE** *Each time you add a new link, you'll need to choose the command again. To remove the code, select the link. Click the Custom Script listed in the Behaviors panel to select it and click the minus (–) sign to remove the custom code.*

**5) Save the document.**

You can close this file.

## CHANGING THE OBJECTS PANEL

The Objects panel is divided into eight panels. There are seven default panels: Characters, Common, Forms, Frames, Head, Invisibles, and Special. Each panel corresponds to a folder within the Configuration/Objects folder in the Dreamweaver application folder. If you look in the Common folder, you'll see an HTML file and a GIF image file for each of the objects in the Common panel. For example, an image.htm file and an image.gif file correspond to the Insert Image object. Some objects also have a JavaScript file ending with the .js extension. Earlier in this lesson, you installed the calendar extension, which placed the Insert Calendar object into a new panel called Goodies on the Objects panel.

The Objects panel is an easy way to insert HTML elements in your page. All the objects included in the Objects panel can be modified to suit your needs. Using only some basic HTML, you can create an object for use in all your documents.

**1) Create a new document. Save it as catcopy.htm in the Lesson_15_Custom/Objects folder.**

In the following steps, you will create a copyright tag line and convert it into an object.

**2) Choose Insert > Horizontal Rule to insert a line across your document and type © Copyright 2000–2001 Compass Adventure Tours. All Rights Reserved.**

You now have the copyright information in your document.

**3) Create a line break by pressing Shift+Enter for Windows or Shift+Return for Macintosh. On the next line, type *Modified:* (including the colon), and then choose Insert > Date.**

The Insert Date dialog box opens.

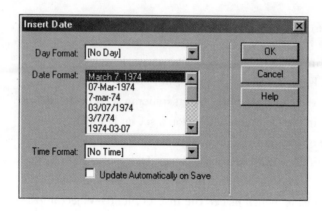

**4) In the Insert Date dialog box, choose Day Format: Thursday; Date Format: March 7, 1974; and Time Format: No Time (default). Check the Update Automatically on Save box and click OK.**

The current date is inserted into your document at the insertion point.

**5) Click the Code View icon on the toolbar to view the HTML. Delete everything in the document except the following (your date line will show the current date):** `<hr> &copy; Copyright 2000–2001 Compass Adventure Tours. All Rights Reserved.<br>Modified:<!-- #BeginDate format:fcAm1 -->Monday, June 21, 2000<!-- #EndDate -->`

In code view, your document will look like the example that follows.

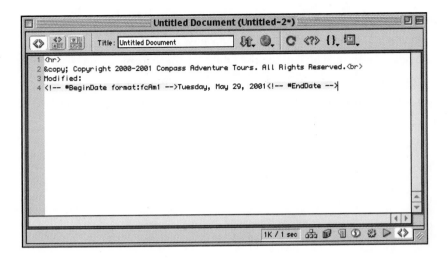

## 6) Click Design View to view your changes.

The document turns gray because you've deleted the <body> tag that contained the white color for the background of the page.

## 7) Save your file as catcopy.htm in the Lesson_15_Custom/Objects folder and quit Dreamweaver.

Do not give the document a title.

After you have created the HTML file, you need an icon that represents the HTML. The icons used by Dreamweaver are GIF files. Some icons have already been created for you to use and are provided on the CD. The icon and the HTML need the same name. In the following steps, you will add your object to the Dreamweaver application.

**NOTE** *To create your own icon for the Objects panel, create an 18 x 18 pixel GIF image in a program such as Macromedia Fireworks. Make sure the name of the GIF image is the same as your HTML file.*

## 8) Using Windows Explorer (Windows) or Finder (Macintosh), open the Lesson_15_Custom folder and locate the Objects folder.

You'll see the file you just created and several GIF files, one of which is named catcopy.gif.

## 9) In the Dreamweaver application folder, open the Configuration/Objects folder and create a new folder within the Objects folder. Name the new folder catcopy.

You can make your own custom object by creating an HTML file and a GIF file and then copying those files into the Objects folder. By creating a new folder within the Objects folder, you create a new panel for the Objects panel.

347

**10) Select the catcopy.htm and catcopy.gif files. Move or copy them both into the catcopy folder you just created and restart Dreamweaver.**

When Dreamweaver restarts, you will see the Objects panel categories now include the new catcopy panel. On the catcopy panel, you'll see a new icon that looks like the copyright symbol. In addition, a new menu item named catcopy appears in the Insert menu. The name of the HTML file is the name of the menu item.

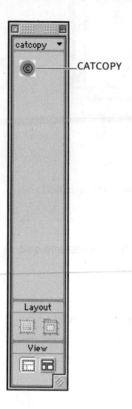

**11) Open a new document and click your new icon on the catcopy panel of the Objects panel.**

The horizontal rule, copyright tag line, and modified date are all inserted in your page.

You can close this file without saving.

**NOTE** *You don't always have to restart Dreamweaver when you load extensions. While in Dreamweaver, Ctrl-click (Windows) or Option-click (Macintosh) the drop-down menu at the top of the Objects panel. Then choose Reload Extensions.*

## WHAT YOU HAVE LEARNED

**In this lesson, you have:**

- Used browser profiles to test individual pages, folders, or an entire site for browser compatibility and find out if there are any errors or unsupported tags (pages 330–332)

- Tested the links in your pages to quickly find any broken links within your site (pages 332–333)

- Created site reports to find common problems in your site such as redundant nested tags and untitled documents (pages 334–335)

- Used the Reference panel to modify the HTML code and create a visual effect with the background image in the browser (pages 335–337)

- Added extensions to expand Dreamweaver's capabilities using the Macromedia Extension Manager and learned where to find more extensions (pages 338–341)

- Used new extensions to change lowercase text to uppercase, create a calender, and get rid of link outlines in the browser (pages 341–345)

- Created your own object and placed it into a new category in the Objects panel (pages 345–348)

# regular expressions

The following table lists special characters in regular expressions and their meanings.

| Type | Description | Example |
|------|-------------|---------|
| ^ | Beginning of input or line | ^T matches "T" in "This good earth" but not in "Uncle Tom." |
| $ | End of input or line | h$ matches "h" in "teach" but not in "teacher." |
| * | The preceding character 0 or more times | um* matches "um" in "rum," "umm" in "yummy," and "u" in "huge." |
| + | The preceding character 1 or more times | um+ matches "um" in "rum" and "umm" in "yummy." |
| ? | The preceding character at most once | st?on matches "son" in "Johnson" and "ston" in "Johnston." |
| . | Any single character except newline | .an matches "ran" and "can." |
| x\|y | Either x or y | FF0000\|000FF matches "FF0000" in BGCOLOR="#FF0000" and "0000FF" in FONT COLOR="#0000FF." |
| {n} | Exactly n occurrences of the preceding character | o{2} matches "oo" in "loom" and the first two o's in "mooooo." |
| {n,m} | At least n and at most m occurrences of the preceding character | F{2,4} matches "FF" in "#FF0000" and the first four Fs in "#FFFFFF." |

| Type | Description | Example |
|------|-------------|---------|
| [abc] | Any one of the characters enclosed in the brackets | [aeiou] initially matches "a" in "apple," "e" in "egg," and "i" in "pig." Specify a range of characters with a hyphen (for example, [a-f] is equivalent to [abcdef]). |
| [^abc] | Any character not enclosed in the brackets | [^aeiou] initially matches "r" in "orange," "b" in "book," and "k" in "eek!". Specify a range of characters with a hyphen (for example, [^a-f] is equivalent to [^abcdef]). |
| \b | A word boundary (such as a space or carriage return) | \bb matches "b" in "book" but nothing in "goober" or "snob." |
| \B | A nonword boundary | \Bb matches "b" in "goober" but nothing in "book." |
| \d | Any digit character. Equivalent to [0-9] | \d matches "3" in "C3PO" and "2" in "apartment 2G." |
| \D | Any nondigit character. Equivalent to [^0-9] | \D matches "S" in "900S" and "Q" in "Q45." |
| \f | Form feed | |
| \n | Line feed | |
| \r | Carriage return | |
| \s | Any single whitespace character, including space, tab, form feed, or line feed | \sbook matches "book" in "blue book." |
| \S | Any single non-whitespace character | \Sbook matches "book" in "notebook" but nothing in "blue book." |
| \t | A tab | |
| \w | Any alphanumeric character, including underscore. Equivalent to [A-Za-z0-9_] | b\w* matches "barking" in "the barking dog" and both "big" and "black" in "the big black dog." |
| \W | Any nonalphanumeric character. Equivalent to [^A-Za-z0-9_] | \W matches "&" in "Jake & Mattie" and "%" in "100%." |

# macintosh shortcuts

You can add, remove, or modify Dreamweaver's keyboard shortcuts by choosing Edit › Keyboard Shortcuts to open the Keyboard Shortcuts dialog box.

## MENU SHORTCUTS

### FILE MENU

| Command | Shortcut |
| --- | --- |
| New Document | Command+N |
| Open a Document | Command+O |
| Open in Frame | Command+Shift+O |
| Close | Command+W |
| Save | Command+S |
| Save As | Command+Shift+S |
| Preview in Primary Browser | F12 |
| Preview in Secondary Browser | Command+F12 |
| Debug in Primary Browser | Option+F12 |
| Debug in Secondary Browser | Command+Option+F12 |
| Check Links | Shift+F8 |
| Quit | Command+Q |

### EDIT MENU

| Command | Shortcut |
| --- | --- |
| Undo | Command+Z |
| Redo | Command+Y |
| Cut | Command+X |
| Copy | Command+C |
| Paste | Command+V |
| Clear | Delete |
| Copy HTML | Command+Shift+C |
| Paste HTML | Command+Shift+V |
| Select All | Command+A |
| Select Parent Tag | Command+Shift+‹ |
| Select Child | Command+Shift+› |
| Find and Replace | Command+F |
| Find Again | Command+G |
| Indent Code | Command+] |
| Outdent Code | Command+[ |
| Balance Braces | Command+' |
| Set Breakpoint | Command+Option+B |
| Edit with BBEdit | Command+E |
| Preferences | Command+U |

## VIEW MENU

| Command | Shortcut |
| --- | --- |
| Switch Views | Option+Tab |
| Refresh Design View | F5 |
| Head Content | Command+Shift+W |
| Standard View | Command+Shift+F6 |
| Layout View | Command+F6 |
| Hide All | Command+Shift+I |
| Show Rulers | Command+Option+R |
| Show Grid | Command+Option+G |
| Snap to Grid | Command+Shift+Option+G |
| Play | Command+Option+P |
| Stop | Command+Option+X |
| Play All | Command+Shift+Option+P |
| Stop All | Command+Shift+Option+X |
| Hide Panels | F4 |
| Toolbar | Command+U |

## INSERT MENU

| Command | Shortcut |
| --- | --- |
| Image | Command+Option+I |
| Flash | Command+Option+F |
| Shockwave | Command+Option+D |
| Table | Command+Option+T |
| Named Anchor | Command+Option+A |
| Line Break | Shift+Return |
| Non-Breaking Space | Command+Shift+Space |

## MODIFY MENU

| Command | Shortcut |
| --- | --- |
| Page Properties | Command+J |
| Selection Properties | Command+Shift+J |
| Quick Tag Editor | Command+T |
| Make Link | Command+L |
| Remove Link | Command+Shift+L |
| Select Table | Command+A |
| Move to the Next Cell* | Tab |
| Move to the Previous Cell* | Shift+Tab |
| Merge Cells | Command+Option+M |
| Split Cell | Command+Option+S |
| Insert Row | Command+M |
| Insert Column | Command+Shift+A |
| Delete Row | Command+Shift+M |
| Delete Column | Command+Shift+- |
| Increase Column Span | Command+Shift+] |
| Decrease Column Span | Command+Shift+[ |
| Left | Command+Shift+1 |
| Right | Command+Shift+3 |
| Top | Command+Shift+4 |
| Bottom | Command+Shift+6 |
| Make Same Width | Command+Shift+7 |
| Make Same Height | Command+Shift+9 |
| Add Object to Library | Command+Shift+B |
| New Editable Region | Command+Option+V |
| Add Object to Timeline | Command+Shift+Option+T |
| Add Keyframe | F6 |
| Remove Keyframe | Shift+F6 |

\* Command is not included in the Modify menu.

## TEXT MENU

| Command | Shortcut |
| --- | --- |
| Indent | Command+Control+] |
| Outdent | Command+Control+[ |
| None | Command+0 |
| Paragraph | Command+Shift+P |
| Heading 1 | Command+1 |
| Heading 2 | Command+2 |
| Heading 3 | Command+3 |
| Heading 4 | Command+4 |
| Heading 5 | Command+5 |
| Heading 6 | Command+6 |
| Align Left | Command+Shift+Option+L |
| Align Center | Command+Shift+Option+C |
| Align Right | Command+Shift+Option+R |
| Bold | Command+B |
| Italic | Command+I |
| Edit Style Sheet | Command+Shift+E |
| Check Spelling | Shift+F7 |

## COMMANDS MENU

| Command | Shortcut |
| --- | --- |
| Start Recording | Command+Shift+X |
| Play Recorded Command | Command+P |

## SITE MENU

| Command | Shortcut |
| --- | --- |
| Refresh | F5 |
| New File | Command+Shift+N |
| New Folder | Command+Shift+Option+N |
| Refresh Local | Shift+F5 |
| Refresh Remote | Option+F5 |
| View as Root | Command+Shift+R |
| Link to New File | Command+Shift+N |
| Link to Existing File | Command+Shift+K |
| Change Link | Command+L |
| Remove Link | Command+Shift+L |
| Show/Hide Link | Command+Shift+Y |
| Show Page Titles | Command+Shift+T |
| Get | Command+Shift+D |
| Checkout | Command+Shift+Option+D |
| Put | Command+Shift+U |
| Check In | Command+Shift+Option+U |
| Open | Command+Shift+Option+O |
| Check Links Sitewide | Command+F8 |

## WINDOW MENU

| Command | Shortcut |
|---|---|
| Objects | Command+F2 |
| Properties | Command+F3 |
| Site Files | F8 |
| Site Map | Option+F8 |
| Assets | F11 |
| Behaviors | Shift+F3 |
| Code Inspector | F10 |
| CSS Styles | Shift+F11 |
| Frames | Shift+F2 |
| History | Shift+F10 |
| HTML Styles | Command+F11 |
| Layers | F2 |
| Reference | Command+Shift+F1 |
| Timelines | Shift+F9 |
| Hide Panels | F4 |

## HELP MENU

| Command | Shortcut |
|---|---|
| Using Dreamweaver | F1 |
| Reference | Shift+F1 |

## CODE EDITING SHORTCUTS

| Command | Shortcut | Command | Shortcut |
|---|---|---|---|
| Select Parent Tag | Command+Shift+‹ | Move Word Right | Command+Right Arrow |
| Select Child | Command+Shift+› | Select Word Left | Command+Shift+Left Arrow |
| Balance Braces | Command+' | Select Word Right | Command+Shift+Right Arrow |
| Select Character Left | Shift+Left Arrow | Move to Start of Line | Home |
| Select Character Right | Shift+Right Arrow | Move to End of Line | End* |
| Select Line Up | Shift+Up Arrow | Select to Start of Line | Shift+Home |
| Select Line Down | Shift+Down Arrow | Select to End of Line | Shift+End* |
| Move to Page Up | Page Up | Move to Top of File | Command+Home |
| Move to Page Down | Page Down | Move to End of File | Command+End* |
| Select to Page Up | Shift+Page Up | Select to Top of File | Command+Shift+Home |
| Select to Page Down | Shift+Page Down | Select to End of File | Command+Shift+End* |
| Move Word Left | Command+Left Arrow | | |

\* Shortcut is available only on the extended Mac keyboards.

# windows shortcuts

You can add, remove, or modify Dreamweaver's keyboard shortcuts by choosing
Edit › Keyboard Shortcuts to open the Keyboard Shortcuts dialog box.

## MENU SHORTCUTS

**FILE MENU**

| Command | Shortcut |
| --- | --- |
| New Document | Ctrl+N |
| Open a Document | Ctrl+O |
| Open in Frame | Ctrl+Shift+O |
| Close | Ctrl+W |
| Save | Ctrl+S |
| Save As | Ctrl+Shift+S |
| Preview in Primary Browser | F12 |
| Preview in Secondary Browser | Ctrl+F12 |
| Debug in Primary Browser | Alt+F12 |
| Debug in Secondary Browser | Ctrl+Alt+F12 |
| Check Links | Shift+F8 |
| Quit | Ctrl+Q |

**EDIT MENU**

| Command | Shortcut |
| --- | --- |
| Undo | Ctrl+Z |
| Redo | Ctrl+Y |
| Cut | Ctrl+X |
| Copy | Ctrl+C |
| Paste | Ctrl+V |
| Clear | Delete |
| Copy HTML | Ctrl+Shift+C |
| Paste HTML | Ctrl+Shift+V |
| Select All | Ctrl+A |
| Select Parent Tag | Ctrl+Shift+< |
| Select Child | Ctrl+Shift+> |
| Find and Replace | Ctrl+F |
| Find Again | F3 |
| Indent Code | Ctrl+] |
| Outdent Code | Ctrl+[ |
| Balance Braces | Ctrl+' |
| Set Breakpoint | Ctrl+Alt+B |
| Edit with BBEdit | Ctrl+E |
| Preferences | Ctrl+U |

## VIEW MENU

| Command | Shortcut |
| --- | --- |
| Switch Views | Ctrl+Tab |
| Refresh Design View | F5 |
| Head Content | Ctrl+Shift+W |
| Standard View | Ctrl+Shift+F6 |
| Layout View | Ctrl+F6 |
| Hide All | Ctrl+Shift+I |
| Show Rulers | Ctrl+Alt+R |
| Show Grid | Ctrl+Alt+G |
| Snap to Grid | Ctrl+Shift+Alt+G |
| Play | Ctrl+Alt+P |
| Stop | Ctrl+Alt+X |
| Play All | Ctrl+Shift+Alt+P |
| Stop All | Ctrl+Shift+Alt+X |
| Hide Panels | F4 |
| Toolbar | Ctrl+Shift+T |

## INSERT MENU

| Command | Shortcut |
| --- | --- |
| Image | Ctrl+Alt+I |
| Flash | Ctrl+Alt+F |
| Shockwave | Ctrl+Alt+D |
| Table | Ctrl+Alt+T |
| Named Anchor | Ctrl+Alt+A |
| Line Break | Shift+Return |
| Non-Breaking Space | Ctrl+Shift+Space |

## MODIFY MENU

| Command | Shortcut |
| --- | --- |
| Page Properties | Ctrl+J |
| Selection Properties | Ctrl+Shift+J |
| Quick Tag Editor | Ctrl+T |
| Make Link | Ctrl+L |
| Remove Link | Ctrl+Shift+L |
| Select Table | Ctrl+A |
| Move to the Next Cell* | Tab |
| Move to the Previous Cell* | Shift+Tab |
| Merge Cells | Ctrl+Alt+M |
| Split Cell | Ctrl+Alt+S |
| Insert Row | Ctrl+M |
| Insert Column | Ctrl+Shift+A |
| Delete Row | Ctrl+Shift+M |
| Delete Column | Ctrl+Shift+- |
| Increase Column Span | Ctrl+Shift+] |
| Decrease Column Span | Ctrl+Shift+[ |
| Left | Ctrl+Shift+1 |
| Right | Ctrl+Shift+3 |
| Top | Ctrl+Shift+4 |
| Bottom | Ctrl+Shift+6 |
| Make Same Width | Ctrl+Shift+7 |
| Make Same Height | Ctrl+Shift+9 |
| Add Object to Library | Ctrl+Shift+B |
| New Editable Region | Ctrl+Alt+V |
| Add Object to Timeline | Ctrl+Shift+Alt+T |
| Add Keyframe | F6 |
| Remove Keyframe | Shift+F6 |

\* Command is not included in the Modify menu.

## TEXT MENU

| Command | Shortcut |
| --- | --- |
| Indent | Ctrl+Alt+] |
| Outdent | Ctrl+Alt+[ |
| None | Ctrl+0 |
| Paragraph | Ctrl+Shift+P |
| Heading 1 | Ctrl+1 |
| Heading 2 | Ctrl+2 |
| Heading 3 | Ctrl+3 |
| Heading 4 | Ctrl+4 |
| Heading 5 | Ctrl+5 |
| Heading 6 | Ctrl+6 |
| Align Left | Ctrl+Shift+Alt+L |
| Align Center | Ctrl+Shift+Alt+C |
| Align Right | Ctrl+Shift+Alt+R |
| Bold | Ctrl+B |
| Italic | Ctrl+I |
| Edit Style Sheet | Ctrl+Shift+E |
| Check Spelling | Shift+F7 |

## COMMANDS MENU

| Command | Shortcut |
| --- | --- |
| Start Recording | Ctrl+Shift+X |
| Play Recorded Command | Ctrl+P |

## SITE MENU

| Command | Shortcut |
| --- | --- |
| Site Files | F8 |
| Site Map | Alt+F8 |
| Get | Ctrl+Shift+D |
| Checkout | Ctrl+Shift+Alt+D |
| Put | Ctrl+Shift+U |
| Check In | Ctrl+Shift+Alt+U |
| Check Links Sitewide | Ctrl+F8 |

## WINDOW MENU

| Command | Shortcut |
| --- | --- |
| Objects | Ctrl+F2 |
| Properties | Ctrl+F3 |
| Site Files | F8 |
| Site Map | Alt+F8 |
| Assets | F11 |
| Behaviors | Shift+F3 |
| Code Inspector | F10 |
| CSS Styles | Shift+F11 |
| Frames | Shift+F2 |
| History | Shift+F10 |
| HTML Styles | Ctrl+F11 |
| Layers | F2 |
| Reference | Ctrl+Shift+F1 |
| Timelines | Shift+F9 |
| Hide Panels | F4 |
| Minimize All | Shift+F4 |
| Restore All | Alt+Shift+F4 |

## HELP MENU

| Command | Shortcut |
| --- | --- |
| Using Dreamweaver | F1 |
| Reference | Shift+F1 |

## SITE WINDOW FILE MENU

| Command | Shortcut |
| --- | --- |
| New Window | Ctrl+N |
| New File | Ctrl+Shift+N |
| New Folder | Ctrl+Shift+Alt+N |
| Open | Ctrl+O |
| Open Selection | Ctrl+Shift+Alt+O |
| Close | Ctrl+W |
| Rename | F2 |
| Delete | Del |
| Check Links | Shift+F8 |
| Exit | Ctrl+Q |

## SITE WINDOW VIEW MENU

| Command | Shortcut |
|---|---|
| Refresh | F5 |
| Refresh Local | Shift+F5 |
| Refresh Remote | Alt+F5 |
| Show/Hide Link | Ctrl+Shift+Y |
| View as Root | Ctrl+Shift+R |
| Show Page Titles | Ctrl+Shift+T |

## SITE WINDOW SITE MENU

| Command | Shortcut |
|---|---|
| Disconnect | Ctrl+Shift+Alt+F5 |
| Get | Ctrl+Shift+D |
| Checkout | Ctrl+Shift+Alt+D |
| Put | Ctrl+Shift+U |
| Check In | Ctrl+Shift+Alt+U |
| Check Links Sitewide | Ctrl+F8 |
| Link to New File | Ctrl+Shift+N |
| Link to Existing File | Ctrl+Shift+K |
| Change Link | Ctrl+L |
| Remove Link | Ctrl+Shift+L |

# CODE-EDITING SHORTCUTS

| Command | Shortcut |
|---|---|
| Select Parent Tag | Ctrl+Shift+< |
| Select Child | Ctrl+Shift+> |
| Balance Braces | Ctrl+' |
| Select Character Left | Shift+Left Arrow |
| Select Character Right | Shift+Right Arrow |
| Select Line Up | Shift+Up Arrow |
| Select Line Down | Shift+Down Arrow |
| Move to Page Up | Page Up |
| Move to Page Down | Page Down |
| Select to Page Up | Shift+Page Up |
| Select to Page Down | Shift+Page Down |
| Move Word Left | Ctrl+Left Arrow |

| Command | Shortcut |
|---|---|
| Move Word Right | Ctrl+Right Arrow |
| Select Word Left | Ctrl+Shift+Left Arrow |
| Select Word Right | Ctrl+Shift+Right Arrow |
| Move to Start of Line | Home |
| Move to End of Line | End |
| Select to Start of Line | Shift+Home |
| Select to End of Line | Shift+End |
| Move to Top of File | Ctrl+Home |
| Move to End of File | Ctrl+End |
| Select to Top of File | Ctrl+Shift+Home |
| Select to End of File | Ctrl+Shift+End |

# index

**browsers**
 and CSS, 235, 239, 256, 330
 detecting users' installed, 129–131
 and DHTML, 129
 and frames, 210–211
 and layers, 212, 216, 224, 229, 304, 310
 opening multiple windows in, 81, 82, 131–135
 previewing pages in, 15–16
 screen space required for, 114
 setting up primary/secondary, 15–16
 and style sheets, 235, 239, 241
 testing pages in multiple versions of, 131, 330, 332
 and timelines, 304, 310
**bulleted list**, 27, 28–29
**buttons.** *See also* specific buttons
 adding to forms, 288–289, 292–294
 creating, 69–71
 modifying, 71
 naming, 70
 states for, 69, 71

# C

**cache**, 14, 62
**Calendar extension**, 342–343
**Call JavaScript behavior**, 176
**cascading style sheets**, 234. *See also* CSS; style sheets
**case, changing**, 341–342
**case-sensitive searches**, 261, 274
**catalog, online**, 180
**Cell Padding/Spacing options, Insert Table dialog box**, 101, 102
**cells.** *See also* tables
 aligning, 96
 copying and pasting, 103–104
 formatting, 97
 merging, 112, 113
 moving between, 102
 preventing word wrapping in, 109
 removing contents of, 104
 resizing, 94–96
 selecting, 106
 setting padding/spacing options, 101, 102
 splitting, 113
**CGI script**, 276–277, 279, 300
**Change Case extension**, 341–342
**channels**, 305, 320, 324
**Character Objects panel**, 40–41
**Check Browser behavior**, 129, 130, 229, 256
**Check In File(s) option, Site window**, 145, 158–160
**Check Links feature**, 332–333
**Check Out File(s) option, Site window**, 145, 158–160
**Check Target Browsers dialog box**, 331
**checkboxes**, 287–288
**Choose Spacer Image dialog box**, 98
**Clean Up HTML command**, 335
**Clean Up Word HTML dialog box**, 47–48
**Clip text field**, 220
**clipping area**, 220
**code-editing shortcuts**, 356, 360
**code inspector**, 43
**Code Navigation feature**, 42
**code view**, 42, 45–46, 63
**collaboration, Web site**, 158, 159, 161
**color picker**, 19–20, 21, 187

**colors**
 applying
  to borders, 61, 109
  to links, 76–77
  to templates, 187–188
  to text, 21, 34
 hexadecimal values for, 19, 20, 76
 saving commonly used, 34–35
 Web-safe, 19–20
**columns.** *See also* tables
 adding to table, 111–113
 changing width of, 101
 copying and pasting, 104
 selecting and modifying, 106–109
 sorting contents of, 109–111
 specifying number of, 101
**comma-delimited files**, 102, 113
**commands.** *See also* specific commands
 keyboard shortcuts for, 353–360
 repeating/undoing, 31
 use of angle bracket (›) in, 2
**Commands menu**, 355, 359
**Common Gateway Interface**, 276. *See also* CGI script
**Common Objects panel**, 48
**Completed folder**, 2
**compression, file**, 56
**Configuration/Objects folder**, 345, 347
**Configuration/Queries folder**, 270
**Connect/Disconnect option, Site window**, 145, 156
**contact information**, 77–78
**content frame**, 205–208
**Convert Layers to Table dialog box**, 231
**Copy command**, 24
**copying**
 cells, 103–104
 text, 23, 24
 URLs, 80
**copyright information**
 creating/converting to object, 345–348
 updating references to, 164–165, 169–170, 174
**CSS.** *See also* style sheets
 browser support for, 235, 239, 256, 330
 converting to HTML, 256–257
 and font size, 33
 and layers, 212
 preserving in library item, 166
 purpose of, 234
 reference material on, 244, 337
**.css files**, 238
**CSS selector styles**, 248–251
**CSS Styles panel**, 237
**custom styles**, 244–247, 266–268

# D

**Date command**, 49
**<dd> tag**, 240
**Define HTML Style dialog box**, 38–39
**Define Sites dialog box**, 13, 153
**definition list**, 30, 241. *See also* <dl> tag
**Delimiter menu**, 102, 113
**demo software**, 3
**Dependent Files dialog box**, 157
**Descending sort**, 110
**design.** *See* Web design
**design notes**, 161–162

design view, 42, 44
Detach from Template command, 191
DHTML, 129, 302
`<div>` tag, 60, 215
`<dl>` tag, 240–241, 246
docking, 11
document. *See also* Web page
    adding animation to, 71–72, 302–303
    assigning title to, 18
    creating style sheet for, 236–239
    finding and replacing text in, 260–262
    linking to, 79–80
    minimizing, 12
    using named anchors in long, 85
    viewing, 42–44
document-relative path, 58, 80
document window, 8
Down Image state, 135, 140
Draw Layer button, 304
Dreamweaver 4
    downloading demo version of, 3
    extending capabilities of, 338–345
    graphics features, 55 (*See also* graphics)
    installing/reinstalling, 3, 13
    interface elements, 8–11
    minimum system requirements for, 5
    purpose of, 1, 6
    updating, 5
Dreamweaver Exchange Web site, 119, 338, 341
drop-down menus, 290–291, 297
`<dt>` tag, 240
DW4_Intro folder, 13, 14
DW4_Lessons folder, 2
.dwt files, 182, 186
Dynamic HTML. *See* DHTML
dynamic link tag, 248

## E

e-mail address
    linking to, 77–78, 146, 299
    validating in form field, 295, 296
Edit Date Format dialog box, 50
Edit Font List dialog box, 32
Edit Grid command, 227
Edit menu, 353, 357
Edit Style Sheet dialog box, 243
embedded style, 235, 253–255
Enable Cache checkbox, 14
encoding, data, 299, 300
end marker, 318
error message, "File Not Found," 332
events, 123, 125–128
Events menu, 127, 128
Excel, 102
Export Styles as CSS File dialog box, 256
Export Table dialog box, 113
Extension Manager, 338–341
extensions, 338–345
    defined, 338
    finding/downloading, 341
    installing, 338–341
    removing, 341
    types of, 338
    using specific, 341–345

## external style sheet

external style sheet
    adding style to, 240–242
    advantages of using, 236
    contrasted with embedded style, 235
    converting to internal, 255–256
    creating, 236–239
    editing, 242–244
    linking to, 251–252
    removing, 255
    using Find and Replace to add, 268–269

## F

Favorites list
    adding colors to, 34–35
    adding images to, 64–66
feedback form, 276, 284–285
fields
    adding to forms, 281–286
    naming, 283
    validating, 295
file management, 12, 142, 144. *See also* Site window
File menu, 353, 357, 359
"File Not Found" message, 332
File Transfer Protocol, 155. *See also* FTP
files. *See also* specific file formats
    adding to Web site, 145–146
    attaching design notes to, 161–162
    for completing lesson projects, 2, 13
    naming, 17, 151
    saving, 16–17, 20, 22
    transferring to/from remote site, 145, 153–157
    updating, 142, 151, 156, 158–160, 164–165, 173, 190–191
Find and Replace dialog box, 260, 270
Find and Replace feature, 258–275
    adding external style sheet with, 268–269
    applying custom style with, 266–268
    looking for name variations with, 274
    purpose of, 258–259
    removing HTML tag with, 262–265
    saving/reusing search criteria, 270–271
    searching document with, 260–262
    searching for regular expressions with, 261, 271–273
Finder, Macintosh, 144
firewall, 155
.fla files, 72
Flash animation, 71–72, 302
Flash buttons, 69–71
Flash text, 50–52
folders. *See also* specific folders
    adding to Web site, 145–146
    naming, 17
    storing lesson files in, 2
font color, 21, 34
font size, 31, 33–34
`<font>` tag, 46, 263, 264, 335
fonts
    changing, 31–33
    readability considerations, 32
    restoring default settings for, 33
`<form>` tag, 278, 299–300
formatting, 31, 36, 234. *See also* HTML styles; style sheets

# Learn Macromedia's hottest software...
## the **Visual QuickStart** way!

## *Visual QuickStart Guides*

***Get Up and Running Fast.*** *Visual QuickStart Guides from Peachpit Press cover Macromedia software and are published in association with Macromedia Press. They are the industry's bestselling series of practical, visual, quick-reference guides. Step-by-step instructions and plenty of screen shots show you how to do the most important tasks and get right to work.*

**Fireworks 4 for Windows and Macintosh: Visual QuickStart Guide**

By Sandee Cohen
ISBN 0-201-73133-9
416 pages • $18.99 U.S.

**Director 8 for Macintosh and Windows: Visual QuickStart Guide**

By Andre Persidsky
ISBN 0-201-70258-4
448 pages • $19.99 U.S.

**Dreamweaver 4 for Windows and Macintosh: Visual QuickStart Guide**

By J. Tarin Towers
ISBN 0-201-73430-3
352 pages • $21.99 U.S.

**Flash 5 for Windows and Macintosh: Visual QuickStart Guide**

By Katherine Ulrich
ISBN 0-201-71614-3
544 pages • $21.99 U.S.

**FreeHand 10 for Windows and Macintosh: Visual QuickStart Guide**

By Sandee Cohen
ISBN 0-201-74965-3
340 pages • $19.99 U.S.
***Available in August***

**Flash 5 Advanced for Windows and Macintosh: Visual QuickPro Guide**

By Russell Chun
ISBN 0-201-72624-6
424 pages w/ CD-ROM • $29.99 U.S.

**macromedia® PRESS**

*www.peachpit.com/mmp*

# Macromedia Press...helping you learn what the Web can be.

## *Training from the Source*

Macromedia's Training from the Source Series is the only series on the market that was created by insiders at Macromedia and modeled after Macromedia's own training courses. This series offers you a unique training approach that introduces you to the major features of the particular software you are working with and guides you step by step through the development of real world projects.

Each book is divided into a series of lessons. Each lesson begins with an overview of the lesson's content and learning objectives and is divided into short tasks that break the skills into bite-size units. All the files you need for the lessons are included on the CD that comes with the book.

**Macromedia Director 8.5 Shockwave Studio: Training from the Source**

By Phil Gross
ISBN 0-201-74164-4
350 pages w/ CD-ROM • $44.99 U.S.

**Macromedia Dreamweaver 4 Fireworks 4 Studio: Training from the Source**

By Patti Schulze
ISBN 0-201-71162-1
400 pages w/ CD-ROM • $44.99 U.S.

**Macromedia FreeHand 10: Training from the Source**

ISBN 0-201-75042-2
480 pages w/ CD-ROM • $44.99 U.S.
*Available August 2001*

**Macromedia Dreamweaver 4: Training from the Source**

By Khristine Annwn Page and Patti Schulze
ISBN 0-201-73135-5
352 pages w/ CD-ROM • $39.99 U.S.

**Macromedia Dreamweaver UltraDev 4: Training from the Source**

By Nolan Hester
ISBN 0-201-72144-9
352 pages w/ CD-ROM • $44.99 U.S.

**Macromedia Flash 5: Training from the Source**

By Chrissy Rey
ISBN 0-201-72931-8
336 pages w/ CD-ROM • $44.99 U.S.

---

## *Other Titles*

**Authorware 5 Attain Authorized**

By Orson Kellogg
ISBN 0-201-35411-X
448 pages w/ CD-ROM • $39.99 U.S.

**Flash and Generator Demystified**

By Phillip Torrone and Chris Wiggins
ISBN 0-201-72584-3
524 pages w/ CD-ROM • $54.99 U.S.

**Director 8 Demystified**

By Phil Gross and Jason Roberts
ISBN 0-201-70920-1
1216 pages w/ CD-ROM
$49.99 U.S.

**Flash 5! Creative Web Animation**

By Derek Franklin and Brooks Patton
ISBN 0-201-71969-X
568 pages w/ CD-ROM • $39.99 U.S.

*www.peachpit.com/mmp*

Macromedia tech support number: 415-252-9080

## LICENSING AGREEMENT

The information in this book is for informational use only and is subject to change without notice. Macromedia, Inc., and Macromedia Press assume no responsibility for errors or inaccuracies that may appear in this book. The software described in the book is furnished under license and may be used or copied only in accordance with terms of the license.

The software files on the CD-ROM included here are copyrighted by Macromedia, Inc. You have the non-exclusive right to use these programs and files. You may use them on one computer at a time. You may not transfer the files from one computer to another over a network. You may transfer the files onto a single hard disk so long as you can prove ownership of the original CD-ROM.

You may not reverse engineer, decompile, or disassemble the software. You may not modify or translate the software or distribute copies of the software without the written consent of Macromedia, Inc.

Opening the disc package means you accept the licensing agreement. For installation instructions, see the ReadMe file on the CD-ROM.